Social Work Research
and Evaluation

SAGE was founded in 1965 by Sara Miller McCune to support the dissemination of usable knowledge by publishing innovative and high-quality research and teaching content. Today, we publish over 900 journals, including those of more than 400 learned societies, more than 800 new books per year, and a growing range of library products including archives, data, case studies, reports, and video. SAGE remains majority-owned by our founder, and after Sara's lifetime will become owned by a charitable trust that secures our continued independence.

Los Angeles | London | New Delhi | Singapore | Washington DC | Melbourne

Social Work Research and Evaluation

Examined Practice for Action

Elizabeth DePoy
University of Maine

Stephen Gilson
University of Maine

Los Angeles | London | New Delhi
Singapore | Washington DC | Melbourne

FOR INFORMATION:

SAGE Publications, Inc.
2455 Teller Road
Thousand Oaks, California 91320
E-mail: order@sagepub.com

SAGE Publications Ltd.
1 Oliver's Yard
55 City Road
London EC1Y 1SP
United Kingdom

SAGE Publications India Pvt. Ltd.
B 1/I 1 Mohan Cooperative Industrial Area
Mathura Road, New Delhi 110 044
India

SAGE Publications Asia-Pacific Pte. Ltd.
3 Church Street
#10-04 Samsung Hub
Singapore 049483

Acquisitions Editor: Nathan Davidson
Editorial Assistant: Heidi Dreiling
Production Editor: Bennie Clark Allen
Copy Editor: Michelle Ponce
Typesetter: C&M Digitals (P) Ltd.
Proofreader: Annie Lubinsky
Indexer: Robie Grant
Cover Designer: Candice Harman
Marketing Manager: Shari Countryman

Printed in the United States of America

Library of Congress Cataloging-in-Publication Data

Names: DePoy, Elizabeth, author. | Gilson, Stephen French, author.

Title: Social work research and evaluation : examined practice for action / Elizabeth G. DePoy, University of Maine, Stephen F. Gilson, University of Maine.

Description: Thousand Oaks, California : SAGE, [2017] | Includes bibliographical references and index.

Identifiers: LCCN 2016000037 | ISBN 9781452259642 (pbk. : alk. paper)

Subjects: LCSH: Social service—Evaluation. | Social service—Research. | Social service—Methodology. | Evaluation research (Social action programs)

Classification: LCC HV40 .D4563 2017 | DDC 361.0072—dc23 LC record available at http://lccn.loc.gov/2016000037

This book is printed on acid-free paper.

SUSTAINABLE FORESTRY INITIATIVE
Certified Chain of Custody
Promoting Sustainable Forestry
www.sfiprogram.org
SFI-01268

SFI label applies to text stock

16 17 18 19 20 10 9 8 7 6 5 4 3 2 1

BRIEF CONTENTS

Detailed Contents

FOREWORD

In 2005, I was invited to make a contribution to *The Encyclopedia of Social Measurement*. The centerpiece of my assignment was to address measurement issues within social work practice and research. I began my work with an historical approach, reading relevant social work meeting minutes from the years 1903 to 1905. In between the lines, I noticed what seemed to be disagreement between social work practitioners and professors regarding the definition of knowledge. In the 1929 edition of *Social Work Year Book* (the precursor of *The Encyclopedia of Social Work)* the difference was no longer hidden.

The disjuncture between research and practice still exists. Practitioners often find research to be dense and irrelevant to the complexity of human experience that is witnessed in the field. For example, practitioners find that research models taught in both undergraduate and graduate school are not feasible to implement in the real world of social work practice. For well over a decade, despite their time consuming conduct in many practice settings, single-system designs have been held in high esteem within the classroom. But, unlike the 1920s, the debate between practitioners and research faculty has become sub-rosa and remains problematic in a context of evidence-based accountable practice.

DePoy and Gilson's *Social Work Research and Evaluation: Examined Practice for Action* serves as a desperately needed bridge between social work research and social work practice. The authors offer the most creative presentation I have read within the last 40 years. The examples within the text become a great catalyst to integrate research, evaluation, and practice. As an unintended consequence of their work, DePoy and Gilson have spearheaded an effort to reduce the tension between social work practitioners and researchers. In the end, their work will improve social work practice and education and create greater harmony between the academic and the practice worlds.

The question becomes: How were DePoy and Gilson able to accomplish this Herculean task? They have written a social work practice guide that focuses on the essentials of systematic thinking and action and have seamlessly woven it into a model for social work knowing and doing. Their model builds on, integrates, and advances beyond the work of many successful authors of past research and evaluation texts. *Social Work Research and Evaluation: Examined Practice for Action* anchors conceptual and praxis components on current thinking in which knowing and doing coexist in a network of practice set in a context of globalism and technology. They creatively marry disciplines that on the surface seem to be unrelated. They link the unlinkable! More than any other authors, DePoy and Gilson stress social work values but they understand that in the tradition of educating researchers, social values are to be bracketed. Consistent with the view that social values are a part of social work research, *Examined Practice* urges social workers in all settings to be part of the knowledge development enterprise, one that is necessary for the credibility and growth of our profession.

Stephen M. Marson, PhD; Retired
Professor of Sociology at University of North Carolina Pembroke;
Current Adjunct Faculty, Wake Forest University
Wake Forest College, Department of Sociology

PREFACE

A number of factors prompted us to write this book. First, as we proceed through the second decade of the 21st century, professional accountability has become increasingly central to social work. Governments in the United States and abroad, insurance companies, and agencies have vigorously emphasized and even developed empirical models, logic modeling, and evidence-based practice. The question "How do you know?" echoes throughout actual and virtual professional social work spaces from diverse audiences, consumers, clients, and customers who previously accepted claims, services, and products on professional authority alone.

Second is the intellectual trend toward pluralism. What we mean by *pluralism* is the acceptance of multiple ways of knowing. Thus, while evidence is requested for social work decisions, actions, and entities, the nature of the evidence is varied. Numbers are compelling but so are narratives, images, objects, and even maps of actual and abstract geographies.

Most important, however, is our own examined practice. Over the years, we have repeatedly heard from our students, colleagues, and clients about the schism between "those who do" and "those who investigate." Yet, in our own work, we have integrated scholarship, teaching, and commitment to our substantive areas of equality of access, full participation, and social justice and have experienced these three areas not only as integrated but as essential in all of our professional roles. In our work, we use the model that we present and illustrate in the book to guide our thinking, activity, and determination of outcome.

Examined Practice is not just a framework to guide social workers in conducting evaluation and research. Rather, it is a logical, systematic model to guide all professional thinking and action within a context of purpose and what is practical in everyday social work practice. *Examined Practice* reminds us to begin at the beginning, at the point of identifying values about what our practices should change, what is needed to achieve the change that we want to see, to look critically at our own activity, and to examine the extent to which, and how, social work produced the change. *Examined Practice* bridges the practice–research separation. The framework embraces diverse theories, action, and sets of evidence from a range of professional and disciplinary perspectives.

Elizabeth DePoy
Stephen Gilson

ACKNOWLEDGMENTS

SAGE Publishing gratefully acknowledges the following reviewers for their kind assistance:

Ashley Austin, *Barry University*

Catherine R. Baratta, *Central Connecticut State University*

Alan A. Bougere, *University of Southern Mississippi*

Jo Brocato, *California State University Long Beach*

Ginny Focht-New, *Widener University*

Richard J. Harris, *University of Texas at San Antonio*

Richard Hoefer, *University of Texas at Arlington*

Ameda A. Manetta, *Winthrop University*

ABOUT THE AUTHORS

Elizabeth DePoy is a professor at the University of Maine School of Social Work, where she has taught research and evaluation methods for 28 years. Her scholarship in social work focuses on methods of inquiry and particularly on integrating research, evaluation, and professional practice. She has coauthored 15 books and over 100 articles and presents her work locally and globally. Her most recent books include *Branding and Designing Disability* and the fifth edition of *Introduction to Research*.

Stephen Gilson is a professor at the University of Maine, where he teaches human behavior in the social environment, diversity theory, and biology for social workers. His own work is informed by systematic inquiry, and thus he is committed to the synthesis of practice and research within social work. Stephen has authored/coauthored 12 books and over 80 articles including *Branding and Designing Disability* and *Evaluation Practice*. He presents his work nationally and internationally.

SECTION I

Chapter 1

INTRODUCTION TO EXAMINED PRACTICE

> *"Social work practice consists of the professional application of social work values, principles, and techniques to one or more of the following ends: helping people obtain tangible services; counseling and psychotherapy with individuals, families, and groups; helping communities or groups provide or improve social and health services; and participating in legislative processes" (NASW, 2016).*

> *"Competency 4: Engage in Practice-Informed Research and Research-Informed Practice:*

> *Social workers understand quantitative and qualitative research methods and their respective roles in advancing a science of social work and in evaluating their practice. Social workers know the principles of logic, scientific inquiry, and culturally informed and ethical approaches to building knowledge. Social workers understand that evidence that informs practice derives from multi-disciplinary sources and multiple ways of knowing. They also*

understand the processes for translating research findings into effective practice. Social workers:

- use practice experience and theory to inform scientific inquiry and research;
- apply critical thinking to engage in analysis of quantitative and qualitative research methods and research findings; and
- use and translate research evidence to inform and improve practice, policy, and service delivery." (CSWE, 2015)

INTRODUCTION TO THE RATIONALE FOR THE TEXT

Over the years that we have been teaching in social work, students often enter research classes with trepidation, fearing the material and questioning the relevance of research thinking and action to practice. Yet, when they complete our classes, they master the logic and precision of inquiry, thought, and action such that they begin to see both not only as mutually informative but as inseparable and thus essential to their professional development. We have therefore written *Social Work Research and Evaluation: Examined Practice for Action* to guide deliberately informed social work practice in which the essentials of systematic thinking and action are seamlessly woven into a model for social work knowing and doing.

It is not surprising that, over the profession's history, research and practice have been somewhat distinct from one another. As reflected in the quotations from the National Association of Social Workers (NASW, 2016) and the Council on Social Work Education (CSWE, 2015) above, practice is characterized as the activation of knowledge, skills, and values, while research and evaluation are both considered to be a set of processes anchored in systematic traditions of science. Moreover, research and evaluation have not only been distinguished from practice but have been differentiated from one another as well.

Models such as evidence-based practice (Stout & Hayes, 2005), evidence-guided practice (Gitterman & Knight, 2013), empirical practice (Nugent, Sieppert, & Hudson, 2001; Grinnell & Unrau, 2011), social work advocate as researcher (Maschi & Youdin, 2012), evaluation practice (DePoy & Gilson, 2003), and critical thinking (Gambrill, 2012) among others have been proposed to bridge the gap between research and practice. So why have we written yet another book explicating a new model? Similar to other models, *Social Work Research and Evaluation: Examined Practice for Action* integrates systematic ways of knowing with social work doing to guide contemporary and informed comprehensive social work in its full diversity of concerns and domains. But examined practice goes further, anchoring its conceptual and practice components on current thinking in which knowing and doing coexist in a network of globalism, technology, and postpostmodern marriage of previous disciplinary strangers (Nealon, 2012). For example, social work and engineering can now partner to systematically conceptualize, determine need, create, and test outcomes of innovations that result in improving the lives and esteem of individuals who need adaptive equipment. Computer programmers and social workers can use the common language of systematic thinking and action to collaborate on web-based health education to reach large populations who were previously unserved. And clinical social workers can engage in thinking and action that result in knowledge accepted as legitimate to advance social work as well as other fields such as public policy and business. These points are exhibited in the exemplars that work throughout the book to illustrate concepts and skills.

Further moving beyond unidirectional evidence-based practice and similar models, examined practice not only applies systematically developed research knowledge to social work practice but also identifies and provides a framework in which social work doing itself, instead of being labeled as practice wisdom (Rubin & Bellamy, 2012) or research informed (Plath, 2013), is a credible, reciprocal avenue for generating research evidence and thus for creating important social work knowing.

Examined practice proposes that all social work doing and knowing are value-based and thus evaluative of the nature of social problems and their resolutions despite the euphemisms and arguments that social work does not focus on identifying and solving problems (Cohen, 2011). For example, as presented in his own words below, Cohen uses the phrase "more desirable future" to supplant the term *problem*. We ask, "more desirable than what?" and point to the "what" as the undesirable or problem to be ameliorated or situation to be changed.

> Throughout its history, social work has been concerned with creating a more desirable future by changing the existing and future conditions of individuals, groups, and communities through planned interventions in social systems and their environments. Viewed in this context, the social work practitioner can be seen as a designer who is concerned with helping clients make choices that will bridge the gap between their present situation and a desired future situation. (Cohen, 2011, p. 341)

Of critical importance to understanding and using examined practice in all parts of social work is the nature of the term *problem*. In examined practice it is defined in the philosophical sense (McCarthy, 2013), denoting not only personal issues and undesirables but inclusive of value-based puzzling situations to be engaged and unraveled by social work. And contemporary models of research such as appreciative inquiry inform an understanding of problems not simply as devalued phenomena but rather as surrounded by resources that can be harnessed to conceptualize, analyze, and engage with them (Cooperrider & Whitney, 2005). Systematic thinking techniques such as force field analysis and codesign, as discussed in Chapter 2, join research methods creating an entry into the process of examined practice. So even problem analysis, the first and most fundamental step in examined practice, integrates logic and values. This marriage erases a major distinction between "pure" or "bench" research and evaluation research, a principle fundamental to examined practice. As illustrated throughout, all research, despite its philosophical tradition, begins with a judgment of what is important to know and then what theoretical lenses will be used, revised, or countered through the process of inquiry. Thus, along with other authors and scholars (Nealon, 2012; Letherby, Scott, & Williams, 2013), we agree that separating values from research is not possible.

As stated by Daniel (2011), "not only is the concept of the value-free ideal impossible to achieve in real life, but so is the overarching notion of objective science at all" (p. 1).

Examining the Name

We have chosen to name this model of social work knowing and doing *examined practice* because of the term's rich history and definitional consistency with the tenets of the systematically conducted social work knowing and doing. The English usage of the word *examine* dates back to the late thirteenth century. It derives from the Latin word *exāmināre*, defined as

1. to weigh, examine, test

2. to observe, test, or investigate (a person's body or any part of it), especially in order to evaluate general health or determine the cause of illness

3. to inquire into or investigate: to examine one's motives

4. to test the knowledge, reactions, or qualifications of (a pupil, candidate, etc.), as by questions or assigning tasks

5. to subject to legal inquisition; put to question in regard to conduct or to knowledge of facts; interrogate: to examine a witness; to examine a suspect (Dictionary.com, 2013)

The noun *practice* dates back to Medieval Latin in which it was used to depict application of knowledge (Harper, 2016). This usage still stands. Thus the name, examined practice, reflects the integration of thinking and doing, systematic scrutiny, and its use in social work.

The Model of Examined Practice

Figure 1.1 presents a schematic of the examined practice model. While the thinking and action processes are presented as circular and sequential for instructional exactitude, we clarify that social work is a fabric of interaction in which each of these steps is permeable, overlapping, and complex, often occurring in a nonlinear fashion. Yet, as depicted below in the foundational principles, deliberation and precision characteristic of research are the obligation of the professional social worker and can be accomplished within daily practice by the intentional and sequential application of the examined practice model.

Although the process is often entered at the "reflexive intervention" point (we detail this step later but at this introductory stage reveal that it is the step in which well-informed social work action occurs), in this book, we propose that all social work activity begins, whether explicit or not, with the identification of a problem or issue to be encountered and then proceeds to the identification of the issues within it that can be addressed in our professional scope. As introduced above and detailed in subsequent chapters, because problems are puzzles calling for resolution or change, they are statements of value (or devalue), and thus, we see the social work enterprise and its knowledge foundation, regardless of how it is worded, as value-based by its inherent purposes.

Once a problem or issue is accepted as relevant and within the scope of social work practice, again a judgment framed by the social work code of ethics, the next steps

Figure 1.1 The Examined Practice Model

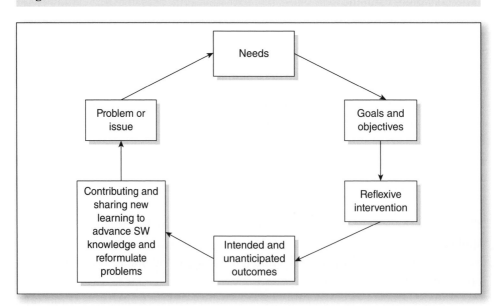

involve determining what is needed to encounter and address the problem, setting the action agenda with explicit and well-informed goals and objectives, enacting carefully scrutinized social work practices, and then assessing the extent to which and how the issue or problem was affected, the need was fulfilled, and the goals and objectives were met. These processes in turn create systematically generated knowledge on which to advance new problem definitions. Thus, throughout all of examined practice, research thinking and action come into play, and knowledge is created.

Primary Principles of Examined Practice

Thinking and action in examined practice are based on four major principles:

1. Social work practice and systematically developed knowledge (following diverse traditions in research) are inseparable.

2. Professional knowledge building and use are value-based and thus evaluative.

3. Research in social work is evaluative of the extent to which and how social problems are encountered and resolved.

4. Engaging in examined practice in all contexts and domains is an ethical obligation for all social workers.

Each of the principles above is discussed and illustrated in detail throughout the book. The first refers to the seamlessness of knowledge and action. In examined practice, social work knowing and doing are reciprocal and equal partners in knowledge generation, in that social work activity is based on legitimately developed knowledge and in turn creates it to inform future practice and so forth.

Principle #2 emphasizes the evaluative nature of social work knowing and doing. This point is critical to understanding the distinction between examined practice and evidence-based practice and similar models that also call on research methods as essential to social work. Examined practice acknowledges and affirms the nature of all knowledge as value-based and thus shaped by and inherent in value. As will be discussed, even knowledge developed with the most rigorous clinical trial research methods is framed by value. The section below on philosophy further clarifies this principle.

The third principle sets out a specific agenda for research in social work. Its primary purpose within the examined practice model is to meet the mission of social work to identify and engage social problems.

Thus, the sequence of examined practice begins with a problem to be defined and addressed and then proceeds to examine the efficacy of social work in problem resolution or change.

The final principle, consistent with the professional and educational mandates of social work, stresses the deontological, or duty-based, ethic of research informing doing with thinking and *vice versa*. The model, therefore, holds the professional accountable for systematic thinking and action, for careful examination of his or her practices, for critical appraisal of the results of professional functioning, and for sharing this knowledge to advance the profession.

Turning to Philosophy

Over the course of history and recorded since the classical works from ancient Greek philosophers, the nature of knowledge has been debated but of course with no consensus as to the true meaning of knowledge. Queries about what constitutes knowledge and how it is acquired remain debated and contested and particularly relevant to thinking about and formalizing examined practice. Because metaphysical philosophical fields shape but are not the focus of this work, in this section we limit our comments to the important points to consider for clarifying social work knowledge and its creative, pluralistic production and use.

First, we take on the debates in social work about what constitutes legitimate professional knowledge. Although there are variations, we see social work primarily divided into a binary of either opposing or promoting evidence-based practice (or its analogues). Adopted from medicine, evidence-based practice has been advanced as a dominant model for informing social work practice. According to Sackett, Rosenberg, Gray, Haynes, and Richardson's (1996) initial definition birthed in the field of medicine, evidence-based practice (EBP) has been described as the "conscientious, explicit, and judicious use of current best evidence in making decisions about the care of individual [clients]" (p. 71).

Although adapted to include professional judgment and client values, the "best" evidence in the model of evidence-based practice still adheres fundamentally to clinical trials methods (which we discuss later). Rubin and Bellamy (2012) identify EBP as "a process for making practice decisions in which practitioners integrate the best research evidence available with their practice expertise and with client attributes, values, preferences and circumstances" (p. 7).

Despite including diverse research methods in their text, Rubin and Bellamy (2012) default to measurement, diagnosis, and deductive logic throughout their work. Moreover, in their definition of EBP, they locate values within the client, sidestepping the age-old fact-value debate.

Opponents of EBP (Cohen, 2011) launch numerous criticisms, most frequently asserting that complexity of human experience in context cannot be characterized or examined comprehensively through the reductionist and nomothetic nature of experimental-type research methods. *Reductionism* refers to the logical structure of breaking down a whole entity into its parts and explaining it in terms of other theories. *Nomothetic* is defined as "the search for general laws or traits" and thus produces research designed to look for within-group commonality and between-group differences (Dictionary.com, 2014).

For example, suppose the social worker is interested in food security for a new immigrant population group. Through a nomothetic reductionist approach, this social worker might define food security (of course from preexisting literature) as high, medium, low, and very low access to sufficient nutrition and then measure it in an immigrant and another nonimmigrant population to see if immigrants were less food secure than their nonimmigrant counterparts. As you can see, this definition of food security is characteristic of reductionism as it proposes an overarching description as access to a preset volume and nutritional status of food and then proposes nomothetic rules for within- and between-group measurements at one of four levels. The experimental-type tradition is discussed and its use illustrated throughout the text. Defined here in brief, experimental-type inquiry is an approach to conducting research based on monism, the tenet that knowledge exists apart from perception and context and thus can only be known by following deductive rules to reduce or ideally eliminate **bias** (DePoy & Gitlin, 2016).

Given the diversity and values of social work, we see the benefit of evidence-based practice in circumstances which call for its purposive use. Yet, we suggest that espousing EBP as the only model for social work knowledge and informed practice is limited by a number of beliefs inherent within it.

First, as stated by Hume (2006) in his "problem of induction" and more recently by Deutch (2011), relying primarily on the past to predict the future is fraught with credibility flaws. Such schemes begin with belief in the truth value of prediction on the basis of prior experience and observation, a claim which cannot be supported by any evidence or reason. So for us, trends of past observation, even when revised as theory verification, should be interpreted cautiously when used to inform expectations, goals, objectives, or other forward-looking thought.

Second is the reliance of reductionist and thus evidence-based strategies on probability theory and the bell curve. These underpinnings and the methods which employ them create knowledge as nomothetic. That is to say, as we discussed above, the aim is to identify within-group similarities and between-group differences. In his most recent work, Orrell (2012) suggested that the story told by the bell curve is one of deceptive beauty. Accordingly, the search for symmetrical order as an aesthetic in both science and math seduces researchers into simplifying and limiting their understandings of the universe that they seek to detail. In agreement, Byers (2011) illuminates a related constraint of positivist models:

> It seems strange to call science a mythology since the story that science tells about itself is precisely that it, an activity pursued by human beings, is objective and empirical; that it concerns itself with the facts and nothing but the facts. . . . And yet science is a human activity. This is an obvious statement but it bears repeating since part of the mythology of science is precisely that it is independent of human beings; independent of mind and intelligence. . . . How do human beings create a system of thought that produces results that are independent of human thought? (p. 7).

Further, given the commitment of social work to celebrate human diversity, allowing knowledge of human difference to languish in essentialism born by methods which seek to homogenize subgroups and distinguish them by a single variable such as ethnicity, gender, or so forth does little to advance the complexity and thus utility of diversity theory and related practice (DePoy & Gilson, 2003).

We have chosen a classical definition of knowledge as a foundational linchpin of examined practice. In the tradition of numerous philosophers before him as far back as Socrates, Goldman defines knowledge "as true belief plus something else" (Kornblith, 2014), with the something else up for grabs depending on the methods and evidence valued by the believer. We do, however, claim that as a profession, social work must delimit the "something else" to systematically derived evidence with claims supported by one or more of the three research traditions discussed in this text. Thus, while the "something else" may be measurement and analysis, other methods of research knowing sit in equal status within examined practice including knowledge as action scrutinized through methods that are characteristic of what is referred to as naturalistic inquiry (Creswell, 2014).

Moreover, different from logical positivist and empirical common denominators that claim full ownership of desirable evidence in evidence-based practice, Kornblith (2014) argues that justification of true belief with measurement and observation is neither necessary nor sufficient for a well-rounded understanding of knowledge. We disagree with his view that they are not necessary but agree with "not sufficient," proposing that pluralistic social work knowing, or knowing in multiple ways, is most pragmatic and potent for our profession. As visited throughout the text, both naturalistic and mixed-method traditions of knowing are indicated for social work. Briefly, naturalistic traditions of knowledge are grounded on diverse philosophical schools, but for the most part, all propose inductive or abductive logical reasoning as the basis for researching phenomena. Naturalistic thinking and action do not see knowledge as distinct from context nor do these approaches seek to "objectively" reveal a singular truth (Creswell, 2014). Within a purposive framework, naturalistic and experimental-type traditions can complement one another (Tashakkori & Teddlie, 2010). All research traditions (experimental type, naturalistic, mixed methods) can be called upon to create social work knowing about what is, why, and how. These types of knowing are now discussed.

Knowing How, Knowing That

The presence and nature of a distinction between "knowing how" (procedural knowledge) and "knowing that" (declarative knowledge) (Ryle, 2009) have been heated debates further informing examined practice. "Knowing that," or the intelligent awareness of a phenomenon and its description, has been differentiated from clarity on the steps of doing, or "knowing how." Within examined practice, knowing how and knowing that are not easily separated, and thus thinking and acting are often indistinguishable sources of knowledge. As we detail throughout, both the doing of practice and the thinking of contemplation overlap and thus are integrated repositories for knowledge generation and its application. This point brings us to a third consideration regarding the nature of knowledge, the role of values in knowing.

In his work on philosophy of mind, Heil (2013) has been very influential in portraying science as value-based. He indicates that science itself is not a whole and singular entity but rather consists of diverse domains of personal interest. Heil's characterization of science therefore creates justification for Letherby et al.'s (2013) claim that research "requires the constant critical interrogation within our personhood in the knowledge production process" (p. 153). Examined practice builds on these ideas, exposing value as inseparable from fact but recognizable with careful and systematic reflection.

Enlightenment thinking proposed that practicing systematic deductive rules for developing knowledge resulted in the generation of truths or facts about the world external to the human that could be differentiated from but never fully understood by the knower. On the other extreme, relativists disagree with this traditional definition of objectivity, asserting that all knowledge is constructed, contextual, and thus subjective. We agree with Letherby et al. (2013), who eloquently stated, "Our descriptions of the world are always partial, selected and filtered by our perceptual apparatus" (p. 6).

This principle is particularly useful and relevant to social work in that Reamer (2013) characterizes "social work among the most value-based of all professions" (p. 3), thus creating a value context in which social work knowing is encased. As asserted by Banks (2012), "Frequently in the social work literature values are distinguished from knowledge, and ethical/moral issues from legal and technical matters. Such distinctions can be useful, as long as it is not implied that knowledge can be value-free" (p. 18)

Expanding beyond the scope of knowledge production discussed by Letherby et al. (2013) and Banks (2012), examined practice is anchored on the tenet that values are inherent in all facets of social work thinking and action including knowledge generation and its use.

The synthesis among fact and value within the scope of social work for us points to a model of social work knowing that is pluralistic, inviting of varied forms of evidence, acknowledging of value and purpose, rigorous, well-reasoned, systematic, integrative of research thinking and doing, transparent, and capable of meeting the value agendas of the profession. In essence, we suggest that value cannot be separated from social work knowing and doing. Therefore, examined practice is proposed as a rigorous evaluative research-based model for social work thinking and action. This point brings us to our final philosophical debate regarding the existence, or not, of a distinction between research and evaluation.

Numerous methodologists and scholars differentiate evaluation from research. Some suggest that because of its purposive, political aims, evaluation is distinct from inquiry. Others such as Trochim (2008) suggest that evaluation is a specialized brand of the research enterprise. He states:

> Evaluation is a methodological area that is closely related to, but distinguishable from more traditional social research. Evaluation utilizes many of the same methodologies used in traditional social research, but because evaluation takes place within a political and organizational context, it requires group skills, management ability, political dexterity, sensitivity to multiple stakeholders and other skills that social research in general does not rely on as much. (Trochim, 2008, p. 1)

Based on the contemporary philosophical understanding that fact and value are interwoven, and that science is not neutral, we see any distinction between research and evaluation as limiting to social work knowledge and informed practice. Social work inquiry is designed to generate knowledge to guide practice and to determine the extent to which and how social work met its goals within the complex contexts of practice. Social work research thus is evaluative of what constitutes problems, how these should be described and approached, the goals and objectives to be achieved, the intended and unintentional influences on knowing and doing in social work, and the assessment of the value of professional action in ameliorating what have been defined as problem areas within the scope of the social work field. To us, preference, value, political acuity, and purpose are not only inherent in this sequence but are explicit. Examined practice is therefore proposed as a pluralistic, dynamic, and carefully scrutinized approach to social work knowing and doing within the context of value, regardless of which tradition of inquiry is used.

ILLUSTRATION OF EXAMINED PRACTICE IN DIVERSE SOCIAL WORK SETTINGS

In this chapter, we introduce you to five scenarios that work with us throughout the book. Each was selected to exemplify the full sequence of examined practice thinking and action in diverse social work arenas.

Exemplars

Exemplar #1—Janice, at the age of 46, an accomplished author, was taken to the emergency department of her local hospital in a semicomatose state. She was diagnosed with a cerebrovascular accident, resulting in right hemiparesis, decrease in visual and auditory acuity on her right side, ataxia, and loss of coordination. She was referred to a clinical social worker for the problem of depression.

Exemplar #2—Dean, a jazz musician in his early 20s, was hospitalized after episodes of delusions of grandeur, in which he was convinced that he could fly. He injured himself in an attempt to fly off the roof of his house.

Exemplar #3—People with low literacy levels are at a disproportionately greater risk for smoking-related illness and fatality.

Exemplar #4—Elders abandon prescribed walking devices, resulting in sedentary lifestyles and related negative consequences of inactivity.

Exemplar #5—As a result of the reasonable accommodation standard of the Americans with Disabilities Act (ADA) and the ADA Amendments Act (ADAAA), workplace accommodations have been insufficient to maintain Elton in his job as janitor. He is unemployed and facing eviction and homelessness.

Because of the scope of methods and the breadth of social work practice, we use additional exemplars as well to illustrate the examined practice model.

ROLES AND RESPONSIBILITIES OF "EXAMINED PRACTITIONERS"

The examined practice framework guides and structures a systematic process whereby professionals themselves, or in concert with others, consistently integrate research into all elements of social work as the primary way to scrutinize the "why, how, what, and results of their own activity." In concert with professional obligation, this approach therefore holds the social worker accountable for systematic thinking and action throughout all phases of social work knowing and doing, for ethically and carefully using existing knowledge to inform practice and for advancing the knowledge base of social work in context and in concert with contemporary human need.

How to Use This Book

The book is divided into two sections. Section I details and illustrates the examined practice model. Each element of the model occupies a chapter along with exemplars from social work thinking and action.

Section II presents detailed research thinking and action. Recall that examined practice proposes that social work knowledge itself is evaluative, and thus Section II focuses on research methods to be used within a value context. Consistent with the pluralistic nature of examined practice, three research traditions, experimental type, naturalistic, and mixed methods, are presented and exemplified using the five exhibits above and other examples.

SUMMARY

In this chapter, we introduced the examined practice model and delved into its philosophical rationale. The four principles that underpin examined practice were specified and described, following which we introduced five exemplars that will be expanded throughout the book. We concluded with a statement of the roles and responsibilities of examined practitioners.

REFERENCES

Banks, S. (2012). *Ethics and values in social work* (4th ed.). New York, NY: Palgrave-MacMillan.

Byers, W. (2011). *The blind spot.* Princeton, NJ: Princeton University Press.

Cohen, D. (2011). Design-based practice: A new perspective for social work. *Social Work, 56*(4), 337–346. doi: 10.1093/sw/56.4.337

Cooperrider, D., & Whitney, D. D. (2005). *Appreciative inquiry: A positive revolution in change.* San Francisco, CA: Berrett Koehler.

Council on Social Work Education (CSWE), Commission on Accreditation, Commission on Educational Policy. (2015). *2015 educational policy and accreditation standards for baccalaureate and master's social work programs.* Retrieved from http://www.cswe.org/File .aspx?id=81660

Creswell, J. (2014). *Research design.* Thousand Oaks, CA: Sage.

Daniel. (2011). *The impossibility of objectivity.* Retrieved from UT Dallas Center for Values at https://www.utdallas.edu/c4v/the-impossibility-of-objectivity

DePoy, E., & Gilson, S. F. (2003). *Evaluation practice.* Pacific Grove, CA: Brooks-Cole.

DePoy, E., & Gitlin, L. (2016). *Introduction to research* (5 ed.). St. Louis, MO: Elsevier.

Deutch, D. (2011). *The beginning of infinity.* New York, NY: Viking.

Examine. (2013). *Dictionary.com.* Retrieved from http://dictionary.reference.com/browse/ examine?s=t

Gambrill, E. (2012). *Social work practice: A critical thinker's guide* (3rd ed.). Oxford, UK: Oxford University Press.

Gitterman, A., & Knight, C. (2013). Evidence-guided practice: Integrating the science and art of social work. *Families in Society: The Journal of Contemporary Social Services, 94*(2), 70–78.

Grinnell Jr., R. M., & Unrau, Y. A. (2011). *Social work research and evaluation: Foundations of evidence-based practice* (9th ed.). Oxford, UK: Oxford University Press.

Harper, D. (2001–2016). *Practice.* Retrieved from Online Etymology Dictionary at http://www .etymonline.com/index.php?allowed_in_frame=0&search=practice&searchmode=none

Heil, J. (2013). *A philosphy of the mind* (3rd ed.). New York, NY: Routledge.

Hume, D. (2006). *An enquiry concerning human understanding.* Stilwell, KS: Digireads.com.

Kornblith, H. (2014). *On reflection.* Oxford, UK: Oxford University Press.

Letherby, G., Scott, J., & Williams, M. (2013). *Objectivity and subjectivity in social research.* Thousand Oaks, CA: Sage.

Maschi, T., & Youdin, R. (2012). *Social worker as researcher: Integrating research with advocacy.* New York, NY: Pearson.

McCarthy, J. (2013). *Some problems of philosophy, empirically considered.* Oxford, UK: Oxford University Press.

National Association of Social Workers (NASW). (2016). *Pratice.* Retrieved from http:// socialworkers.org/practice/default.asp

Nealon, J. (2012). *Post-postmodernism.* Stanford, CA: Stanford University Press.

Nomothetic. (2014). *Dictionary.com.* Retrieved from http://dictionary.reference.com/browse/ nomothetic

Nugent, W. R., Sieppert, J. D., & Hudson, W. (2001). *Practice evaluation for the 21st century: Research, statistics, & program evaluation.* Belmont, CA: Brooks/Cole.

Orrell, D. (2012). *Truth or beauty.* New Haven, CT: Yale University Press.

Plath, D. (2013). Organizational processes supporting evidence-based practice. *Administration in Social Work, 37*(2), 171–188.

Reamer, F. (2013). *Social work values and ethics* (4th ed.). Columbia University Press.

Rubin, A., & Bellamy, J. (2012). *Practitioner's guide to using evidence-based practice* (2nd ed.). Hoboken, NJ: John Wiley.

Ryle, G. (2009). *The concept of mind: 60th anniversary edition.* New York, NY: Routledge.

Sackett, D. L., Rosenberg, W. M., Gray, J. A., Haynes, R. B., & Richardson, W. S. (1996). Evidence based medicine: What it is and what it isn't. *BMJ, 312*(7023), 71–72.

Stout, C. E., & Hayes, R. A. (2005). *The evidence-based practice: Methods, models, and tools for mental health professionals.* Hoboken, NJ: John Wiley

Tashakkori, A., & Teddlie, C. (2010). *Handbook of mixed methods in social and behavioral research* (2nd ed.). Thousand Oaks, CA: Sage.

Trochim, W. (2008). *Introduction to evaluation.* Retrieved from http://www.socialresearchmethods .net/kb/intreval.php

Chapter 2

PROBLEMS, ISSUES, AND NEEDS (WHAT, WHY, HOW, WHEN, WHERE)

DEFINITION OF TERMS

In this chapter, we examine the nature of social work problems and issues and illustrate specific techniques that can be used to identify, analyze, and clarify problem statements. The problem statement is the entry point for all thinking and action processes in social work given that the field is committed to advancing human well-being or what Aristotle and contemporaries such as Sen (2009) and Nussbaum (2013) refer to as human flourishing. Of particular note is the potential for the thinking techniques that we illustrate here to integrate and make complementary agendas and perspectives that may seem unconnected and in opposition to one another. Therefore, careful and systematic formulation of the problem statement is critical not only in illuminating the complexity of social work problems and concerns but in providing the structure for discussion, analysis, and social work responses that advance tolerance and pluralism (DePoy & Gilson, 2007; Kukathas, 2003).

Unlike many evidence-based frameworks that do not differentiate problem and need, we see these two processes as distinct from one another. A **problem** is a conceptual-value assertion of what is undesirable and/or in need of attention and change, while a **needs statement** is a systematically supported pathway that guides specific actions necessary to engage, examine, verify, and resolve all or part of the problem as it is stated. Problem definition is therefore precise but is not a research enterprise. It is simply a value statement of what needs to change. Need statements define how the change should occur and thus can be are investigated by research thinking and action as we discuss below (DePoy & Gilson, 2009).

Begin, for example, with the following problem statement about Janice (Exemplar #1):

As a result of functional losses resulting from a cerebrovascular accident (CVA), Janice is depressed.

In this statement, what is undesirable? Both the cause (CVA) and the result (depression) are implicated. Conversely, by stating what is desirable, a problem statement directly or indirectly indicates what is valued. Now we reword the previous problem statement to illustrate:

With assistance to address functional limitations, Janice is likely to adapt.

In this statement the desirable (adaptation) is identified as desired outcome of assistance. CVA is an undesirable as well but has already occurred and thus cannot "unoccur." Yet, this diagnostic condition should not necessarily be omitted from an expansive problem statement as it may provide knowledge for social work in areas beyond work with individuals. We illustrate this point later in the chapter in our discussion of mapping strategies.

Now consider one more example to illustrate the value-based nature of problem statements.

> People with low literacy levels are at a disproportionately greater risk for smoking-related illness and fatality.

Two undesirables (smoking related illness and fatality) are stated with two implied (low literacy and smoking). Because of the complexity of this problem statement, desirables can be phrased in numerous ways, including the following examples:

- Smoking prevention reduces illness and fatality.
- Smoking prevention and cessation information should be accessible to people with diverse literacy levels.
- Literacy should be improved.

Although problems are often considered as entities outside and apart from those who conceptualize them, consistent with contemporary thinking, problems are contextually embedded and individually defined. Thus, a problem statement exists on a continuum from personal through social, emerging from the values and interests of those who are naming the problem (Best & Harris, 2013).

Consider an illustration from exemplar #5—As a result of the reasonable accommodation standard of the ADA and ADAAA, workplace accommodations have been insufficient to maintain Elton in his job as janitor. He is unemployed and facing eviction and homelessness.

First, consider accommodation. Employers might consider the cost and effort of accommodation excessive and burdensome, while for Elton, who requires such responses in order to remain employed and earn a living, accommodation would be a solution, not a problem. Attorneys may not find insufficient accommodation problematic but rather as an opportunity for work. The taxpayer who bears the cost of public assistance may see the employer as the problem, given that the employer's acceptance of the fiscal burden would decrease unemployment and potentially the numbers of people supported by public safety nets.

Thus, problems are differentially articulated by each person who defines them. So how would social workers locate and decide which problem statements fall within their purview and which do not? While professionals address problem statements that affect different levels of concern, from individuals through cultural phenomena, Eitzen, Zinn, & Smith (2012) claim that a problem becomes public and of concern to social work when it attracts political and social attention and is positioned within the public and professional arenas of justice, fairness, well-being, and resource allocation. Thus, a problem statement in itself is not generated through research, but systematic thinking informs and clarifies problems as we discuss later in this chapter. Problems are axiological or value-based claims, not empirically generated knowledge.

Consider obesity as an example. Diverse weights have characterized human populations throughout existence, but claims of how much people should weigh and why have been contested only within recent history (Gilman, 2008). Using current vernacular, people have been overweight and obese for eons, but only within the past 2 centuries has the professional world focused its attention on obesity prevention and treatment (Gilman, 2008). The conversations about the need for a healthy diet and exercise have been ramped up as the economic, employment, public health, and, to some extent, personal costs of obesity are realized and documented (Vigarello & Delogu, 2013).

Similarly, although people have smoked throughout human history, smoking has only gained significant political and professional attention as a "problem" over the past 50+ years, particularly in the United States. But, as just illustrated, defining obesity and smoking as problems to be eliminated has negative consequences to those who do not agree (Gilman & Zhou, 2004). For example, states in which tobacco is grown derive economic benefit from it, and thus, the smoking prevention itself may be an economic problem in such states.

Thus, a well-developed problem statement in which values are clarified is essential for social workers to identify the desirable outcomes of their actions and then enact evaluative thinking and action to determine the extent to which they succeeded. Further, without clarifying a problem, as discussed later in this chapter, the rationale for what is being done by social work intervention is unclear. Problem statements articulate the reason that social workers practice and state the changes that should occur as a result of what we do.

Ideally, social work seeks to influence and/or resolve issues and problems by addressing all or part of what is needed to change the problem in a valued direction. However, with the action orientation so characteristic of contemporary social work practice, it is not unusual for practitioners to move to activity that is believed to "work." Unfortunately, the problems to be addressed are too frequently omitted from intentional thought and communication. The questions of "works" to do "what" and "how" are not possible to answer without a clear problem explication. While well-meaning in efforts to quickly remediate problems and diminish negative consequences, the omission of the thinking step of problem clarification opens the door not only to **error** but also to inability to be accountable for illustrating the value of social work in resolving or even addressing the social problems for which the profession exists (Alkin, 2013; Preskill & Catsambas, 2006).

Each year, we ask our students to conduct interviews with practicing clinical social workers to ascertain the problems/issues/concerns addressed in practice and to identify how professionals know that their clinical activities are effective in producing desired outcomes. It is not unusual to find that most practitioners have no formal mechanism to evaluate intervention success, no clearly articulated problem/issue/concern for which their practice is initiated, or any systematic evidence to support their clinical action agenda. Thus, the efficacy of counseling over other forms of intervention cannot be empirically or logically supported since the purpose for the clinical social work intervention is not precisely articulated. Moreover, even in popular news media, the benefit of counseling and "talk therapies" to clients is challenged (Carey, 2015).

Consider Janice, for example. Her first clinical encounter following her illness occurred with a social worker who chose Jungian theory to guide her intervention. The problem as articulated by Janice, however, did not lend itself to this approach, as we discuss later. The social worker failed to clarify the problem for which Janice sought help, and thus the social work intervention failed.

Now, consider the public health issue of smoking prevention efforts as an example. As part of a national effort to reduce tobacco and other substance use and dependencies in the United States, the National Association of Social Workers developed a professional credentialing program to certify alcohol, tobacco, and other drugs social workers (NASW, 2016). Inherent in this initiative are several value-based principles that frame substance abuse as a problem for some groups. The following are some examples:

1. Tobacco and other substance abuse is an undesirable behavior with undesirable causes, correlates, and consequences.

2. Tobacco and other substance abuse should be prevented.

3. Tobacco and other substance abuse should be prevented by social work intervention.

As reflected in the work of Eitzen et al. (2012), none of these claims are research statements. Moreover, the value statements above are certainly not relevant or useful to corporations that produce and sell cigarettes and other tobacco products.

Now consider the statement below, justifying the credentialing approach undertaken by NASW. This excerpt references research as the basis for credentialing, but as discussed below, is actually a need statement minus a clear problem.

In 1998, NASW conducted a survey of its membership, in which respondents clearly identified the need for and a strong level of interest in NASW establishing and offering a national certification program in areas of social work specialization. NASW is pleased that this program helps NASW members in today's competitive workplace attain

1. Enhanced professional and public recognition

2. Increased visibility as specialized social workers

3. Association with a select group of specialized social workers who have attained national distinction. (NASW, n.d., p. 1)

There is a disconnect between the inferred "problem" related to substance abuse as harmful, listed above, and the action strategy of credentialing. Nowhere in the NASW materials that proposed licensing "specialist" social workers for practice with substance abuse did a problem statement appear that mentioned any undesirable circumstance associated with the lack of a specialty credential. The problem is inferred as inadequate workforce development in the third statement only (Association with a select group of specialized social workers who have attained national distinction), yet the extent to which professional activity can effect a change in substance abuse behavior or even if substance abuse was the problem to which certification was directed is unclear (Lemmens, Oenema, Knut, & Brug, 2008). Skeptics suggest that credentialing has little to do with alcohol, tobacco, and drug abuse prevention (CASA, 2013) but rather is a planned effort for providers to garner economic recognition and advantage through training fees and carving out and branding expertise in the context of a reimbursable professional activity, ergo the need for specialization. If the problem statement had focused on what was missing without credentialing, NASW would have countered this criticism before it got out of the gate.

THINKING PROCESSES OF PROBLEM AND ISSUE CLARIFICATION

By social problems, we are referring to the problem statements that social workers identify and address within their scope of concern. Although it may seem simple to specify a problem, precise problem clarification is an intricate task that requires careful and exacting thinking processes. Look at the examples below to illustrate some of the common mistakes made in problem statements.

First, Consider Vague Problem Specification

The first and most basic error is the failure to articulate a problem statement at all. By examining the myriad examples of "the problem" of substance abuse already discussed, it is simple to see how broad, complex, and different this phenomenon is to those individuals and groups who are concerned with it. Thus, stating that substance abuse is a problem does not do any substantive work in articulating the nature of the problem, its causes, and its consequences and thus areas for social work intervention and **outcome**.

Just consider the diverse ways in which "tobacco abuse" is defined and seen as a problem or not. We recently returned from a trip to Eastern Europe in which, unlike in many states in the United States, cigarette smoking remains an accepted public behavior rather than a "substance abuse" problem. Cigarette smoking is allowed and frequently observed in public spaces including restaurants, buildings, and even some hospital areas. But one need not look internationally to illustrate the vagueness of the "tobacco use problem" since, in the United States, the nature of tobacco abuse is also differentially defined depending on context, values, and perspectives. From a public health perspective and the recent "Real Cost" campaign launched by the U.S. Federal Drug Administration in early 2014 to combat smoking (Goszkowski, 2008; Kaplan, 2014), any tobacco use is considered problematic.

Consider, for example, the effort in New York City to elevate the legal age for buying cigarettes from 18 to 21:

> The proposal would make the age for buying cigarettes and other tobacco products the same as for purchasing liquor, but it would not prohibit people under 21 from possessing or even smoking cigarettes. (Hartocollis, 2013)

Implied is that purchase would deter use, but use or even possession is not considered illegal under this scheme. So while health and social service professionals may consider tobacco use and its negative health consequences as the "problem," vendors and owners of smoking establishments might view the strategy of delimiting the pool of product purchasers more problematic than the risks of smoking. Moreover, tobacco use is not a unitary phenomenon nor accepted by all as a problem given the large body of systematic inquiry identifying the income, age, gender, and class correlates of tobacco use and laying bare the contextual nature of defining tobacco use as a problem.

Another Common Mistake Related to Vague Problem Definition Is Failure to State the Scope and Complexity of a Problem

Consider why tobacco use would be problematic. Who smokes, what are the consequences, which consequences can be tolerated by whom, where, and when, and so forth? Why does the problem as initially stated even exist? In the statement "tobacco use is a problem," none of these elements is even broached. How each person hears and interprets tobacco use thus shapes the nature of the problem and is relative and individual.

Stating a Problem in Terms of a Preferred Solution Is Another Error That Frequently Occurs

As illustrated above, the solution stated in Principle #2, "tobacco and other substance abuse should be prevented," is an outcome preference statement since it speaks to what should happen rather than what is problematic. By articulating Principle #2, the only solution is prevention, narrowing the range of responses to a singular focus.

The logical and conceptual difficulties typical of many problem statements are vast and too numerous to cover here. We refer you to literature on cognition and logic to further explore conceptual errors that may contribute to vague and ill-defined problems (Kane & Trochim, 2006; Reike, Sillars, & Peterson, 2012, Walton, 2013). To avoid being limited by an inadequately stated problem, let us illustrate a powerful tool, problem mapping. This process comprises thinking strategies to conceptualize and clarify complex problems from multiple value perspectives as we demonstrate below.

Problem mapping is based on the technique of concept mapping first popularized by Novack in the 1970s (Novack, 2010; Kane & Trochim, 2006). Simply put, concept mapping is the visual representation of relationships among concepts or ideas. According to Kane and Trochim (2006), concept mapping is a cognitive operation that falls under the rubric of "structured conceptualization" in which a logic sequence can be traced, documented, and visually represented. Concept mapping techniques have been used in multiple areas including but not limited to business, healthcare, policy, education, and design (Novack, 2010; Schmehl, 2014).

Within examined practice, concept mapping is a technique for "social problem mapping." This method is a purposive thinking and visualization strategy that links disparate views of what is a problem, its causes, and its consequences together for the purpose of identifying areas and opportunities for professional activity, collaboration, and evaluation. To briefly illustrate the benefit of problem mapping in forging conceptual and human collaborations, let us revisit the prevention strategy of workforce development.

A simple problem map as shown in Figure 2.1 on page 24 would have been useful in locating workforce development within the larger context of tobacco and other abuse prevention. Moreover, problem mapping is a useful tool in drawing out logical and incremental expected or hoped-for outcomes and their assessment approaches when the initial problem statement is vague or too large to be assessed.

The two-step method has proven very useful not only to expand the thinking process about social work problems and issues but to identify values, chart a direction for subsequent thinking and action processes in examined practice, and ultimately to bring disparate conversations and perspectives together to advance understanding and tolerance to which social work is committed.

To interpret this diagram, look at the text boxes and directional arrows. The three concepts are sequentially linked beginning with limited formal education, which is necessary for workforce development. The argument that limited research and knowledge are necessary to prevent tobacco and other substance abuse is compelling and thus would have made sense if positioned in a problem map. Furthermore, scrutinizing outcomes at any point in the map becomes relevant to evaluating prevention of tobacco and other substance abuse, even if prevention cannot be directly observed and measured (DePoy & Gitlin, 2015). For example, suppose you selected insufficient knowledge as the part of the problem to tackle. You then implement an educational program and test the knowledge and skills obtained by the participants. If they have acquired the knowledge that is deemed to be important for prevention, you have made an important improvement in prevention as you have addressed one of the causes of substance abuse. So without measuring actual reduction in substance use, you can verify that part of the problem has been resolved and can move on to tackle other parts of this complex issue. We now turn to a detailed presentation and discussion of problem mapping.

Clarification of the Problem: Mapping and Force Field Analysis

Problem clarification consists of two sequential thinking processes: mapping followed by force field analysis. Both are structured thinking tools (DePoy & Gilson,

Figure 2.1   Education and Substance Abuse

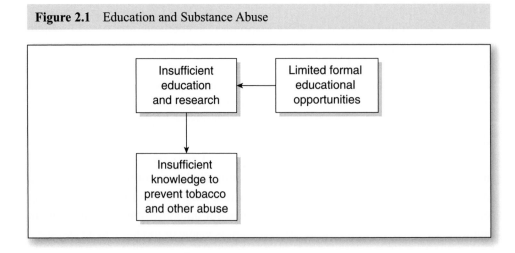

2007), but each has a different scope and purpose. Together, they make a powerful thinking team. Depending on purpose, force field analysis may be omitted, particularly when the scope of the problem is local, delimited, or specific to an individual client.

Problem mapping is a thinking process through which problems, no matter how they are initially conceptualized and/or stated, can be expanded, grounded in value, and be awaiting activation from acceptable professional sources. Problem mapping is a superb tool to assist social workers to identify the context in which their thinking and action take place, to specify problem parts and sequences, to illuminate what part of the problem can be addressed within the scope of social work, to identify collaborations with others, and to set the path for the next step of direct analysis of what might be needed to do so.

Through problem mapping, one enlarges a problem statement beyond its initial conceptualization by asking two questions repeatedly: "What caused the problem?" and "What are the consequences of the problem?" In Figure 2.1, only one causal question was posed. The map, while useful, was incomplete.

Now, consider this problem statement in Figure 2.2 to illustrate the full process.

To conduct problem mapping, first conceptualize a problem as a river, as in Figure 2.2.

The initial problem statement articulated in the diagram is your first step into the river to pick up one rock. The water flowing to that rock from upstream

Figure 2.2   Cigarette Smokers Continue to Smoke Despite the Evidence That Smoking Is Harmful

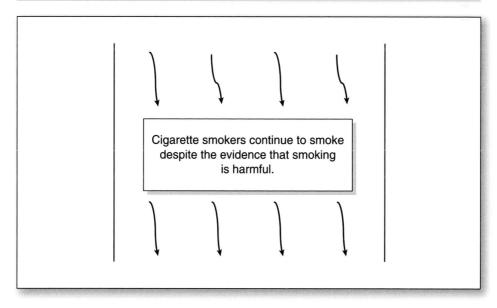

Cigarette smokers continue to smoke despite the evidence that smoking is harmful.

shapes the rock, the initial problem statement, while the rock itself influences the water and river that flows from it. The downstream waters are therefore the consequences, or in this analogy, what happens as a result of the rock. Therefore, looking upstream we see causes; looking downstream, consequence. Thus, the flow of ideas from above the initial statement shapes the problem and the flow away from the initial idea is influenced by the problem statement. Using the example, only six of many possible causes of the problem stated in Figure 2.2 are listed below:

1. Cigarette smokers may not be aware of all of the negative primary, secondary, and tertiary health and environmental consequences of smoking.

2. Cigarette smokers may not believe assertions about the negative primary, secondary, and tertiary health and environmental consequences of smoking.

3. Cigarette smokers do not care about the negative primary, secondary, and tertiary health and environmental consequences of smoking.

4. Nicotine is extremely addictive.

5. Advertising promotes smoking as "chic."

6. Cigarettes are available and legal for purchase for adults over the age of 18.

Mapping upstream again from the initial set of causal statements, explanatory sources are expanded even further. Only consider several causes of the first tier causal statement #1 (cigarette smokers may not be aware of all of the negative primary, secondary, and tertiary health and environmental consequence of smoking) as an example for now.

1. There is insufficient information available to the public about the negative primary, secondary, and tertiary health and environmental consequences of smoking.

2. Available information to the public about the negative primary, secondary, and tertiary health and environmental consequences of smoking is not accessible to many, including those with low literacy.

3. The placement of information available to the public about the negative primary, secondary, and tertiary health and environmental consequences of smoking is not efficacious, and thus does not reach a large spectrum of individuals.

4. Smokers ignore information about the negative primary, secondary, and tertiary health and environmental consequences of smoking.

Map upstream one more level using statement #3 (the placement of information available to the public about the negative primary, secondary, and tertiary health and environmental consequences of smoking is not efficacious, and thus does not reach a large spectrum of individuals) from above to consider these three causes:

1. Provision of widespread information about the negative consequences is expensive and time consuming.

2. Provision of information about the negative consequences is limited by tobacco companies and lobbyists.

3. Dissemination of information about the negative consequences of smoking is a task that requires special skills.

Revisit the discussion above about prevention workforce development in which the connection between the problem and the activity was missing in action. Using problem mapping reveals at least one logical thinking trail that resulted in the chosen strategy to address part of the expanded problem statement (Cigarette smokers continue to smoke despite the evidence that smoking is harmful). Thus, rather than guessing at why workforce development was undertaken, the problem mapping approach articulates the logical and axiological material.

Now look downstream at consequence mapping, illustrated below with only five of many possible consequences.

1. Cigarette smoking causes lung damage.

2. Cigarette smoking causes health damages to nonsmokers.

3. Cigarette smoking creates excessive refuse.

4. Cigarette smoking is expensive.

5. Cigarette smoking carries a negative stigma in some social groups.

Now, through asking the question again (What are the consequences?) of the first tier of consequences, mapping further downstream occurs. For illustration purposes, look at some second tier consequences related to the initially articulated consequence: Cigarette smoking causes lung damage. Only three of many consequences are posited here:

1. Lung damage compromises health, leading to illness and premature death.

2. Lung damage interferes with daily function.

3. Lung damage is costly in lost productivity and excessive health care costs.

Figure 2.3 illustrates the full problem map just created. Each box above the initial problem is a broad answer category to what caused the problem. As demonstrated above, creating the problem map is an iterative (repetitive) process. Once the first-tier causes of the problem are identified, continuing to ask the question "What caused the cause of the problem?" and so on will result in reaching cultural and/or social value statements. Below the initial problem statement, repeatedly asking the questions "What are the consequences?" and "consequences of consequences" and so forth contracts the scope from broad cultural cause to the impact of the problem on individuals. The problem map therefore expands the problem statement from cultural-social causes to personal impact and values, providing many different places to target professional activity, as well as topical areas for further inquiry and specification.

As illustrated in the map, there are many causes and consequences related to and emergent from the initial problem statement, some of which are addressed by multiple professional groups, some by social work exclusively, and some by none. For example, physical health issues would be the primary province of

Figure 2.3   Smoking Problem Map

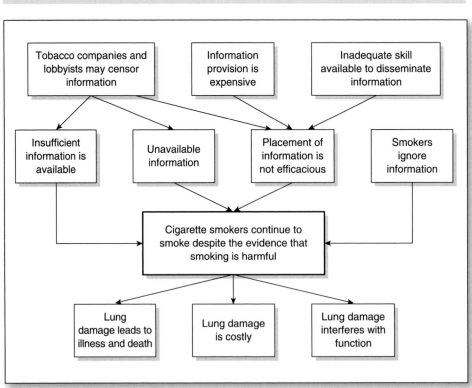

public health and social work providers, while information access would be the concern of multiple social work, educational, health, and business professionals. Issues related to social stigma might be the purview of social work in concert with advertisers, public health professionals, community organizers, and school personnel, while policy and legislative allowance for tobacco production and consumption would be the concern of macrosocial workers, legislators, and lobbyists. Counseling individuals would be undertaken by clinical social work, perhaps even by those especially credentialed for substantive abuse practice. Certainly, the cost of a pack of cigarettes is not a direct action agenda of social work or of health providers but could be tackled indirectly through legislative and social action.

Using the problem mapping technique, the initial task of each professional is to identify the elements of an issue presented that are within his or her professional scope, skills, and resources. However, a second and critical use of problem mapping is collaboration. By locating one's professional activity within a broad analytic context, social workers can visualize the potential contributions and collaborative opportunities of others outside of their own professional groups and seek productive interdisciplinary relationships that can only enhance and hasten complex problem resolution. Once the scope of the problem and the points of action are identified in the problem map, planning through force field analysis can be conducted. We turn to that topic now.

Force Field Analysis

Force field analysis is a planning tool developed by Lewin (1951) in the 1940s. This classical planning approach was based on "holistic psychology," which suggests that a network of factors affects an individual's decision-making process (Hustedde & Score, 1995, p. 5). Lewin (1951) was interested in the influence of phenomena and their subsequent actions on factors such as government, the kind of work an individual did, family members, and personal ambitions.

Lewin demonstrated force field analysis thinking through elaborate diagrams of "life space" or "psychological space" pertaining to and affecting individuals (Hustedde & Score, 1995, p. 5). These diagrams appeared as a series of directional vectors depicting the nature and strength of the influence of relevant factors (driving and restraining) on the object of change. Driving factors are those which advance the issue while restraining forces limit it. Identifying these factors provides visual guidance for intervention. So if you want to maintain or expand your issue, the driving forces would be important to use. Conversely, decreasing or eliminating the issue or circumstance would warrant use of restraining forces. Since its inception, force field analysis has been widely used in diverse professional domains including but not limited to business, psychology, education, economics, social science, and public health and community planning (Accel, 2013). As evidence of its value, force field analysis software and online tools have become increasingly popular to guide the analytic process (Mindtools, 2016; Skymark, 2013). Across these fields, there are several basic models of force field analysis, all which tend to share common elements (DePoy & MacDuffie, 2004).

The first commonality is the use of force field analysis for problem identification, analysis, and goal setting. A second use is the thinking process of applying a relevant body of information to the identification of restraining and driving forces that impact each problem segment. Third, all models share the step of identifying which influences and resources can be targeted for action (Skymark, 2013). Thus, at its basic level, force field analysis includes a clear definition and dissection of influences, both positive and negative, on a specified part of a mapped problem (Skymark, 2013).

Of course, in addition to shared characteristics, the scholarly literature and web resources on the use of force field analysis as a planning tool to frame and structure change reveal variations of Lewin's original model. The beauty of force field analysis is that it provides a simple, comprehensive, yet compelling diagrammatic picture of identified influences that maintain and/or impact a situation at a given moment. Through force field analysis, assessment and change can be systematically planned if the following three areas are addressed: (a) a multilevel analysis of an issue or problem, (b) inclusion of pluralistic information and evidence from numerous **variables** to examine the influences affecting a situation, and (c) an analysis of the factors that serve to affect **stability** and change in a situation (DePoy & MacDuffie, 2004). If these three elements are addressed, force field analysis can be used to enhance organization and specificity so that reaching issue-specific change goals captures complexity, and resources can be exploited, thereby simultaneously decreasing impediments to change.

Given its history and diversity, force field analysis is a power tool for further clarifying and honing the scope of the problem to which social work activity is directed. Force field analysis is an excellent thinking strategy in identifying primary and secondary targets of change; resources both existing and needed to enhance problem resolution; barriers to be avoided, diminished, or eliminated; and stakeholders who can accelerate social change.

Where does one begin? Review the problem map in Figure 2.3 above. The social worker would identify targets for change depending on purpose, expertise, professional scope, timing, and context. Look at the choices of causal statements below within the scope of social work and other collaborating professions.

There is insufficient information available to the public about the negative primary, secondary, and tertiary health and environmental consequences of smoking—*social work, public health, health education*

Available information to the public about the negative primary, secondary, and tertiary health and environmental consequence of smoking is not accessible to many, including those with low literacy—*social work, technology experts, technology corporations*

The placement of information available to the public about the negative primary, secondary, and tertiary health and environmental consequences of smoking is not efficacious and thus does not reach a large spectrum of individuals—*advertising and marketing, public health, social work*

Smokers ignore information about the negative primary, secondary, and tertiary health and environmental consequences of smoking—*public health and social work and health providers, insurance industry*

Now look at a force field analysis for the following causal statement:

Available information to the public about the negative primary, secondary, and tertiary health and environmental consequence of smoking is not accessible to many, including those with low literacy.

Once the statement is selected it becomes activated and functions as a center point of analysis to identify the factors that contribute to maintaining the problem, those that do or have the potential to make it worse, and those that could be harnessed to remediate the problem in part or in total. Although force field analysis can be done by a single individual, it is frequently conducted as a group activity (Mindtools, 2016; DePoy & MacDuffie, 2004). Collaborative work can enhance the process by bringing diverse evidentiary and experiential sources to bear on the analysis (Accel, 2013). However, decisions about who is involved and the specifics of the process are dependent on purpose.

Following the clarification of the problem, participants in the analysis identify the driving (positive) and restraining (negative) forces that maintain the problem as is, and thus if carefully and skillfully manipulated, would affect movement toward the desired goal of alleviating part or all of the problem as stated. In professional social work action, systematic evidence enters the process at this point. Each force and its magnitude should be well supported by credible knowledge such that uncertainty is eliminated.

How the analytic process is staged and conducted depends on purpose, resources, and context. In the example below, members selected for the force field analysis group were asked to consider their own experiences and knowledge as evidence for identifying influences on the problem statement. There were many forces identified by the group, but for illustrative purposes, we illustrate with just the six driving and restraining forces that follow:

Driving Forces

1. The potential and diversity of electronic information delivery systems

2. Reasonable costs of disseminating information on the internet

3. Extensive information already existing on the negative consequences of smoking

Restraining Forces

1. Diverse methods of information consumption among the target population

2. Limitations of print material for the diverse target population

3. Lack of skilled professionals who can make information available in multiple formats

Once forces have been identified, each is then rank ordered to represent its perceived importance in maintaining the status quo (DePoy & MacDuffie, 2004; Accel, 2013). This step identifies the strongest and least potent force candidates to use in social action.

Looking at need and action planning based on the driving and restraining forces identified in the two lists, rank order and analysis of each reveals that all are important and can be engaged and/or addressed. Further, one or more professional groups might collaborate with social work to develop a strategy for the creation and dissemination of accessible educational information about smoking consequences enlisting the driving forces and minimizing or eliminating the restraining forces. However, as presented in the next chapter, in the examined practice model, action would be initiated only after the conduct of a full systematic needs assessment to determine what strategies are needed and what goals and objectives are to be achieved by social work action.

A two-phase approach to problem identification using mapping and force field analysis is depicted in Table 2.1. See also Figure 2.4, which follows.

In this example, a value of 6 was assigned on a scale between 0 and 10 (10 denoting the problem or issue being as bad as it can get, and 0 denoting that the problem is no longer active). The rating scale is not static or prescribed and thus

Table 2.1 Steps in Two-Phase Force Field Analysis

Phase 1: Preparation —Problem statement is clarified through constructing a problem map and identifying the arena for change.

Phase 2: Conducting the Analysis— Identify the magnitude of the problem and place it within a grid illustrating its severity.

Step 1: Based on multiple sources of knowledge, identify and visually depict driving and restraining forces.

Step 2: Each force is rank ordered as a target for intervention from most important to those that will not be addressed at all.

Figure 2.4 Visual Depiction of the Force Field Analysis

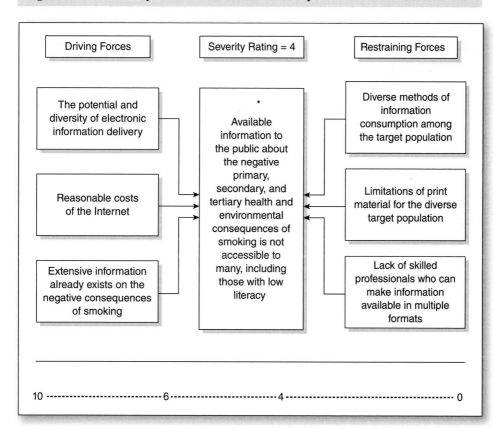

can be selected based on purpose and context. In this example, the 0 to 10 range was useful since it is amenable to incremental quantification and simple translation into percentages over the course of the examined practice sequence. Although

Figure 2.4 is a rudimentary map, so to speak, of the thinking processes of social workers and other key informants, it provides what Tufte (2001) suggests is beautiful evidence. That is to say, the visual grounds the concepts within a context, and depending on purpose and resources, force field analyses can be represented with a full range of complexity to simplicity, with various visuals integrated to communicate the process. In Figure 2.4, the location of the active problem statement between 0 and 10 denotes its magnitude, and the length of the arrows denotes the contribution of each vector to the maintenance of the phenomenon. This simple diagram provides a rich visual tapestry to guide subsequent action, through identifying barriers and resources to be addressed in needs assessment, planning, and professional activity. In addition, the construction of a visual image provides the basis for assessing and representing movement and change against the initial understandings of the active problem.

GROUNDING NEEDS IN PROBLEM AND ISSUES TO BE RESOLVED

Once a problem or social issue has been expanded through mapping (and force field analysis if it is used), systematically determining what is needed to address the part of the identified problem as scope of practice follows. Before exploring need in detail, revisit the distinction between problem and need. As discussed above, a problem is a value statement about what is undesirable or targeted for change.

Distinct from a clarified problem or issue, a need statement is an action claim supported by research thinking and action, linked to all or part of a problem, which specifies what conditions and social work activity are indicated to prompt the desired change. The identification of need involves the purposive use of one or more of the three traditions of inquiry. Experimental-type methods verify need while naturalistic traditions are best suited to discovery. The needs assessment may be conducted by the social worker or obtained from research literature.

Consider what could happen if need is not clarified and the social worker moves from a problem immediately to an action. As providers, we might assume that we know the needs of a **population**, group, or individual and skip this step. Dean's experience illuminates the dangers of such an omission.

Dean, a jazz musician in his early 20s, was hospitalized after he sustained a complex fracture of his left hip. When interviewed in the emergency department, Dean reported that he believed that he could fly and was injured in an attempt to take off from a second story window in his home. Dean was immediately placed on the short-term psychiatric floor of the general hospital where he was seen by the mental health care team. During his intake interview with the social worker, Dean indicated that he had some experience with cocaine and other "recreational drugs" but not within the past few weeks. He reported previous episodes of believing that he could fly. After a routine work-up, Dean was referred to substance abuse rehabilitation. There, he was started on risperidone for the treatment of delusions and enrolled in substance abuse counseling with a social worker. In efforts to avoid future injury, Dean complied with all recommendations. Yet, over the next 3 months, he gained 20 pounds, was anxious, and was unable to concentrate on practicing or performing music. At 4 months into his treatment, Dean, fully compliant with his intervention plan, once again was hospitalized for fractures sustained in a fall as he tried to fly out his second story window.

What went wrong for Dean? One might assume that he engaged in substance abuse while in treatment. However, in addition to the failure to expand the problem statement (injury in an attempt to fly off the roof of his house) to causes and consequences, what was needed to help Dean was poorly investigated and accepted without sufficient systematic support. Because of his career as a musician and history of recreational drug use, other causes of delusional thinking were not seriously considered until the second episode. Had the social worker and health care team conducted a comprehensive needs assessment, they would have learned that Dean had a long history from childhood of the same delusion of flying capability. Causes other than drug abuse should have been investigated. Dean was finally diagnosed with a seizure disorder, medicated properly, and discharged from substance abuse treatment.

As noted above, at this stage of the examined practice sequence, the social worker may already have access to systematically developed and supported information on which to formulate need, or one may conduct needs assessment research to clearly delimit and identify need. In the example of Dean, a comprehensive research-based approach to move beyond supposition would have been indicated, and alternative needs other than substance abuse intervention could have been found in the literature.

A need statement should specify who is (are) affected by the problem, how, what changes are desired, what specific part of the problem is in need of change, what strategies are needed to create the change, the desired degree of change, and how one will recognize that the change occurred. In examined practice, need is based on systematically derived knowing from a full range of credible primary or secondary sources.

But why is knowledge created by research used as the legitimate basis for professional social work knowing at the needs assessment stage? As illustrated by Dean's story, besides the error of assuming without verifying one's hunches, another issue is important to acknowledge. Knowing through research, no matter what position one takes about the value of different types of knowing (Byers, 2011), clarifies both the nature of evidence on which a claim of need is based and the logical thinking trail, so to speak, of how evidence was used to support or derive this claim. Evidence and its interpretation are thus transparent and open for audit. Given the clarity and capacity in systematic inquiry to follow knowledge derivation and use, a well-supported need statement displays within it the evidence for what it claims as the means to address a problem. Moreover, knowing why, how, who, what, and when about a need determines direction for goal and objective development as well as for intervention strategy.

Think back to the workforce development and credentialing example and what evidence might be compelling enough to direct fiscal resources to support this strategy over others as an avenue for prevention of substance abuse. One set of evidence that might be used is research on professional curricula requirements and the rationale for credentialing across disciplines. As an example, investigation of relevant practice from nursing contributes to this body of knowledge, given nursing's regular approach of developing and credentialing specialties, one being substance abuse and addictions prevention (IntNSA, n.d.). A second convincing set of data emerges from investigating the judicial system, which determines expertise in a particular content area in part on formal credentialing (Segal, 2008).

In any needs assessment, formal research strategies, previously and well-conducted studies, and logically scrutinized practice comprise the knowledge base upon which professionals, scholars, researchers, policy makers, and funders communicate about and come to consensus of need. The use of research thinking and action therefore not only allows funding, policy, and professional decisions to be made on values (as would be the case if the problem statement solely were used for allocation decisions) but also adds a set of support both credible and essential to the professional world to warrant and justify tackling value-based undesirables (DePoy & Gilson, 2007).

How does one therefore decide how to proceed with systematic examination of need? First and foremost is clarification of the purpose of assessing need. Purpose guides the magnitude and nature of needs assessment thinking and action. For example, in seeking to inform a successful intervention with Dean, the social worker might do the following:

1. Consult the research literature on factors other than substance abuse leading to delusions

2. Obtain more complete and systematic social and personal history data, thereby amassing a comprehensive data set on which to make clinical decisions

Yet, in Exemplar #3 (People with low literacy levels are at a disproportionately greater risk for smoking-related illness and fatality), what was needed to improve access to smoking cessation and prevention information required a more extensive and collaborative process such that a research team was involved in planning a needs study. Given the complexity, a mixed-method inquiry was undertaken (we detail this research tradition later in the text). The results revealed the need for low-literacy web-based information that could easily be translated by automated text to speech in aural formats. The team therefore proceeded to meet the need through innovative web design and dissemination of this tool (Gilson & DePoy, 2009).

Once purpose is clarified, the three questions in Table 2.2 below further hone the methods through which systematic needs assessment is conducted.

What Is Known About a Need?

To ascertain what is already known about need, a comprehensive information review is indicated. As we discuss in Chapter 7, reviewing information can be a huge and daunting task. To make it potent, purposive, and manageable, approaching review both practically and systematically is warranted. At minimum, the social worker critically considers the general knowledge presented about need to determine the current level of theory development, the explicit and implicit value base, the methods used to generate the knowledge, the degree to which this knowledge is relevant to the scope of the needs assessment, and the extent to which the knowledge is applicable to the **target**(s) of change. Existing resources may suffice to systematically define need, but if not, knowledge has to be synthesized, applied in a manner different from what is advanced in the literature, or developed anew. At that juncture, research is indicated.

Nature of Knowledge

A major consideration in determining what is known about the need and its linked problem statement is the nature of knowledge. By nature of knowledge, we mean the level of theory development, how this theory has been generated and how it has been supported. Consistent with methodological literature (DePoy & Gitlin, 2016;

Table 2.2 Developing Systematic Assessment

What is known about a need?
What else needs to be known and how?
What limitations are imposed on needs assessment by resources and time?

Rubin & Bellamy, 2012), systematic knowledge can be divided into three levels of theoretical development: descriptive, relational, and causal/predictive. These incrementally complex levels are anchored on research thinking and action in both naturalistic and experimental-type inquiry briefly defined in Chapter 1 (DePoy & Gitlin, 2015) and discussed in detail in Section II.

Descriptive Knowledge

This level of knowledge provides an understanding, illumination, and detailing of a phenomenon by answering the question "What is it?" (Mertens, 2010). The essential characteristics, examples, nonexamples, and borderline cases of the phenomenon emerge from a descriptive process. From empirical description, what the phenomenon is and what it is not should be clear. What is and what is not a need therefore can be clarified and understood. Descriptive knowledge can be produced by both naturalistic and experimental-type inquiry or by mixing traditions.

As an example, if the social worker is satisfied with the definition and relevance of current theory and practice knowledge, and is seeking to assess the magnitude of need, experimental-type strategies would be appropriate. However, if entirely new understandings of the need are indicated, naturalistic approaches to develop new theoretical tenets would be undertaken. Think of Exemplar #4 (Elders abandon prescribed walking devices, resulting in sedentary lifestyles and related negative consequences of inactivity). According to the research conducted by Bateni and Maki (2005), functional ineffectiveness is a major reason that elders do not use prescribed walking aids. However, Kennedy (2016) challenges this claim, suggesting that abandonment creates an opportunity for innovation in thinking and action. Relying on experimental-type traditions to examine what has already been successful in meeting a goal would therefore not be useful since novelty and newness are not hallmarks or aims in this research tradition.

Relational Knowledge

Once a phenomenon is described, its relationship to other factors and/or contexts can be ascertained. What factors are present and/or change as the phenomenon appears and changes? How strongly are two or more factors associated? What is the direction of the association? What is the web of association? This level of knowledge begins the process of expanding understanding beyond knowing "what" something is to knowing "how" something relates to or is embedded in something else. Thus, a statement of need moves beyond a unitary descriptive lens to begin to construct how need is distributed, related to other needs, embedded in contextual factors, influenced, and ranked in priority. Moreover, understanding how phenomena relate to one another may shed light on how each will change as specific needs are met and addressed. For example, consider Exemplar #5 (As a result of the reasonable accommodation standard of the ADA and ADAAA, workplace accommodations have been insufficient to maintain Elton in his job as janitor. He is unemployed and facing eviction and homelessness.) Inquiry to understand the context and associated factors that prevented Elton's retention on the job revealed his recent exacerbation of Parkinson's Disease, resulting in difficulty walking. An examination of the evidence suggested that Elton's employer, responding to Elton's use of a rolling walker, assumed that he would be required to erect expensive ramps inside and outside of the building. The second and most illuminating influence revealed by systematic interview was employer and employee ignorance of other accommodation strategies so that Elton would be able to navigate the small building. Assuming a single descriptive reason (use of wheeled mobility device) for Elton's inability to do his job resulted in his unemployment, which was legally sanctioned within the undue financial hardship clause in the ADA.

Typically, experimental-type research has been used to examine relationships, based on the notion that in order to relate something to something else, both "somethings" must be clearly understood. However, as naturalistic traditions become more widely valued, these methods, too, can reveal important and complex relationships that may be overlooked with the deductive quantification that is the foundation of **experimental-type design**. Of particular note is the value of naturalistic inquiry in revealing the natural setting. One caution about relational knowledge is in order. "Association is not causation" is a phrase that we have often heard and too frequently do not heed. When associations are found, causal inferences cannot be implied by them without further appropriate research thinking and action. As an example, Dean both had prior experience with cocaine and was injured because of delusions. These two factors are related in that both are part of Dean's experience, but as we learned, substance abuse was not the cause of Dean's delusions.

Predictive/Causal Knowledge

As explicated by the category name, this level of theory development answers the question of "why?" Once phenomena are related, seeking explanations for cause as a basis for further understanding need and positing goals that address the "why" rather than the "what" or "how" of a need are warranted. Looking at the host of strategies through which causal relationships are examined, note that **true-experimental design** is the most widely accepted and valued method of supporting causal claims (DePoy & Gitlin, 2016). However, as discussed later in the text, naturalistic strategies can be used to produce understandings of cause as well within natural settings (Reiss, 2009). Consider Exemplar #3. Because of the conceptual distance between digital inequality and maintenance and thus prevention of substance abuse, it is not likely that an experimental design itself would be able to support a direct causal relationship between the two. However, through mixing experimental-type and naturalistic traditions, a contextual understanding of the following causal relationships was developed (Gilson & DePoy, 2009):

1. Access to prevention knowledge contributes to healthy decision making.

2. Limited access to information does not provide individuals with information on which to make informed substance use decisions.

3. Limited access to information in the rural state in which the needs assessment was conducted is caused by limited English literacy and inability to comprehend electronic information.

Scope of Knowledge

Equally important as answering what is known about need is the relevance of content to the specific part of the problem delimited. Does the existing knowledge describe the social worker's domain of concern; apply to the population who owns, identifies, or is concerned with the problem; address policy specific to the problem, and so on? The experimental-type thinking strategy of identifying the extent to which existing knowledge informs need within those boundaries is a critical step in needs assessment. As an example, to determine what would be needed for Elton to resume employment, knowledge about simple ergonomics and navigation methods used by other small businesses for employees who experience changes in mobility would be valuable and thus would have been at least one avenue to guide social work action.

This point leads us to the second thinking strategy relevant to needs assessment, that of identifying what else in addition to the knowledge found in the literature needs to be known and how?

What Else Needs to Be Known and How?

At first blush, the "what else" question seems to default to naturalistic inquiry as a means to develop new knowledge. And while this systematic tradition is often incredibly productive, it is joined by numerous other sources of information.

As discussed in Chapter 1, a major and underused source of social work knowing is social work practice itself, providing that practice is thoughtfully and systematically characterized through research thinking and action. (Reflexive intervention is one way to assure that the repository of practice knowledge is well developed and considered as a credible source of social work evidence.)

A second approach to discovering what is not known is to consult diverse fields and forms of knowing outside of what has traditionally been considered to be the social work knowledge base. Consider the enduring "knowing power" transmitted in art, music, film, literature, and so forth. As an example, Cohen (2012), a photographer, and Miller (2010), a material culture theorist, have been unexpected sources in informing what could be needed for many elders to accept and use mobility devices. Their systematic research in this visual field highlights the role and importance of "things and objects" as well as style in creating positive personal and public identity. Along with knowing derived from theoretical and artistic counterparts of Cohen and Miller (Candlin and Guins, 2009; Pullin, 2009), a literature and artifact review crafted the rationale to support research which unearthed the role of appearance and perceived stigma created by medicalized appearing mobility equipment typically prescribed for mobility support. Thus, in addition to functional disappointment, or for many by itself, appearance was empirically revealed as the major barrier that needed to be overcome in order to promote adoption and use of mobility devices by those who needed them for safety, balance, and function (DePoy & Gilson, 2014).

What Limitations Are Imposed on Needs Assessment by Resources and Time?

This question must be answered to guide needs assessment. What use are the best-laid plans if they cannot be implemented? Frequent reasons for omitting needs assessment from social work action include limited time and inadequate resources to take busy social work practitioners away from social work doing. So rather than neglecting the step of determining what is needed to resolve or address a social work problem and thus falling prey to ineffectual practice, creative needs assessment strategies that fit within resources and time should be the goal. Collaboration with those who have both the time and expertise for needs assessment may be indicated. For example, social work educators often are seeking sources of data to guide their research agendas. Or field students who are conducting required research for their degree completion can be called upon.

SUMMARY

This chapter has covered significant ground. In it, the discussion began with the nature of problems, strategies for clarifying them, and then an overview of the step of determining what is needed to influence problems in a desired direction. Section II delves into the "how" of needs assessment as the chapters explore and detail research thinking and action using the three primary inquiry traditions.

The main points in this chapter are as follows:

- The distinction between problem and need is a critical element of examined practice.
- Problem statements are assertions of value.
- What is considered to be a problem may differ among diverse groups and individuals.
- Expansion and clarification of problem statements using the tools of problem mapping and force field analysis provide the precise scaffold for understanding what social work activity and collaboration are necessary to influence a social problem in a valued direction.
- Understanding need involves the conduct of systematic approaches crafted with purpose, resources, and time in mind.

REFERENCES

Accel. (2013). *Force field analysis*. Retrieved from www.accel-team.com

Alkin, M. C. (2013). *Evaluation roots: A wider perspective of theorists' views and influences* (2nd ed.). Thousand Oaks, CA: Sage.

Bateni, H., & Maki, B. (2005). Assistive devices for balance and mobility: Benefits, demands, and adverse consequences. *Archives of Physical medicine and Rehabilitation, 86*, 134–145.

Best, J., & Harris, S. (2013). *Making sense of social problems*. Boulder, CO: Lynn Reinner.

Byers, W. (2011). *The blind spot*. Princeton, NJ: Princeton University Press.

Candlin, F., & Guins, R. (2009). *The object reader*. London, UK: Routledge.

Carey, B. (2015, October 20). New approach advised to treat schizophrenia. *The New York Times*. Retrieved from http://nyti.ms/1LAjHnm

CASA. (2013). *The polemics of certification and credentialing*. Retrieved from http://www.casa-stpete.org/blog,the-polemics-of-certification-and-credentialing

Cohen, A. S. (2012). *Advanced style*. New York, NY: PowerHouse.

DePoy, E., & Gilson, S. (2007). The bell-shaped curve: Alive, well and living in diversity rhetoric. *The International Journal of Diversity, 7*, 254–259.

DePoy, E., & Gilson, S. (2009). *Evaluation Practice*. New York, NY: Routledge.

DePoy, E., & Gilson, S. F. (2014). *Branding and designing disability*. Abingdon, Oxon, UK: Routledge.

DePoy, E., & Gitlin, L. (2015). *Introduction to research: Multiple strategies for health and human services* (5th ed.). St. Louis, MO: Mosby.

DePoy, E., & Gitlin, L. (2016). *Introduction to research*. St. Louis, MO: Elsevier.

DePoy, E., & MacDuffie, H. (2004). Force field analysis. *Journal of Health Promotion Practice, 5*, 306–313.

Eitzen, D. S., Zinn, M. B., & Smith, K. E. (2012). *Social problems* (12th ed.). Englewood, NJ: Prentice Hall.

Gilman, S. (2008). *Fat: A cultural history of obesity*. Malden, MA: Polity.

Gilman, S., & Zhou, X. (2004). *Smoke: A global history of smoking*. London, UK: Reaktion Books.

Gilson, S., & DePoy, E. (2009). *Tobacco access portal project*. Retrieved from http://ccids.umaine.edu/research-projects/completed/tap

Goszkowski, R. (2008, March 21). *Among Americans, smoking decreases as income increases*. Retrieved from http://www.gallup.com/poll/105550/among-americans-smoking-decreases-income-increases.aspx

Hartocollis, A. (2013, October 30). New York raising age to buy cigarettes to 21. *New York Times*. Retrieved from http://www.nytimes.com/2013/10/31/nyregion/new-york-approves-law-to-raise-tobacco-purchasing-age-to-21.html?_r=0

Hustedde, R., & Score. (1995). *Force-field analysis: Incorporating critical thinking in goal setting*. Milwalkee, WI: Community Development Society. Retrieved from http://files.eric.ed.gov/fulltext/ED384712.pdf

International Nurses Society on Addictions (IntNSA). (n.d.). Retrieved from http://www.intnsa.org

Kane, M., & Trochim, W. (2006). *Concept mapping for planning and evaluation*. Thousand Oaks, CA: Sage.

Kaplan, K. (2014, February 4). FDA emphasizes 'real costs' of smoking in campaign aimed at teens. Los Angeles Times. Retrieved from http://www.latimes.com/science/sciencenow/la-sci-sn-fda-real-cost-anti-smoking-campaign-20140204,0,3002785.story#axzz2smTBTw4Z

Kennedy, P. (2016). *Inventology: How we dream up things that change the world*. New York, NY: Eamon Dolan/Houghton Mifflin Harcourt.

Kukathas, C. (2003). *The liberal archipelago: A theory of diversity and freedom*. Oxford, UK: Oxford University Press.

Lemmens, V., Oenema, A., Knut, I., & Brug, J. (2008). Effectiveness of smoking cessation interventions among adults: A systematic review of reviews. *European Journal of Cancer Prevention, 17*(6), 535–544.

Lewin, K. (1951). *Field theory in social science*. New York, NY: Harper and Row.

Mertens, D. (2010). *Research and evaluation in education and psychology: Integrating diversity with quantitative, qualitative, and mixed methods*. Thousand Oaks, CA: Sage.

Miller, D. (2010). *Stuff*. Malden, MA: Polity.

Mindtools. (2016). *Force field analysis*. Retrieved from http://www.mindtools.com/index.html

National Association of Social Workers (NASW). (2016). *The Certified Clinical Alcohol, Tobacco, and Other Drugs Social Worker (C-CATODSW)*. Retrieved from https://www.socialworkers.org/credentials/specialty/c-catodsw.asp

National Association of Social Workers (NASW). (n.d.). *Information booklet with application and reference forms. Certified Clinical Alcohol, Tobacco, and Other Drugs Social Worker (C-CATODSW): For the experienced MSW substance abuse counselor*. Retrieved from https://www.socialworkers.org/credentials/applications/c-catodsw.pdf

Novack, J. D. (2010). Learning, creating, and using knowledge: Concept maps as facilitative tools in schools and corporations. *Journal of e-Learning and Knowledge Society, 6*(3), 21–30. Retrieved from http://www.je-lks.org/ojs/index.php/Je-LKS_EN/article/viewFile/441/433

Nussbaum, M. (2013). *Creating capabilities: The human development approach*. Cambridge, MA: Belnap.

Preskill, H. S., & Catsambas, A. T. (2006). *Reframing evaluation through appreciative inquiry*. Thousand Oaks. CA: Sage.

Pullin, G. (2009). *Disability meets design*. Boston, MA: MIT Press.

Reike, R., Sillars, M., & Peterson, T. (2012). *Argumentation and critical decision making*. New York, NY: Pearson.

Reiss, J. (2009). Causation in the social sciences: Evidence, inference, and purpose. *Philosophy of the Social Sciences, 39*(1), 20–40.

Rubin, A., & Bellamy, J. (2012). *Practitioner's guide to using evidence-based practice* (2nd ed.). Hoboken, NJ: John Wiley.

Schmehl, P. (2014). *Introduction to concept mapping in nursing.* Burlington, MA: Jones and Bartlett.

Segal, D. (2008). The growing admissibility of expert testimony by clinical social workers on competence to stand trial. *Social Work, 53*(2), 153–163.

Sen, A. (2009). *The idea of justice.* Cambridge, MA: Belknap Press.

Skymark. (2013). *The new nexus 7.* Retrieved from http://www.skymark.com/resources/tools/force_field_diagram.asp

Tufte, E. (2001). *The visual display of quantitative information* (2nd ed.). Cheshire, CT: Graphics Press.

Vigarello, G., & Delogu, C. J. (2013). *The metamorphoses of fat: A history of obesity.* New York, NY: Columbia.

Walton, D. (2013). *Methods of argumentation.* New York, NY: Cambridge.

Chapter 3

SETTING GOALS AND OBJECTIVES FOR REFLEXIVE INTERVENTION

O nce a clear, well-reasoned, and credible understanding of need is achieved, the action process of setting goals and objectives to guide reflexive intervention can be initiated. Recall that reflexive intervention is the action part of social work during which the practitioner systematically assesses his or her practice. We proceed sequentially beginning with goals and objectives and follow with reflexive intervention.

EMERGENCE OF GOALS AND OBJECTIVES FROM NEEDS STATEMENT

Goals and objectives provide the structure for professional action and clarify desired outcomes at one or more time intervals. The action process of goal and objective formulation is critical as it is the first step in which specific accountability criteria are set.

Goals are broad statements about the ideal or "hoped for" (Coley & Scheinberg, 2013). They look forward in time to general "desirables." Thus, goals are not simply value statements but rather are tethered to problem resolution because they emerge directly from articulated problems and what has been supported by previous or conducted research that reveals what is needed to effect the problem. Goals guide what should be accomplished and changed through social work activity. Because this model of social work is purposive throughout its entire thinking and action processes, goals are purposive as well. Expected goal attainment can range from immediate to the long-term and can be simple or complex. Consider the following exemplar of the tobacco prevention project.

As illustrated in Chapter 2, the problem of inaccessible public health information was selected as the locus for change. Consistent with the purpose of assuring that information was not only accessible but also free and always available, and informed by the force field analysis, the social worker collaborating with an interdisciplinary team proceeded to examine and verify need using a mixed-method inquiry. The methods are detailed in Section II. Results revealed the need for innovation using technology and automation such that the driving forces were optimally exploited.

An intermediate goal therefore was articulated:

Use information technology to translate existing smoking cessation and prevention information into multiple accessible formats.

Long-term goals included the following:

Improving the availability and use of substance abuse prevention information.

In the example above, the direct relationship between need and goal is seen in the intermediate goal of expanding access to information using contemporary technology. The long-term goals of information dissemination and improvement in the availability of public health knowledge are linked directly to the part of the problem statement that addresses the "undesirable" of inadequate public health knowledge. Note that decreasing smoking was not articulated as a goal to guide this social work activity since it cannot be controlled and thus cannot be promised as an outcome of the intervention. We return to this important point later in this chapter.

Because goals are broad statements of what is desired, how the goal will be attained and how the social worker will know that it has been attained must be specified. These two elements are the purposes of objectives and frame the nomenclature for three types of objectives: process, outcome, and output objectives. The completion of all three can be researched while goal attainment cannot.

Objectives are therefore operationalized goal statements. The process of operationalization has several steps. First, it involves specifying a definition in words of a **concept** or what is referred to as a lexical definition. Operationalization involves the translation of the words in the lexical definition into action, observation, ascertainment, and/or measurement (DePoy & Gitlin, 2016). For example, tobacco abuse is a concept defined in words (lexically) as the unhealthy use of tobacco products. Operationalizing the concept of tobacco abuse could be done in several ways. For example, counting the daily cigarette consumption and setting an unhealthy quota is one method. Observing the number of cigarette packs purchased by an individual is another, albeit indirect. Diagnosing the negative effects of tobacco use on health would be an alternative operational definition. Or simply asking for a self-report is frequently used to measure the concept of tobacco abuse.

Goals are abstractions of what is desirable. Objectives provide the action steps on how, when, and who will do what to achieve goals and how it can be known that they are achieved. Recall that we indicated that goals cannot be operationalized because they are vague value statements. Thus, the challenge in establishing objectives is to make sure that they are operationalized so that they will provide information to determine if, how, when, and what effort was required to attain the goal. Objectives that specify actions (how) are process objectives, and those that specify outcomes (what resulted) are outcome or summative objectives. Output objectives refer to "descriptive indicators of what the specific activities generate" (Knowlton & Phillips, 2013, p. 7). So if the expansion of smoking cessation information was only made available in text format, the goal of expansive, multimethod access would not be achieved.

Process (also called formative or monitoring) objectives state what activities will be done, how, when, and by whom, while outcome (summative) objectives delineate how one will know success in producing a desired result from what was done. Both types of objectives are derived from goals statements (Coley and Scheinberg, 2013). Outputs specify products.

Consider the example of using information technology to translate existing smoking prevention information into multiple accessible formats. Table 3.1 presents process objectives, and Table 3.2 lists primary outcome objective. Outputs are exemplified in Table 3.3.

Outcome (summative objective) for intermediate goal: Use information technology to translate existing smoking prevention information into multiple accessible formats.

There are several important points to note in these objectives. First, they are time sequenced. Second, some are process objectives, one is summative, and one

Table 3.1 Process Objectives

Intermediate Goal Statement: Use information technology to translate existing smoking prevention information into multiple accessible formats.

Objectives

1. Determine expertise to be assembled
2. Convene project team
3. Develop a work and funding plan
4. Identify the content to be disseminated
5. Develop automated literacy translation software
6. Link the text translation software to text to voice and language translation portals
7. Pilot test the system
8. Conduct focus groups to determine website design preferences
9. Develop website design
10. Pilot test website
11. Revise website based on pilot test findings
12. Host formal website and disseminate it widely to diverse user audiences

Table 3.2 Primary Outcome Objective

Diverse users of all reading levels will access and consume information on the website.

Table 3.3 Output

The website will be produced.

is an output. Third, each objective can be assessed according to the degree of its completion. Later in the chapter, these points are further detailed. But for now, examine and analyze how goals and objectives structure the sequence of professional activity and create a platform for directing attention to a particular source of evidence to be used to assess objective completion. Process objectives are those that will be used to guide monitoring and **formative evaluation** or, in the examined practice model, the comprehensive process of reflexive intervention. Outcome objectives are used to determine summative value of professional action. Output objectives relate to concrete product or service or effort that can be costed out and entered into a cost-benefit analysis (Knowlton & Phillips, 2013). The objectives as stated in this example are not "measurable" until the source of evidence and the way the evidence will be used to assess objective completion are articulated.

Some definitions of objectives specify that they must be measurable as stated (Coley and Scheinberg, 2013); however, we do not agree. First, not all objectives will or should be measured. All will be *assessed* using research approaches, but some may be assessed in ways that do not use numbers as **indicators**. As an example, affective response to a mobility device is typically observable and narrative, but not numeric. So while changes in affect can be proposed and assessed, the assessment scheme may not be expressed in numbers. Or consider Janice's progress. Her life satisfaction and engagement may be systematically examined through narrative rather than numbers.

Second, objectives provide a structure for reflexive intervention. Until these points are examined in more detail, suffice it to say that objectives are critical statements about action processes and expectations that provide the foundation for reflexive intervention and **outcome assessment**. The objectives in Table 3.4 on page 50 present a structure for the action processes and outcomes necessary to attain the intermediate goal of using information technology to translate existing smoking prevention information into multiple accessible formats in the Tobacco Access Portal (TAP) example.

But how are these objectives ascertainable? As stated above, the "how" is not specified in either the left or middle column and thus needs to be crafted using research thinking and action that follow one or more of the traditions of inquiry. The right column in Table 3.4 adds this detail. The table

1. links each objective to a success criterion,

2. identifies evidence on which to assess the criterion, and

3. creates a timeline to assess the timely completion of each professional action.

Table 3.4   Intermediate Goal Statement for the TAP Project: Use Information Technology to Translate Existing Smoking Prevention Information Into Multiple Accessible Formats.

Objectives	Timeline	Assessment Strategy
1. Determine expertise to be assembled	Month 1	Areas of expertise identified and names assembled
2. Convene project team	Months 1–3	Agreements and team assignments completed
3. Develop a work and funding plan	Months 3–12	Funding and work plan for prototype completed
4. Identify the content to be disseminated	Month 12	All materials are completed and documented
5. Develop automated literacy translation software	Month 12–18	Complete and host prototype website
6. Link the text translation software to text to voice and language translation portals	Month 18	Completion of linkages
7. Pilot test the system	Month 18–22	Conduct mixed-method trials
8. Conduct focus groups to determine website design preferences	Months 18–22	Complete focus groups with diverse users and report
9. Develop website design	Month 22–24	Finalize design and functionality
10. Pilot test website	Months 24–28	Test functionality, preference, and use in diverse user groups
11. Revise website based on pilot test findings	Months 28–30	Complete web design and navigation in response to pilot testing
12. Host formal website and disseminate it widely to diverse user audiences	Month 30+	Completely functional website hosted, tracking analytics and broad dissemination Design research on web use and tobacco prevention learning in target populations

Thus, the structure of examined practice is set for the action, for the determination of which action process addresses each objective, and for the delineation of when and the extent to which objectives are successfully achieved. The thinking process of specifying objectives begins to illustrate how distinct parts of interventions can be monitored, linked to outcomes, and thus generate social work knowledge.

The specification of process objectives thus provides the guidance to systematically reflect on professional action. Building on Schon's (1983) classic work, the term "reflexive intervention" was therefore coined to denote our ideal approach to professional activity as one in which careful and informed scrutiny through research thinking and action is not only possible but an essential part of all professional activities, products, services, and entities.

Illustrating the thinking process of establishing objectives to accomplish a long-term goal, look above at Objective 12. Derived from the needs assessment, a long-term goal was specified: Improve the availability and use of substance abuse prevention information. Objective 12 and its measurement look forward to developing inquiry to examine the extent to which these objectives were met and the goal achieved. The output objective in Table 3.4 specifies what and how many (one) services or products (the TAP website) will be produced.

So far, the general thinking process of relating goals to objectives has been illustrated. However, many different goals and objectives can be formulated to achieve the same need. We now move to the action processes of translating needs into goals and objectives.

DERIVING GOALS FROM NEED STATEMENTS

As illustrated, even in the presence of a clear and well-documented needs statement, many goals can be relevant to the same statement. Once again, consider the example of the TAP project. What if the need were crafted to target tobacco companies to develop alternatives to tobacco such as the multiple herbal substitutes for nicotine (Montesines, 2008)? This approach addresses the same needs statement of tobacco smoking prevention and cessation but from a differing perspective. Each strategy has its advantages and limitations, and none is the "correct" or "incorrect" way to structure the aim of a professional entity. Some are within the domain of social work, and others are not. For example, crafting antismoking legislation would not be a social work function whereas testimony and advocacy would be actions in which social workers engage.

How are needs translated into goals? There is no simple answer or formula, but there are action processes and principles that guide this step. As in all steps in examined practice, values and purpose within the scope of social work frame how need is translated into action. If the social worker were committed to corporate accountability, social action to pursue this agenda would be indicated. However, if agency purpose and social work values centered on the right of access to health information, automated web translation of the large body of prevention knowledge would be preferred.

Second, the context for social work action delimits goal setting. If, for example, the social worker is an employee of a public health agency, expanding accessible public education might be more aligned with the agency mission than macro action necessary to influence corporate social change.

Third, the literature or previous professional experience may provide systematic guidance for goal setting. As an example, the research literature on positive outcomes of increasing health literacy is compelling and thus may form the foundation for the goal of expanding access to knowledge that informs an individual's choices and health decisions.

Fourth, what limitations and advantages are provided by resources? If, for example, the social worker did not have programming expertise or access to computer science colleagues, web-based accessibility would not be feasible. Fiscal resources must also be considered. Comparative costs may thus shape goals.

ACTION PROCESS OF CRAFTING PROCESS OBJECTIVES

To develop sound process objectives, the program goals should be clear, and the financial, time, material, and human resources must be known. Objectives and their success criteria are then specified to guide reflexive intervention and illuminate how successful attainment of objectives can be known. Table 3.5 presents a set of guidelines for the action process of writing process objectives. These type of objectives form the foundation for reflexive intervention by precisely structuring what is to be done.

Table 3.5   Action Process Guidelines for Writing Process Objectives

1. Each objective must be derived directly from one or more goals.
2. Process objectives must be time sequenced.
3. Only one activity per objective should be described so that it can be directly assessed.
4. The objective should identify what, who, when, and how an activity will be enacted to result in an outcome.
5. Statements of objective must be clear and unambiguous.
6. Process objectives must be written such that the expected time of completion can be specified in assessment of the objective.
7. Process objectives are purposive.
8. Process objectives must consider resource limitations.
9. Process objective completion must be assessable by collection and analysis of systematic evidence without looking at outcomes.
10. Accountability (who does what) is specified by process objectives.

ACTION PROCESS OF CRAFTING OUTCOME OBJECTIVES

Outcome or summative objectives specify successful outcome criteria (what benefits or changes resulted from or followed completion of process objectives). They also structure how success will be conceptualized and demonstrated. Similar to process objectives, outcome objectives are clearly stated, with each addressing a single desired outcome of an intervention. Outcome objectives also provide the structure for timing of outcomes. That is, outcome objectives indicate when an outcome should occur and at what level. Thus, crafting outcomes states what is expected as reasonable, but not impossible due to factors that cannot be controlled or even anticipated. Recall that the Tobacco Access Portal did not specify a decrease or the elimination of smoking as an outcome. While desirable for the smoker, the provision of information cannot promise to produce this outcome. And while abstinence may be the object of all prevention and cessation interventions, quitting smoking cannot be the success criterion for the project because it is not within the social worker's capacity to control the behavior of others. Outcome objectives therefore are shaped by the purposes and type of the intervention and what can be achieved or feasibly changed. Thus, all outcomes should be designed to make a change in the problem map in one or more cause or consequence, but may not eliminate the problem as it is initially stated.

Revisit the outcome objectives in the TAP project once again. Each specifies who will do what or what will happen as a result of a professional action. Note that outcome objectives do not specify how the activity will be organized (since this job belongs to process objectives). Rather outcome objectives lay out what should occur after and/or as a result of professional action and for whom and how outcomes can be known (some through measurement and others through nonnumeric forms of systematic assessment.)

There are several important considerations in developing outcome objectives. Table 3.6 presents guidelines for crafting outcome objectives.

Not surprisingly, outcome is not easy to assess. The causal links between professional action and outcome often are challenging to investigate due to the limitations of systematic strategies available to do so. Keep this point in mind when developing outcome objectives so that formalized expectations are not unattainable or unable to be assessed. Sound outcome objectives are those that make sense for social work attention, are within the scope of social work practice, are consistent with the expertise held by the "doers," are possible, and provide the structure to examine the links between project and outcome.

Table 3.6   Guidelines for Writing Outcome Objectives

1. Specify the desired results of the project, and translate into objectives that detail each result.
2. Link outcome objectives to one or more goals.
3. Clarify the desired impact of social work action by including as appropriate, what, who, when, and where in the objective statement.
4. Delimit both the scope and the nature of the impact so that it can be known through systematic research using one or more of the inquiry traditions.
5. Write each objective so that it provides the structure and rationale for the selection of data collection and analytic techniques that can best reveal the nature and degree of desired impact.
6. Do not promise what cannot be delivered.

CHARTING OUTPUTS

Output objectives specify parameters of products, services, or reach. In social work, outputs often are framed in terms of how many clients are seen, service hours provided, educational sessions delivered, publications produced, and so forth. Within examined practice, as discussed in this chapter and in Chapter 4, output objectives are used both in reflexive intervention and in the assessment of the outcomes of a social work action. As an example, the TAP output objective specified one product, the website, to be developed during the reflexive intervention phase. The "how much/how many" question sets the stage for evaluating cost on the basis of productivity. Consider the clinical social worker who sets an objective to provide 50-minute sessions to five clients daily over a 5-day work week. This social worker can then look at the ratio of time to dollars generated to determine the fiscal efficiency of social work practice and then examine how many sessions produced the desired change outcome.

Grounding Social Work Activity in
Goals and Objectives: Reflexive Intervention

Once goals and objectives are formally established, the social work action agenda is set in motion. Looking back in the examined practice sequence, goals and objectives are designed to fulfill one or more of the systematically supported needs that arise from a broad problem statement. Because examined practice incrementally builds each subsequent step on the expanded problem, and given the definition of a problem as a statement of value, all actions are therefore value-based. Reflexive intervention is thus a series of activities contained within the value framework articulated in the problem statement. The term *reflexive* refers to practice action that is carefully and systematically scrutinized such that what was done, by whom, with whom, to whom, and how are linked to why and thus form a credible and useful source of social work knowledge. This application of research strategies to the systematic monitoring of action is one primary element that distinguishes reflexive intervention from other models of social work activity.

The term *reflexivity* is used in naturalistic research to indicate the thinking process in which investigators identify the influences they bring to a study and to the analysis that shapes the knowledge derived therefrom (Gilgun, 2010). Schon (1983) was well known for his work on the "reflective practitioner," one who routinely examines professional activity in the service of learning from doing. Expanded beyond individual learning and applied to social work action, reflexivity within the intervention phase describes social work action in which professionals individually and collectively are engaged in a systematic examination of their work, resources, use of self, and other influences on professional process, outcome, and thus, social work knowledge. Moreover, because Lyon, Mollering, & Saunders (2012) have associated reflexivity with trust, the critical importance of reflexivity in all professional social work domains is intended to engender trust and confidence from within and outside of one's professional group.

From the reflexive intervention perspective, research thinking therefore does not cease or pause during the implementation of social work action. A hallmark of professional practice ostensibly is precise decision making based on systematically derived evidence (Freidson, 2001). Reflexive action not only guides social workers to use this organized approach to decision making but directs the professional to seek credible feedback from the actual professional activity itself, as well as from examination of use of self in and other factors that bear on one's practice (DuBois & Miley, 2013). Thus, unlike the professional whose practice is skill based and intuitive, the social worker who applies the principles of reflexive intervention carefully and seamlessly integrates research into studying the implementation of goals and objectives through systematically monitoring all phases of "doing." That is not to say that practice wisdom and intuition do not occur. They do, but in examined practice, the social worker makes it a point to be well aware of the bases from which he or she is making decisions, identifying the nature of each, and then going one step further to formalize them using research thinking and action. Then he or she carefully looks at all activity to obtain clarity about what was done, how, and why. Careful thought about practice is the key to generating knowledge from social work action.

Consider the following example. Dean's assumed need for psychiatric and substance abuse intervention produced the goals of his sobriety and the outcome objective of elimination of substance-produced delusions. Reflexive intervention, however, revealed that despite Dean's compliance, his regular attendance and engagement in substance abuse counseling, the outcome objective was not met. The social worker used this knowledge to identify the failure of the intervention strategy and of the outcome objective. This careful monitoring led to obtaining additional data on which to craft an alternative need statement. Once revised, the need for medical intervention was established and appropriate goals and objectives were recrafted.

In concert with the trends for professional accountability (Dekker, 2007; Freidson, 2001), systematically investigating need and grounding goals and objectives on logically derived principles are warranted. Moreover, reflexive intervention guides translation of research-based knowledge into practice and in turn legitimates knowledge-generated practice.

Selection of an Approach—Translating Goals and Objectives Into Action

By the time the social worker has reached this action phase of examined practice, it is likely that he or she will have a good idea of what action processes will occur. Supported by the theoretical approach and skills basis for action, each of the previous steps provides a firm knowledge foundation to inform choice of action process. Yet, because of the social work propensity to take immediate action to decrease suffering, it is not uncommon for social workers to move to "doing" without articulating a systematic rationale for professional work (Reamer, 2013). This absence, however, does not mean that a sound justification does not exist. Using examined practice, social workers have the logic tools and structure to identify and communicate their reasoning in a deliberate and transparent manner such that professional action is not only accountable but also builds on and advances professional knowledge.

Look again at the discussion of force field analysis presented in Chapter 2. Using this strategy in problem clarification is an excellent tool through which to further sharpen and delimit the problem focus of social work intervention and to set the foundation for integrating research into subsequent activity. Recall that the initial step involved stating a problem, estimating its severity, and then looking at the forces (driving [positive] or restraining [negative]) that influence the extent to which a problem remains the same, increases, or decreases in severity (Accel, 2013; DePoy & MacDuffie, 2004).

At this point in the examined practice model, force field analysis serves yet another function: identifying specific actions to achieve goals and objectives. To use force field analysis to plan specific strategies, the thinking processes presented in Chapter 2 are applied to a specific objective rather than to a broad problem statement. Even if force field analysis is not used, engaging in a similar systematic thinking approach enhances specificity and clarity about why an action is selected to achieve a particular outcome, what resources can be used, and what is expected as the outcome of social work doing. By using a systematic approach to action planning, the link between objectives and action processes is deliberate, well communicated, and available for investigation. The social worker both knows and can explain the relationship among objectives, activity, and outcome. The chapters in Section II on outcome assessment expose the difficulty in using research for attributing outcome to professional activity in total or in part. Therefore, the more clarity and specificity in how actions are planned to accomplish goals and objectives, the easier and more useful outcome assessment will become.

Consider this example from the force field analysis informing TAP. A major restraining force, "diverse methods of information consumption among the target population" identified the failure of a single approach to providing public information. Sharing information in text only format excluded too many individuals who do not learn well through reading at the literacy level characteristic of the presentation of current information. The action agenda of expansive access to information was therefore clarified, as was the outcome objective of improving access for diverse knowledge consumers, preparing the social worker to use research for evaluative purposes.

Sequential guidelines for selecting an examined approach to professional action are listed in Table 3.7. Note that we always begin with the problem.

The detail by which the guidelines in Table 3.7 are addressed will be an important determinant in the degree to which one can ultimately attribute changes in outcome to social work activity. We examine this point in greater detail later in the text. Now let us turn to systematic reflexive intervention processes.

Table 3.7 Sequential Guidelines for Selecting an Examined Approach to Professional Action

1. Be clear in the problem statement. To whom does the problem belong, whose values are represented in the statement, which part of the problem is to be addressed, and which stakeholder groups are concerned with the problem?

2. Consult and keep the needs assessment research in mind when planning action. What is needed by whom and why, what is the scope of need, what disagreements exist among stakeholder groups about what is needed, and who can fill the need as articulated? How do you know?

3. Be sure that goals and objectives clearly emerge from and respond to the full scope of need as articulated and supported by research evidence used in the needs statement.

4. Use a systematic thinking process to plan action strategies, based on a sound research- and/or theory-informed rationale that will be conducted to achieve goals and objectives.

5. Consider the purposive, organizational, and resources context of social work activity.

6. Clearly articulate the action processes of social work activity, being sure to detail the temporal sequence, distinct action processes, and outcomes expected from each aspect of intervention.

7. Clearly link each action process to one or more objectives that it is designed to accomplish.

SYSTEMATIC REFLEXIVE INTERVENTION PROCESSES

Reflexive intervention consists of three important evaluative processes: **monitoring**, cost analysis, and analysis of external influences on social work process and outcome.

Monitoring

"Monitoring is the art of collecting the necessary information with a minimum effort" (Gudda, 2011, p1). Applied to social work doing, reflexive monitoring involves using research thinking and action to promote awareness of self in context such that scrutiny and clear documentation of what was done, how it was done, and the resources used can be detailed and applied to knowledge generation and practice advancement. Systematically answering "who, what, why, when, where, and how" questions is a good way to monitor social work action processes. Consider Exemplar #5 (As a result of the reasonable accommodation standard of the ADA and ADAAA, workplace accommodations have been insufficient to maintain Elton in his job as janitor. He is unemployed and facing eviction and homelessness). Recall that the social worker, in constructing a problem map found that the employer assumed that he would be required to build ramps inside and outside of the building. Fearing the cost, the employer opted not to construct the ramps under the undue financial hardship clause of the ADA resulting in Elton's unemployment. In this case, the social worker identified two major needs: immediate response to Elton's fiscal hardship and long-term educational action for small business owners. Many other needs related to this complex tangle of rights, fiscal responsibilities, and human need could have emerged from a convoluted, complex problem map. However, within the scope of social work expertise and agency function, individual client need was initially targeted. The ultimate goal of returning Elton to his previous gainful employment was set with specific objectives of finding workplace accommodations that would be within the budget of the employer and could be shared by Elton when he was rehired.

Cost Analysis

Borrowed from economic research and the for-profit arena, cost analysis is becoming increasingly important for understanding and communicating the economic value of social work knowledge and practice to diverse audiences. As stated by Lamy (2013),

We can estimate the benefits of our efforts calculating how much those . . . efforts are worth to the families that need them as well as to the rest of us, as members of the broader society.

Benefit cost analyses in the social services has put us light years ahead in under-standing the impact of our social programs. (pp. 5–6)

Numerous models of estimating costs have been developed in the for-profit sector and now in the nonprofit arena including benefit-to-cost ratio, social return on investment, and so forth (Lee et al., 2012). Although there are differences in defini-tions of cost and benefit, as well as the equations to calculate them, what all attempt is the justification of cost related to outcome, thereby allowing for economic com-parisons of different approaches. Within logic models that were introduced previ-ously, costs and resources of conducting activity are typically referred to as inputs. Just as a quick reminder, outputs name productions of activity (i.e., number of coun-seling sessions, people accessing websites, etc.). Outputs are distinct from outcomes, defined as what occurs or follows from an action (Knowlton & Phillips, 2013).

Revisit Elton, for example. The inputs of social work effort involving time and cost of finding and informing Elton's previous employer could be calculated using time, supplies, equipment, and expense equations. Outputs could be specified as the number of visits to the employer and trials of access equipment. Determining the cost of immediate outcome would certainly involve what resources were nec-essary and used to return Elton to gainful employment. However, the long-term cost benefits even for this one client would be substantial if Elton remained employed, paid taxes, did not require safety net support, and so forth.

Analysis of External Influences on the Intervention Process and Outcome

There are numerous influences on social work, including but not limited to political, economic, social, cultural, population-based, geographic, virtual, expressive, intellectual, fiscal, and technological factors (DePoy & Gilson, 2012). Thus, within the reflexive intervention process, it is essential to be as expansive and analytic as possible in investigating all the factors that may impact both the outcome of and knowledge generated from social work activity. Once again, con-sider the issues that impact social work practice with Elton. Beyond the typical considerations of policy and resources, simply including attitudes and unsubstan-tiated beliefs about cost on the part of both the employer and Elton were major factors influencing the goals, objectives, and methods of intervention. Without attending to those influences, it is not likely that Elton would have a chance to be rehired. And while Elton's maintenance job requires his presence at the work site, simple technological solutions would be useful in reducing his physical effort. Targeted to Elton's ability to enter, leave, and move around throughout the work-place, the social worker, working online with an access consultant, was able to find inexpensive, lightweight portable ramps for Elton's walker that easily provided access even when stairs were present. The total cost of this access feature was $143, and because it was purchased for Elton, the employer did not have to spend additional funds to keep Elton employed.

USING THE THREE TRADITIONS (EXPERIMENTAL-TYPE, NATURALISTIC, MIXED METHODS) IN REFLEXIVE INTERVENTION

As discovered above when looking at thinking processes of reflexive intervention, the purpose, scope, and practical constraints encountered by the social worker, as well as the **audience** who will receive, read, evaluate, and use the findings, are important determinants in selecting the most beneficial research strategy to capture and transmit practice knowledge. Given the professional, systematic, and deliberate nature of examined practice, relying on the thinking and action process of the three major research traditions is a valued way for professionals to systematically structure and communicate reflexive intervention such that it informs the social worker about the nature of his or her activity, identifies areas for improvement, and ultimately adds to the knowledge base of social work.

Using Experimental-Type Traditions

Although reflexivity is often aligned with naturalistic inquiry, experimental-type designs are both useful and prevalent in studying this phase of examined practice. Unlike outcome assessment, reflexive intervention does not seek cause-and-effect relationships between professional efforts and their results (DePoy & Gilson, 2007). Remember, looking at cause requires that one knows what occurred. So when outcome has not yet happened and is not yet assessed, causal claims are irrelevant. At this phase, it is therefore valuable to use descriptive designs that can identify what was done, what resources were used, and the contextual and internal influences on the intervention process. According to Whitney, Trosten-Bloom, & Cooperrider (2010), reflexive intervention, if enacted systematically, is informative beyond simply being a process of self-examination.

Because of its aims to standardize and/or characterize within-group similarities and between-group differences, experimental-type thinking is indicated when the social worker wants to know about comparisons, the behavior and characteristics of groups of individuals, groups of groups, and/or groups of other units of analysis. It may, for example, be possible that the social worker wants to know if and how diverse genders experience interventions differently. In this case, experimental-type methods that are capable of comparing gender-specific groups would be warranted at the reflexive intervention stage.

Although experimental-type reflexive action answers many questions, inquiries about context and uniqueness of process cannot always be captured by measurement. Naturalistic or mixed-method studies would thus be indicated for these purposes.

Using Naturalistic Traditions

Complexity, flexibility, narrative, and induction, to a greater or lesser extent depending on the specific design, are essential elements of naturalistic inquiry (Fetterman, 2010; DePoy & Gitlin, 2011). The naturalistic tradition is extremely valuable in reflexive processes in that it provides a vehicle through which information can be garnered, even if this information has not been previously theorized or considered prior to the intervention (Patton, 2012). The complexity of description in naturalistic inquiry also lends itself to specifying nuance related to different contexts of social work action. Naturalistic methods are extremely valuable both in describing the richness of an intervention and in providing data about its context.

Of course, the use of both traditions provides the flexibility, depth, and breadth to systematically characterize and examine social work for multiple purposes including the generation of evidence-based practice, as well as understanding the uniqueness of use of self in context. Mixed-method thinking and action, if possible, are thus ideal for reflection, discovery, and accountability.

Using Mixed-Method Traditions

Mixing methods, in our opinion, is most desirable in all examined practice but particularly in reflexive intervention. Integrating approaches allows for multiple forms of data collection and analysis necessary to obtain complex and diverse knowledge upon which to generate immediate ideas for improving practice, for developing evidence-based practice, and for identifying areas for future study and development. Moreover, mixed methods engage multiple interest groups and use of diverse strategies and ways of knowing.

SELECTING A TRADITION—GUIDING QUESTIONS

To select a systematic approach in reflexive intervention, given the multitude of factors to consider, the questions in Table 3.8 provide guidance. The answers to these questions will help structure reflexive intervention within an examined practice framework.

These guiding questions can be valuable tools for finding a viable, systematic, and "doable" strategy for reflexive intervention.

Table 3.8   Guiding Questions for Selecting a Systematic Tradition for Reflexive
Intervention

1. What is the question to be answered by research?
2. What are the purposive considerations (e.g., monitoring, examining cost, developing evidence to inform future practice approaches in the same domain, different domain, etc.)?
3. What are the practical constraints—time, resources, context (e.g., acute, time-limited intervention, community-based intervention, etc.)?
4. What target audiences will benefit from the knowledge derived? In what way?
5. How will each best be able to consume and use the knowledge to improve the intervention, and create knowledge?

ILLUSTRATION

Elton provides an illustration for this chapter.

The initial problem statement: As a result of the reasonable accommodation standard of the ADA and ADAAA, workplace accommodations have been insufficient to maintain Elton in his job as janitor. He is unemployed and facing eviction and homelessness. Figure 3.1 presents the problem map expanding this statement such that its complexity can be understood and needs can be investigated.

As discussed previously, the two statements were the immediate problem areas within the scope of the social work domain chosen as the focus for intervention by the social worker. Note that the employer lack of knowledge formed a long-term agenda as discussed in subsequent chapters. While formal force field analysis was not indicated to address the employer's concern with high cost of accommodation, the social worker still used this thinking strategy to identify driving and restraining forces to further elucidate the issue. The increasing variety, production, and availability of adaptive equipment was determined to be a major driving force and thus was factored into needs assessment. In the needs assessment, literature on equipment was therefore examined revealing a large choice of inexpensive products that were unknown to the employer. The goal guiding intervention was gainful employment for Elton with specific objectives of

Figure 3.1   Problem Map

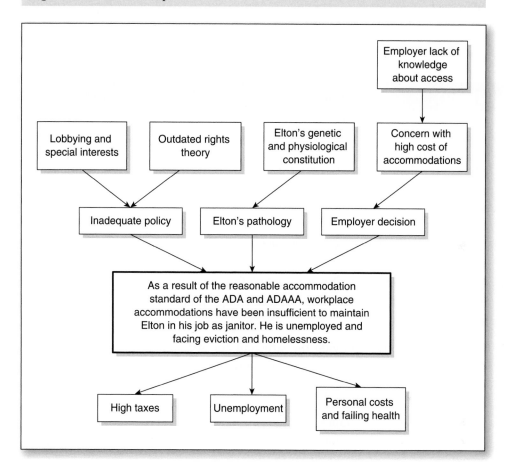

1. compiling a list of options, costs, and funders for accommodations;

2. sharing resources with the employer; and

3. negotiating Elton's return to work.

While potentially seamless, reflexive intervention revealed that this simple intervention was complicated by the employer's reluctance to rehire Elton because of fear that Elton would become ill and engender significant costs. Documenting this barrier, the social worker revised the objectives to include education about Parkinson's disease for the employer and a 6-month trial period during which time the social worker would stay engaged in the workplace in case plans needed to be renegotiated. As a long-term agenda, the social worker identified a problem to be addressed: small business employers' lack of knowledge about access. Specific reflexive methods are discussed in Section II.

SUMMARY

In this chapter, we examined two major elements of examined practice: setting goals and objectives and reflexive intervention. Both were illustrated as steps following but carefully linked to problem and need. A brief discussion of the three research traditions was then presented as the bedrock for generating knowledge within the context of active intervention.

The main points in this chapter are as follows:

1. The action process of goal and objective formulation is critical to the examined practice model because it forms bridges among problem, need clarification, and accountability.

2. Goals and objectives provide the structure for social work action and identify desired outputs and outcomes at one or more time intervals.

3. Goals are broad statements about the ideal or "hoped for."

4. How the goal will be attained and how its attainment can be known are the purposes of objectives and frame three types of objectives: process, outcome, and output.

5. Process (also called formative or monitoring) objectives state what will be done, when, and by whom.

6. Outcome (also termed summative) objectives identify success criteria.

7. Outputs are productions that occur and are typically used to calculate cost to benefit ratios.

8. There is a set of action process guidelines for extracting goals from needs statements and for writing objectives to address goals. In doing these tasks, one must consider purpose, resources, constraints, and values.

9. Reflexive intervention involves the translation of goals and objectives into social work action and concurrent systematic scrutiny.

10. Experimental-type, naturalistic, and mixed-method traditions of inquiry each have unique uses in reflexive intervention.

11. Mixed-method design is the most complete and versatile approach to reflexive intervention.

12. Diverse participants are interested in the answers to different and varied questions in the intervention process.

13. Selecting an approach to reflexive intervention is dependent on purpose, resources, audience, and expected use of the knowledge derived from systematic examination.

REFERENCES

Accel. (2013). *Force field analysis*. Retrieved from www.accel-team.com

Coley, S. M., & Scheinberg, C. A. (2013). *Proposal writing: Effective grantsmanship* (Sourcebooks for the human services; 4th ed.). Thousand Oaks, CA: Sage.

Dekker, S. (2007). *Just culture: Balancing safety and accountability.* Burlington, VT: Ashgate.

DePoy, E., & Gilson, S. (2007). The bell-shaped curve: Alive, well and living in diversity rhetoric. *The International Journal of Diversity, 7*, 254–259.

DePoy, E., & Gilson, S. F. (2012). *Human behavior theory and applications*. Thousand Oaks, CA: Sage.

DePoy, E., & Gitlin, L. (2016). *Introduction to research* (5th ed.). St Louis, MO: Elsevier.

DePoy, E., & MacDuffie, H. (2004). Force field analysis. A model for promoting adolescent involvement in their own health care. *Journal of Health Promotion Practice, 5*(3), 306–313.

DuBois, B. L., & Miley, K. K. (2013). *Social work: An empowering profession.* Pearson.

Fetterman, D. (2010). *Ethnography step by step* (3rd ed.). Thousand Oaks, CA: Sage.

Freidson, E. (2001). *Professionalism, the third logic: On the practice of knowledge.* Chicago, IL: University of Chicago Press.

Gilgun, J. (2010). *Reflexivity and qualitative research.* Kindle Edition.

Gudda, P. (2011). *A guide to project monitoring & evaluation.* Bloomington, IN: Authorhouse.

Knowlton, L. W., & Phillips, C. C. (2013). *The logic model guidebook: Better strategies for great results.* Thousand Oaks, CA: Sage.

Lamy, C. (2013). *American children in poverty.* Lanham, MD: Lexington.

Lee, S., Aos, S., Drake, E., Pennucci, A., Miller, M., & Anderson, L. (2012, December 4). *Return on investment: Evidence-based options to improve statewide outcomes April 2012 update.* Retrieved from http://www.wsipp.wa.gov/pub.asp?docid=12-04-1201

Lyon, F., Mollering, G., & Saunders, M. N. (2012). *Handbook of research methods on trust.* Northampton, MA: Edward Elgar.

Montesines, P. B. (2008, Jan 19). *Herbal cigarette may help smokers quit.* Retrieved from http://newsinfo.inquirer.net/breakingnews/metro/view/20080119-113485/Herbal-cigarette-may-help-smokers-quit

Patton, M. Q. (2012). *Essentials of utilization focused evaluation.* Thousand Oaks, CA: Sage.

Reamer, F. (2013). *Social work values and ethics* (4th ed.). New York, NY: Columbia University Press.

Schon, D. (1983). *The reflexive practitioner.* New York, NY: Basic Books.

Whitney, D., Trosten-Bloom, A., & Cooperrider, D. (2010). *The power of appreciative inquiry* (2nd ed.). San Francisco, CA: Berrett-Koehler.

Chapter 4

EXPLORING OUTCOMES

DEFINITION OF TERMS

The word *outcome* is defined as

> a final product or end result; consequence; issue
>
> a conclusion reached through a process of logical thinking

something that follows from an action, dispute, situation, etc.; result; consequence (Dictionary.com, 2013)

From these definitions, outcome is synthetically conceptualized as something that
follows from a process of logical thinking and action. Note that outcome may not
be directly attributable to social work activity, and thus, as we discuss in detail, the
strongest approaches for exploring outcomes are sometimes creatively choreo-
graphed with multiple methods of inquiry. Consider the Tobacco Access Portal
(TAP) project in which health information and attitude change toward tobacco use
were the desired outcomes. Even in the event that both outcomes were achieved,
determining if the TAP website was the reason that the change occurred is difficult
to do. Many other factors could be responsible for such outcomes, even when not
reported by the client. Because of this difficulty and the need to investigate and
communicate the benefits of social work, well-developed outcome knowledge to
ascertain what social work activity produced or facilitated not only meets the purposes of benefiting direct recipients of social work service but further contributes
to the knowledge base informing the profession.

Outcome assessment in examined practice can be an expansive task, both seeking knowledge about the extent to which planned goals and intended objectives
were achieved as well as revealing unanticipated occurrences that resulted from or
followed social work action. It may be a deliberate step or seamlessly woven into
the full sequence of examined practice. Consider the difference between assessing
the outcome of clinical practice and examining outcome in the elder mobility
project. Clinical social workers monitor outcomes of intervention on a regular
basis even as part of a clinical session whereas in the elder mobility project, outcome assessment was a planned study.

As illustrated by Dean, unintended outcomes can range from extremely positive
to very harmful and thus are essential to study in either planned or integrated outcome assessment. Outcome assessment is therefore defined as the set of thinking
and action processes to examine and verify what occurs as a result of or following
voluntarily or involuntarily exposure/participation to/in a purposive social work
process.

PURPOSES OF OUTCOME ASSESSMENT

Of course, a primary purpose of outcome assessment is to systematically investigate and document the benefits of social work activity and indicate for whom
these benefits occurred. This aim not only justifies social work but equally
important is a determination of who else beyond the targeted social work service

consumers were affected and how. Thus, assessment of both planned and unintended occurrences are contained within outcome assessment.

Consider the TAP website project. Recall that it was initially targeted to low-literacy English speakers. Interestingly, in conducting research on website use, we found that immigrants who had high levels of literacy in their native languages were the most frequent but totally unanticipated user group. Coming to the United States as smokers and finding the habit both expensive and stigmatizing, outcome research revealed that the literacy translation website provided multiple unintended features and benefits to this group. First, low-literacy English text was easier to read and digest than text on higher-literacy sites. However, low-literacy English text had another major benefit. It increased accuracy in automated translation to other languages through sites such as Babelfish and Google translate. Text to speech was also more accurate and clear when a lower reading level was used in narrative. Without examining unintended consequences, this expansive outcome and learning would not have been discovered or available to similar social work information dissemination efforts.

WORTH OF SOCIAL WORK

In his seminal and contentious paper Fischer (1973) asked the question "Is casework effective?" sending the profession into a major debate about the worthiness of social work practice in clinical contexts. In a metareview of numerous studies, Fischer (1973) concluded that social casework was not effective and cautioned, "the issue of effectiveness of practice always must be of paramount concern to the profession and cannot be brushed aside" (p. 7).

This work challenged the value of social work because outcome was not supported through the conduct of clinical trials (remember that clinical trial methods are the gold standard of evidence-based practice). Although there were many criticisms, rightfully so, of Fischer's work, he brought awareness and immediate attention to the critical importance of illustrating the worth of professional practice through systematically investigating the extent to which social work activity produced its desired and articulated outcomes.

In examined practice, outcome assessment takes on a broader methodological scope than the clinical trial approach suggested by Fischer (1973). Yet, we agree that demonstrating the worth of social work should remain of utmost concern both as our professional duty as well as for our very survival and growth. Thus, researching outcome must use rigorous methods to delve into social work efficacy and worth. We address the issue of worth in more detail below. But for now, just consider the worth-accountability link.

Three definitions of *worth* (Dictionary.com, 2013) shed light on its role and determination in examined practice:

1. Usefulness or importance, as to the world, to a person, or for a purpose

2. Value, as in money

3. A quantity of something of a specified value

Therefore, outcome assessment once again illuminates the role of values in social work. Not only is value internal to practice, but through outcome assessment, the importance and purposiveness of social work within the larger context of policy, services, and funding are communicated beyond professional boundaries. Answering questions about accountability is thus critical to demonstrating the worth of social work.

Thus, explicit in outcome assessment is the display of the value of social work, again affirming the value element throughout the totality of social work and thus the wisdom of using evaluation research as the inquiry approach for social work knowing. Because this point highlights outcome assessment as thinking and action beyond its typical notion of demonstrating a cause-and-effect relationship between effort and outcome, systematic outcome research methods can move beyond this single aim in several ways.

First, outcome assessment is linked not only to what happened as a result of intervention but glances further back in the examined practice sequence to examine the extent to which the identified needs were met to address the targeted problem focus. Second, outcome assessment, while maybe not including a wide scope in specifying success criteria, reminds the social worker to think more broadly within the problem map. In other words, how did a change in one part of the map influence other areas? If outcome assessment is limited only to the investigation of causal relationships between intervention and intended result using traditional quantitative methods, understanding outcomes as well as methods for accountability and worth would be significantly limited (Patton, 2012). Evaluative research is thus further supported as the model for social work knowledge within examined practice.

Finally, whether we like it or not, we need to be accountable as paid workers. Social workers earn a living doing "something" and thus need to show that we are doing it and producing what is promised. We already introduced the caution not to promise what we cannot deliver and will revisit this critical point throughout the book. So outcome assessment in examined practice examines the extent to which attainable results were achieved and what factors influenced this phenomenon.

Essential Elements of Outcome Assessment

More than other areas discussed in the examined practice sequence (perhaps with the exception of needs assessment), outcome assessment is typically a function of a research process, as its primary aim is to study, discover, and document the results of social work activities in terms which are acceptable in professional literature. Yet, recall that if possible and purposive, outcomes should be considered more broadly than the named desirables. First, promises should not be made if they cannot be achieved. Consider substance abuse treatment for a moment. The social worker who promises that clients will remain sober after or even during treatment as a result of social work intervention sets the client and the profession up for failure. Given that social work cannot control the behavior of individuals, such aims cannot stand as outcomes despite their desirability. Incremental steps which have been associated with sobriety, such as readiness, can be promised (Connors, DiClemente, Velasquez, & Donovan, 2013). With this point in mind, two distinctions within outcome assessment are proposed. First and foremost are the essential aims of outcome assessment, to examine the degree to which viable outcome objectives were established, met, and attributable to social work activity. But second, and critical to advancing social work knowledge, is the examination of unanticipated influences and outcomes following a partial or completed social work action. Knowing not only what was achieved as planned but also what unexpected phenomena occurred rounds out the complexity of social work knowledge, providing the opportunity for new **theory** to be developed and tested and setting a course for an ongoing evaluation research agenda to expand social work knowing.

The TAP project provides a clear illustration. The data-based documentation of its unanticipated benefit to immigrants whose first language is not English has many implications not only for the expansion of web-based knowledge to non-English speakers but to support the use of automated language translation in diverse social work venues. Informed by this knowledge, we used Google translate in our social work classes to make dense readings more accessible to students from Saudi Arabia whose first language was Arabic.

The essential elements of outcome assessment are listed on page 72 in Table 4.1, while Table 4.2 lists the broader parts of outcome assessment that may or may not be present in each outcome assessment process. What is included in outcome assessment is dependent on context, purpose, and resources.

For example, consider Elton. While education of the employer and, in the future, broader small business owner education regarding accommodation options may be stipulated and measured as primary outcomes for sequential social work activity, it is unlikely that the social worker will engage in a complex analysis of

Table 4.1　Essentials of Outcome Assessment

1. Establishment of viable outcomes
2. Value-based
3. Systematic inquiry using one or more of the three traditions of research
4. Linking reflexive intervention to outcomes—process, output, and outcome

Table 4.2　Broader Elements of Outcome Assessment

1. Investigation of problem resolution and/or change
2. Contribution to professional knowledge base
3. Cost analysis

the extent to which policy change is influenced by the educational intervention or the benefit-to-cost ratio of returning one person to work. If feasible, this knowledge would be extremely valuable to demonstrate the broad impact of social work action but more likely would be part of a collaborative research agenda rather than the responsibility of a practitioner whose focus is not on those parts of social work.

Value-Based Social Work Practice

Given the value-based underpinning not only of examined practice but of all social work activity (Reamer, 2013), as we noted above, outcome assessment is value-based as well because this part of the examined practice model measures what should have changed or stayed the same. Moreover, what did not change that should have resulted from a social work effort is a value statement implying success or not. Note that the word *should* is a preference or opinion about what is desired. Thus, outcome assessment both details and examines the extent to which what is valued and desired occurred following or as a result of an intentional action. In the examined practice model, the desired outcome is a change in the problem statement in one or more directions; reduction or elimination of a problem; change in understanding, status, or influence on targeted issues; and so forth. Remember that social problems that create the rationale and focus of social work doing and outcomes are statements of value even if they are framed as areas to be changed using strengths-based philosophy (Corcoran, 2008).

Furthermore, methodologies (how these desired outcomes are measured and/or assessed with numeric or nonnumeric data and what denotes success in this assessment scheme) are action processes that are dependent on values and opinions. As discussed in action processes in the next chapter, keep in mind that in examined practice, unlike other models such as evidence-based practice, belief in efficacy, alliance with the social worker (Ardito & Rabellino, 2011), and investigator purpose may be major driving influences in the choice of methods even though these movers and shakers of research often go unspoken. Consider Janice as an example. One of the factors that produced a negative outcome and thus termination of intervention with the first social worker was the lack of alliance or trust in the social worker's plan of action.

SYSTEMATIC INQUIRY USING ONE OR MORE OF THE THREE RESEARCH TRADITIONS

As detailed in Section II, outcome assessment uses diverse research techniques to examine the relationship between professional efforts and outcomes in multiple domains. In outcome assessment, the design used should, in its basic configuration, focus on investigating the link between a social work activity and what follows, even if it is not feasible to use true experimentation to attribute assessed outcome to social work doing. This task can be done in many ways from designing and conducting complex inquiry to systematic monitoring built into social work in a seamless fashion.

Knowledge management, an emergent field of practice within the digital age, has been suggested as a good approach for outcome assessment purposes (KM World, 1998–2016). This field integrates multiple forms of knowing into a systematic database, available for mining through diverse forms of research. As an example, an automated self-reporting system combined with clinical notes scanned into the database followed Dean's attendance, progress, and health in his substance abuse program, revealing that despite compliance, he did not attain the outcome of being seizure-free. Thus, measurement of the objective was seamless with no additional effort required to obtain data. The knowledge management system in place provided the opportunity to ask questions of the information within it, revealing the failure of the intervention in time for needed change in the social work action plan. In Section II, we detail each research tradition, specific strategies, and their uses in outcome assessment.

Linking Reflexive Intervention to Outcomes—Process, Output, and Outcome

In the examined practice model, measurement of post-intervention variables and/or documentation of desired outcomes in themselves are insufficient to depict the breadth and depth of outcome. A clear articulation of the activity and its parts, and an attempt to examine which actions of a total social work effort related to or influenced a result are necessary not only for a complete assessment but, equally important, for contributing to the repository of social work knowledge detailing practice efficacy. This point is critical when considering both intended and unintended outcomes of social work activity. Without reflection necessary for specification of the parts and processes of social work intervention, it is not possible even to begin to uncover what social work produced or influenced as an outcome. Thus, the reflexive intervention phase is essential to developing a full complement of social work knowledge as it links outcome to what was done.

Consider Elton once again. Suppose in anticipation of a legal action, Elton's employer surfed the Internet to find inexpensive ways to accommodate Elton. If employer knowledge was the only outcome measured, attributing Elton's employment to social work effort would thus be inaccurate. Simple strategies to attribute outcome to social work activity, such as asking the employer to detail the sources through which he obtained his knowledge, would be indicated here in the absence of both the capacity or the need to conduct experimental-type research.

Now consider the TAP project. Twelve process objectives were framed to achieve the following output objective:

> Diverse users of all reading levels will access and consume information on the TAP website.

Simply assuming that all process objectives led to this outcome would not be warranted given the multiple factors that could have been responsible for the discovery of this website by its users, including serendipity. Carefully evaluating the attainment of each of the process objectives in reflexive intervention not only provides evidence of the completion of each, by whom, and when but provides an important and easy-to-follow **audit trail** to chronicle progress in the development and dissemination of the electronic information. Thus, even in the absence of a systematic evaluation research design, a convincing argument can be made to link process to output. At the end of the chapter, we revisit this exemplar to illustrate.

Measuring Intended Outcome Attainment Using Experimental-Type Methods

Measurement is defined as "the act or process of ascertaining the extent, dimensions, or quantity of something" (Dictionary.com, 2013). Explicit in measurement is the establishment of a numeric standard for comparison. So if the social work purpose of outcome assessment warrants comparison of individual progress to a previous state, individuals to others, groups to groups, and so forth, experimental-type traditions are useful and indicated. As already discussed, experimental-type strategies, specifically true experimentation, are the primary thinking and action processes that support evidence-based practice and thus must be used when the social worker aims to develop information for this body of knowledge.

The four discrete action elements listed in Table 4.3 comprise experimental-type outcome assessment, regardless of purpose or research design.

Review the discussions in Chapter 1 and in Section II on the logical foundation of true-experimental design. Recall that experimental-type thinking is anchored in logical positivism, a philosophical view that positions truth as a singular phenomenon, outside of one's opinion and only discoverable by following specific logico-deductive rules and sequences (detailed in Chapter 9). Within the experimental-type tradition, the ultimate aim is to eliminate bias, or unintended influences on a study, such that one can be reasonably assured that the outcome was a direct result of professional action.

To achieve the ideal of attribution of outcome to intervention through research in this tradition, the gold standard of true experimentation is used. The thinking and action processes in this strategy are detailed in Section II. Of particular note is the value of true-experimental design, if properly structured, to generate knowledge that is both predictive and generalizable beyond the immediate inquiry. Here we revisit the TAP project to illustrate.

Of course, when using examined practice, all steps from the articulation of the problem statement to reflexive intervention precede outcome assessment. Now, suppose the long-term objective of positive attitudes toward smoking cessation is the focus of this outcome query. The formal evaluation research question to be answered using experimental-type thinking and action is

To what extent did access and use of the website produce positive attitudes toward smoking cessation?

Table 4.3 Four Action Processes in Experimental-Type Outcome Assessment

1. Based on summative (outcome) objectives, articulate definitions expressed in words of desired outcomes and criteria for success. These desired outcomes comprise the variables to be measured.
2. Delineate the exact assessment questions.
3. Design the structure of assessment action processes with attention to field constraints.
4. Conduct the outcome assessment inquiry with attention to purposive, ethical, field, and resource delimitations.

To structure conditions in which this question can be answered, groups with and without access to the website would have to be created. The social worker accomplished this comparative structure by randomly selecting first wave participants and then staggering participation rather than eliminating it altogether for other groups. (Randomization is explained further in Section II.) Thus, the outcome objective could be measured at two intervals for both groups, before anyone was exposed to the website and then after only one group accessed and used it. By using a waiting list, the social worker was able to follow the rules of true experimentation (laid out in Section II) while being assured that this intervention would be available for all users in the long run.

As alluded to above, structuring true experimentation is not simple. Because of its complexity and the frequent barriers to conducting such outcome studies in social work, true experimentation is not often feasible unless intentionally planned and well-funded in advance. Furthermore, in many instances, examined practice presents ethical and practical challenges to structuring true experimentation to measure outcomes, as it requires the condition of "withholding" social work action from a control group altogether or for a time period in order to test differences between the presence and absence of an intervention that may be valued as useful. However, if purposive, it is not only possible but indicated to use experimental-type thinking in outcome assessment even if true-experimentation action processes cannot or should not be conducted. Affirming the attitudinal changes toward smoking through experimental-type measurement provides valuable and compelling evidence for the expansion of web-based health knowledge dissemination.

When structuring methods to investigate the cause of outcomes is not feasible, thinking and action still involving measurement but in different configurations can be implemented. These approaches are fully explained in Section II. Consider the example from the TAP project once again. Rather than staggering participation, the social worker could have developed and placed a survey on the website, testing user knowledge gained, and then asking respondents the sources of their current fund of knowledge. The combination of a post-test knowledge measure and self-report of attribution can provide strong evidence of the degree of knowledge acquisition and the sources through which this new information was acquired. Thus, combining various methods is an excellent systematic approach to examining outcome and its causes when attribution cannot be directly assessed through true experimentation.

Qualifying Intended Outcomes Using Naturalistic Inquiry

Naturalistic traditions provide an alternative and/or a complimentary approach to experimental-type designs for assessing outcome. Thinking and action processes in this tradition respect the contextual nature of social work activity and thus often are used to gain a complex understanding of outcomes within time and place. As noted in Chapter 1, naturalistic designs are not concerned with generalizing outcome assessment results to broader populations and thus are well considered for evaluative research. Many practitioners who do not look at outcome for the purpose of developing evidence-based practice knowledge find this tradition valuable for informed practice and for establishing relevance and viability for similar contexts. Thus, the typical criticism of naturalistic design, that it is context-specific and idiosyncratic, is not pertinent to examined practice unless an explicit purpose of outcome assessment is to broaden the results of an evaluative study to a population represented by the tested **sample**.

The use of naturalistic inquiry can be powerful not only to characterize what has happened following an intervention but also to ascertain why and to identify nuances in outcome that are related to specific characteristics of the social work activity including context, interaction, and other influences. Moreover, because naturalistic inquiry is pluralistic and inductive or abductive in its logic structures, complexity can be characterized and depicted in both activity and outcome. Studying complexity is an excellent way to advance social work theory that can then be tested in diverse contexts beyond that from which the theory was developed.

Consider Janice for example. Studying her interaction with the clinical social worker could have been valuable in developing a theoretical approach to working with newly injured clients or others such as Janice who lost significant function due to illness.

In order to use naturalistic strategies to uncover cause-and-effect linkages between action and outcome, data analytic approaches that move beyond description are indicated (see Chapter 12). As discussed in Chapter 11, there are numerous methods in this tradition that lend themselves to theory development and thus are useful for documenting causal relationships. Note that these findings are specific to context and thus not predictive unless tested more broadly through experimental-type research. A major advantage of naturalistic inquiry is its flexibility, allowing the social worker to change systematic approaches even before the process is completed. So it may be possible to begin with the aim of description and then move to a study design that generates theory.

Returning to the TAP project, once it was noted on the website survey that an unanticipated population, immigrants with limited English literacy, were frequent users, a request for participation in an open-ended interview was posted for the purposes of discovery. Findings from that interview revealed the value of this website to an unexpected population as well as the efficacy of low-literacy English in automated translation to alternative languages and formats. As such, new theory was developed for application and testing in expansive contexts.

Examining the Complexity of Intended and Unintended Outcomes Using All Traditions

Mixed-method forms the third tradition of systematic evaluation research thinking and action. As we have indicated, if possible and purposive, this approach to outcome assessment provides the richest data not only for determining the immediate, unique outcome of a single social work effort but also for adding comprehensive and complex knowledge to social work knowing. As an example, adding the naturalistic element of interview to the experimental-type assessment of the TAP project provided further evidence about both anticipated and unexpected outcome and causes.

Investigation of Problem Resolution/Alteration

In essence, all aspects of the examined practice model refer to the extent to which an identified problem has been addressed, reconceptualized, altered, or resolved in part or in total as a result of or following a professional intervention. Assessment of outcome allows the social worker to make well-informed judgments about the impact of social work on social problems and issues of concern because each step of the sequence derives from the problem statement.

Because all of the exemplars illustrate this point, we will not reiterate an illustration here.

Contribution to Professional Knowledge Base

Although outcome assessment is traditionally and primarily initiated for the purpose of ascertaining the success and worth of a social work intervention or effort in achieving its goals and objectives, systematic outcome assessment contributes to the overall professional knowledge base, in the ways listed in Table 4.4.

Table 4.4 Outcome Assessment as Knowledge Building

1. Allows for replication and future planning of successful professional efforts based on empirical evidence
2. Provides knowledge for comparison of social work actions
3. Provides feedback for knowledge and advancement of professional practices
4. Allows for prediction of future outcomes
5. Contributes to empirical professional knowledge
6. Contributes to social work theory

Table 4.5 Typical Targets of Outcome Assessment

Direct targets: Smokers, potential smokers

Indirect targets: Nonsmokers exposed to secondhand smoke; friends, families, coworkers, and so on

The professional: Health care providers, computer programmers

The professions: Public health, computer science, health education, health literacy

The global community: All concerned with health and equality of access to health knowledge

Administrators: Workplace administrators responsible for smoking policy, health insurance, and so on

Policymakers and policy: Public health policy, state and national health and information access rights policies, health insurance policy

For evaluative as well as knowledge and theory building purposes, outcome assessment applies to numerous groups. Refer to Table 4.5 for only some exemplars of the broad range of populations who benefitted from outcome assessment in the TAP project.

COST OF INTERVENTIONS

Although cost analysis is a major concern of reflexive intervention, it is also an essential part of outcome assessment in that cost analysis focuses on the balance of inputs and outputs and thus is a fiscal determination of efficiency and worth (Spolander, 2012). Although this type of inquiry may seem simple at first glance, estimating the costs and benefits of an action is a complex task.

The bulk of cost measurement typically occurs within reflexive intervention and monitoring. As discussed previously, preceding and during social work activity, cost schemes are developed and enacted. Similar to theorizing cost as more than financial currency necessary to fund social work, benefit is complicated and variable as well. Benefits for whom, in what form, and how operationalized are major considerations in deciphering the comparative fiscal worth of social work interventions (Thyer, 2009; Spolander, 2012). Cost analysis in outcome assessment is therefore an important determination of worth and in large part of the continuation or not of a social work approach.

Consider the exemplar of Elton discussed above. If costs of returning Elton to work are balanced against benefits just for him, the ratio of cost to benefit could be much smaller than expanding scrutiny of monetary benefits to the employer, taxpayer, and so forth. However, as discussed by Thompson (2010), considering the avoidance of vocational rehabilitation or expenditures for welfare support would change the cost-benefit equation not only for Elton's immediate situation but also for additional populations and circumstances as well.

SUMMARY

In this chapter, outcome assessment was defined, discussed, and illustrated. Following a conceptual discussion and sequential location of this step within the examined practice model, how outcomes inform the other parts of the model were discussed and linked to each research tradition.

The main points in this chapter are as follows:

1. Outcome assessment should examine intended and unintended outcomes and influences on the social work process.

2. Outcome is difficult to attribute to social work action, and thus, creative systematic thinking and action are necessary.

3. Outcome assessment is evaluative.

4. Outcome assessment may be a deliberate step or one that is integrated into daily practice activity.

5. There are multiple purposes for conducting outcome assessment.

6. All outcome assessment is value-based and should examine the extent to which the problem that generated social work action was changed following or as a result of practice.

7. Accountability and worth are two primary functions of outcome assessment that are both ethical requirements and necessary for professional survival and growth.

8. Social work should only promise and assess outcomes that can be accomplished.

9. Knowledge management systems provide an excellent model for seamless outcome assessment.

10. Traditions can be used or integrated to answer outcome questions.

11. The scope of outcome can range from assessing a single effort to creating evidence-based interventions for broad use.

12. Cost-benefit analysis, although part of reflexive intervention as well, is an important part of assessing the fiscal worth of social work.

REFERENCES

Ardito, R. B., & Rabellino, D. (2011). Therapeutic alliance and outcome of psychotherapy: Historical excursus, measurements, and prospects for research. *Frontiers in Psychology*, 270. doi: 10.3389/fpsyg.2011.00270

Connors, G. J., DiClemente, C. C., Velasquez, M. M., & Donovan, D. M. (2013). *Substance abuse treatment and the stages of change* (2nd ed.). New York, NY: Guilford.

Corcoran, J. (2008). *Groups in social work.* Boston, MA: Allyn & Bacon.

Fischer, J. (1973). Is casework effective? A review. *Social Work, 18*(1), 5–20.

KM World. (1998–2016). *Knowledge management.* Retrieved from http://www.kmworld.com

Measurement. (2013). *Dictionary.com.* Retrieved from http://dictionary.reference.com/browse/measure?s=t

Outcome. (2013). *Dictionary.com.* Retrieved from http://dictionary.reference.com/browse/outcome?s=t

Patton, M. Q. (2012). *Essentials of utilization focused evaluation.* Thousand Oaks, CA: Sage.

Reamer, F. (2013). *Social work values and ethics* (4th ed.). New York, NY: Columbia University Press.

Spolander, G. (2012). *Successful project management in social work and social care: Managing resources, assessing risks and measuring outcomes.* London, UK: Jessica Kingsley.

Thompson, C. (2010). *Able-minded.* Retrieved from https://www.homewoodhumansolutions.com/docs/HSreport_10.pdf

Thyer, B. (2009). *The handbook of social research methods* (2nd ed.). Thousand Oaks, CA: Sage.

Worth. (2013). *Dictionary.com.* Retrieved from http://dictionary.reference.com/browse/worth?s=t

Chapter 5

SHARING EXAMINED PRACTICE TO GENERATE SOCIAL WORK KNOWLEDGE

Unlike many social work practice and/or research frameworks, sharing knowledge is one of the essential elements of examined practice. But what should be shared and how are not agreed upon despite the numerous scholars, researchers, and practitioners who are calling for the formalization and consistent advancement of social work knowledge (Brekke, 2012; Gray, 2008; Trevethick, 2008).

In this chapter, we begin with definitions. We then follow the guidance from Lau (2004): "organizations need to know what, how, why, where, and when to use their knowledge," detailing how each element fits within the knowledge-sharing element of the examined practice model.

DEFINITION OF TERMS

What is meant by sharing and dissemination?

To share is defined as "to use, participate in, enjoy, receive, etc., jointly" (Dictionary.com, 2015).

Dissemination refers to "the act of scattering or spreading widely, as though sowing seed; promulgating extensively; broadcasting; dispersing" (Dictionary.com, 2015).

Both processes are active and intentional. Collectively, both suggest a climate of openness and receiver benefit in the form of enjoyment or germination. Finally, both terms reflect the examined practice spirit of expanding knowledge beyond the "social work self" or the immediate practice environment.

EXAMPLES OF SHARING KNOWLEDGE

A seminar that we attended several summers ago functions as the first example. Unexpected learning is a precious gem to be discovered, and we therefore impart an essential lesson learned that speaks to the nature of knowledge within and among varied groups. This seminar on using qualitative research methods to investigate disability and work issues was designed to bring those who were well known in the field together with those who were relatively new to the topic or the research tradition. Each participant was asked to prepare a short description of a current or future project on which he or she was working or wanted to work. The dissemination of knowledge in the week-long seminar was intended to shape participants' projects for implementation. Among the attendees were attorneys, policy makers, philosophers, educators, and health providers. Although nothing new or innovative about methodology or content relating to disability and work was presented, the lesson learned from that week was invaluable and now serves to inform examined practice: Because standards of evidence and venues for talking to diverse interested parties and audiences differ so greatly within and across fields, communicating knowledge is a puzzle with multiple dimensions.

As presented in the next section of this chapter, many definitions of knowledge, **science**, and professions exist and in large part are dependent on what is considered by different interest groups to be legitimate evidence. Applied to dissemination, this action process must be purposive and framed by an understanding of what the audience will value as accessible, comprehensible, and believable.

So what was learned quite some years back came to roost in crafting this purposive model of systematic thinking and action in social work and provides a segue to the second exemplar, an excerpt from a social work blog site (Rose, 2013) on a contemporary issue.

I recently heard the sad tale of a friend's 88-year-old mother who had received one of those "too good to be true" phone calls. She was told she had won thousands of dollars, and all she needed to do was allow a courier to pick up several hundred dollars from her to secure her prize.

Fortunately she called her son. But by then the callers were threatening her that the courier was on his way and she'd better have the money available.

Once her son heard that, he called police. They responded by tracing the call . . . to Trinidad! They handled the threatening scammers and she was relieved of her fear.

I wondered what information might be available to others who are advising families whose elders might have a bit of impaired judgment. I found this article on Fraud.org that can be very helpful. It is well-written and contains easy-to-follow bullet points.

For example, you can tell older people that they should report any calls such as these to family and/or law enforcement:

- **A promise** that you can win money, make money, or borrow money easily;
- **A demand** that you act immediately or else miss out on this great opportunity;
- **A refusal** to send you written information before you agree to buy or donate;
- **An attempt** to scare you into buying something;
- **Insistence** that you wire money or have a courier pick up your payment; and,
- **A refusal** to stop calling after you've asked not to be called again.

Unfortunately, my friend's mother's experience was not uncommon.

While the excerpt above does not display research or reflect logico-deductive methods of inquiry held as the standard for evidence-based practice, Rose (2013) shares critically important knowledge for social workers to acquire in order to prevent major assaults against elders. Note that the evidence for intervention lies in grey literature, not research. Grey literature refers to "publications that are non-conventional, fugitive, and sometimes ephemeral" (Greylit.org, n.d.).

Nevertheless, the conversational tone of storytelling in the blog is both inviting and informative, leaving the reader to evaluate the relevance of this narrative for his or her practice use and further investigation. Moreover, the blog highlights the limited empirical literature on scamming elders and thus begs for social work attention and research.

SHARING SOCIAL WORK KNOWLEDGE

As we have discussed throughout the text, there are competing claims about the nature of knowledge itself and the type of knowledge that social work should use as its foundation. As an example, Brekke (2012) suggests that social work should be developed as a science through empiricism.

> We can define a science as a combination of theory and systematic empirical method, rooted in an ontological and epistemological context, and applied to a defined set of phenomena. When a discipline describes, derives, or advocates a set of theories and empirical methods, it has begun to define itself as a science. (Brekke, 2012, p. 256)

He reminds us that other professions are underpinned and even defined by their advancement of "scientific" knowledge. By *science*, Brekke (2012) is referring to knowing through methods of inquiry that rely on measurement.

We agree that enhancing the scientific reputation of social work is one major reason for the development and dissemination of knowledge by social workers. However, within the examined practice model, science as defined by Brekke (2012) is not the only way to build knowledge. More consistent with the definition of knowledge in examined practice, and thus what should be shared, are ideas presented by Bell (2012) and Rasmussen (2011). Bell proposes a model of knowledge for social work that is both comprehensive and imaginative. In order to develop a truly comprehensive knowledge base that addresses people in the twenty-first century, social work needs to further reflect, reimagine, and reform its view of what constitutes knowledge and move to a more contemporary theory of knowledge.

Consider co-design as an example of contemporary knowledge building. Borrowed from industry and business, codesign is a new and emerging method in social work based on the tenet that client populations not only are cognizant of their own issues and needs but also may have the most viable strategies not yet considered by professions. Thus, client populations are recruited to work alongside professionals to develop solutions to social problems. Using this type of method in the example of mobility device abandonment, elders were asked to provide their viewpoints not only about the barriers to using mobility equipment but also to suggest how to decrease and eliminate the causes of abandonment.

On another note, Rasmussen (2011) reminds us of the value of capturing and disseminating social work "doing" within the canon of social work knowledge. Therefore, knowledge can and should come from many different and varied sources. Moreover, the cooperation of these assets enriches the knowledge generated as collaboration brings multiple perspectives to bear on a single problem.

Regardless of the source, the knowledge created must be systematic with the basis of claims clearly articulated. It is because of its systematic, research-based nature throughout all thinking and action processes, that the examined practitioner generates legitimate professional knowledge to meet both Brekke's (2012) call to science and Bell's (2012) and Rasmussen's (2011) urgency for social work to develop and disseminate knowledge useful for knowing both within and outside of the profession. As we repeatedly emphasize, the common denominator for knowledge lies in its systematic logic conforming to one of the three major traditions of research.

THE SCIENCE-INTUITION DEBATE

As lightly grazed in our previous discussion on evidence-based practice, there has been significant discussion about the role of intuition in social work activity and the extent to which empirical approaches interfere with one's ability to be spontaneous and intuitive. This heated debate is centered on whether or not intuitive knowing is acceptable for formal sharing and thus public assertion of its role in the canon of social work knowledge. Given the multiple and competing definitions of intuition, accepting intuition as credible knowledge for social work is dependent on how one defines intuition. Confounding the acceptance of intuition as a viable way of professional knowing is in large part its wide expanse of definitions, spanning a continuum from nonrational awareness to knowing informed by science yet to be articulated (Luoma, 2010).

Within the examined practice model, pulling knowledge from thin air, from guessing, or from feeling, without exploring its roots, is unacceptable, does not qualify for professional knowledge, distinguish itself for inclusion in credible social work knowledge, or even remotely form the basis for intervention and desired outcomes. A clear and well-reasoned rationale must be present in order for knowledge to qualify as valued within the profession of social work. Using the latter definition above, there is much room for using and then formally sharing intuition in examined practice, providing that the source for claims is transparent and conforms to methods within the research traditions.

"What" is shared as knowledge in examined practice is thus pluralistic in its generation and nature of evidence but must reflect the basic structure and processes of systematically supported claims.

WHY SHARE?

This question identifies purpose and precedes any consideration of the remaining questions. As discussed throughout the text, there are multiple reasons for sharing beyond, including the traditional approaches of disseminating evidence for the purpose of informing the profession of social work. As addressed in answers to when and what to share, certainly the advancement of the profession and its knowledge base is a primary purpose for developing and exchanging social work knowing. However, knowledge is always in flux. It is possible that sharing knowledge is both a professional duty as well as practical.

For example, faculty in schools of social work may hold publishing knowledge as important for stability in their careers, while the clinical social worker's reason for communicating knowledge may be to acquire new, well-supported techniques to assist a unique client in meeting his personal goals. Others may choose to express provocative ideas to advance social work knowing. Or perhaps empirical validation of one's ideas and actions in itself is the reason for social workers to share. Each purpose begins to shape the structure, location, and timing of knowledge dissemination.

As an example, revisit the Tobacco Access Portal (TAP) project. Several purposes frame the dissemination strategy. First, in order to produce the website, funding was necessary. However, in the long term, the substantive public health information remained free, but the programming methods were kept as proprietary. So in order to successfully obtain funding, the problem statement, compelling systematic evidence that the website would fill an essential unmet need, and plans on how the project would be carried out were shared through a research grant proposal format. However, limited technical information was made available in order to walk a line between privacy and adequacy of information for judgment and a favorable funding response.

Second, because this project was and remains central to our own professional activity and research agendas, a second purpose of dissemination was contributing to professional knowledge. Third, and most important, was the purpose of improving equality of access to public health information for all population segments and individuals. So the multiple scholarly, outcome, and proprietary purposes guided strategies for the timing, locations, and formats for knowledge dissemination in this project.

WHEN TO SHARE?

When not to share knowledge is well articulated and to some extent much clearer than when to share. Diverse codes of **ethics** used by social workers guided by several ethical models prohibit distribution of knowledge in instances where client confidentiality and protection of human subjects would be violated (NASW, 2013; Department of Health, Education, and Welfare, 1979).

Consider the harm from stigma that could have been sustained by Dean if information about him had been available during his enrollment in substance abuse intervention. Knowing when and when not to divulge knowledge is a professional obligation not to be taken lightly. But this chapter is about sharing for the purpose of advancing social work knowledge. So when is the best time to share? Once again, purpose and benefit are the two criteria on which to judge when to publicize one's knowledge.

As introduced above, prior to any social work activity, a primary purpose for sharing knowledge and/or plans for developing formal knowledge is to craft proposals to conduct social work activity (DePoy & Gitlin, 2016). Proposals are prepared for many reasons: to seek approval and funding for a study, to seek support and resources for implementing social work programs, or even for recruiting collaborators in a knowledge-generating project. As an example, the TAP project was not yet initiated when knowledge about its target problem, need, intended methodology, and expected outcomes were formalized and conveyed to potential collaborators as well as prepared as a formal proposal to seek funding from potential grant-making sources. Failure to extend knowledge that shaped this project beyond the social workers who conceptualized it would have halted its progress before it ever was initiated.

Many social work researchers and practitioners await the termination of an inquiry or program to determine its outcomes and worth before they disseminate what was learned. Yet, we have found that discussing emerging knowledge during its birth and development is often illuminating. Clinical social work supervision has been a staple of knowledge exchange since early in the history of social work (Smith, 1996–2011). As characterized by Smith (1996–2011), who critically analyzed this form of interaction, supervision during the course of social work activity can be both formative and corrective, depending on the context.

Similarly, but in a scholarly domain, Jaheil (2012) regularly organized formal sessions in which incomplete theory and knowledge development on broad topics of disability are invited for presentation and criticism.

A particular emphasis is given on the plurality of scientific approaches and knowledge (theoretical, applied, grounded in the experience of disability) provided by this research area. It is an open intellectual society and welcomes all who have an interest in disability without exception or particular orientation. Established with a focus on Europe, the society welcomes scholars from all parts of the world.

The AESDR Conference is envisaged as an annual event that will enable dedicated research scientists, young researchers and doctoral students to present their work. It aims to provide a forum for a broad spectrum of disability research as well as a place to make contacts and exchange ideas (Jaheil, 2012).

These sessions are jewels not only to the audience hearing new knowledge but also for presenters who benefit from a village of thinkers providing critical feedback.

Combining sharing theory and inquiry with systematic practice knowledge is much more potent than using each on its own. To some extent, knowledge management (Booth, Purdy, Ward, & Lindsay, 2010) subscribes to this type of synthesis, albeit primarily through electronic organization, archiving, and interaction. While knowledge management theory and practice have grown and become diverse, this relatively new field (see KMworld.com) operates on using three divisions of knowledge: explicit, implicit, and tacit. For most models the three should be available at all times such that all with knowledge access can benefit from each type. Table 5.1 defines each element in the typology.

Explicit knowledge is exemplified by formal research reports and program descriptions while implicit knowing of the same material is that which is held but not articulated beyond the social worker. The tacit knower does not identify or communicate what is known, nor is the source retrievable.

Consider the social work clinician. Explicit clinical knowledge would include evidence-based practice, techniques, theory, and research. The implicit clinical knower with some thought and effort would be able to delve into his or her fund of knowledge to retrieve the source of knowing. The tacit knower would do what feels right in clinical practice without being able to answer questions about why and on what knowledge the interaction is based.

Knowledge management is relatively new to social work (Leung, 2007). Frequently, this field is met with opposition due to its reliance on technological methods to archive and make knowledge available. For social workers who view knowledge primarily as process, electronic repositories do not always receive enthusiastic responses (Leung, 2007). However, within examined practice, knowledge management provides an important but only a partial model for expanding knowledge beyond the knower. Consistent with the definition of legitimate social

Table 5.1 Typology of Knowledge Within the Field of Knowledge Management

Explicit: information or knowledge that is set out in tangible form

Implicit: information or knowledge that is not set out in tangible form but could be made explicit

Tacit: information or knowledge that one would have extreme difficulty setting out in tangible form work knowing presented in Chapter 1, examined practice limits professional knowledge to that which is systematically generated through one or more of the three traditions of research. While valuable for discussion, sharing tacit knowledge is only supported when the sources of knowledge and its substance can be revealed and articulated. Thus, within the examined practice model, sharing knowledge at the tacit stage is premature for inclusion in the formal professional body of social work knowledge. What knowledge management theory and practice do contribute to social work are the principles of availability, pluralism of evidence, and substantiated thought and action.

Consider Dean once again. If a broad repository of knowledge was available and made interactive, its use by the social worker may have led to well-investigated and supported practice and research experience on Dean's neurological condition. The guesses and assumptions that linked him to an inaccurate social work response, substance abuse intervention, would therefore have been avoided.

Unfortunately, too many practice innovations and studies (some displaying Brekke's [2012] notion of science and others consistent with alternatives) remain private, placed on physical or virtual shelves, and thus unavailable to those who would benefit from the thinking and action of others. Thus, if systematic social work knowledge is not disseminated, an essential part in the sequence of examined practice and a function critical for social work efficacy are lost.

WHERE TO SHARE?

Over the last decade, where to make knowledge available to others has been an expanding universe. Traditional venues remain viable and relevant. As discussed below in answering the "how" question, conferences, journals, and books are seats of formal social work knowledge. Yet, the virtual world has created such an opportunity for disseminating and acquiring knowledge that this time period in history is referred to as the Information or Digital Age. Traditional print and face-to-face exchange have been translated into e-publications and virtual video meetings and other online media. In this digital climate, almost all schools of social work in the United States, Western Europe, and many in other areas of the globe disseminate the content of their programs and host their applications in online formats. Moreover, it is now becoming common for schools of social work to hold coursework online. As of November, 2015, Council on Social Work Education listed 39 MSW programs offering virtual graduate programs (CSWE, 2015), stating that it was only a partial roster.

In the blog example by Rose (2013), immediate access to information and its sources in electronic format were available for all who have digital opportunity.

Web resources such as social networks and academic sites (Researchgate, academia.org., Digital commons, etc.) create the venues for posting and sharing knowledge in the making. Unlike print journals in which production processes delay the static display of current knowledge sometimes by 2 years, electronic sources provide a buffet of information sites with immediate dissemination of current knowledge, albeit in many forms. Moreover, commentary on the knowledge is frequently invited, providing a forum for virtual scholarly and knowledge communities to develop. Cautious, critical, and judicious appraisal of the knowledge on these sites creates significant opportunity for sharing and obtaining state-of-the-art, rigorous social work knowing.

Answers to the where question do not remain static, as they change with the evolving virtual world. Because of the expansive and unstable scope of sharing opportunities, Table 5.2 lists just some guiding questions to assist the social worker in deciding on where to share knowledge.

A final consideration in answering where knowledge can be shared relates to intellectual property. Traditional forms of knowledge dissemination such as print publication most often carry a copyright identifying the "owner" of the ideas, data, and so forth presented (Hyde, 2010). As discussed by Hyde (2010), who himself claims ownership of a model to respond to what is a contentious and complex issue, considering who profits from dissemination must be part of the intellectual property equation. In teasing out and taking a position on one's "thought" ownership, the placement of one's knowing is critical to consider. Is copyright important to the thinker, to the doer? Under what circumstances? What is to be shared? Why? What is ethical practice to guide sharing? How do we both collaborate and avoid theft of our ideas? Adding the answers to these questions about intellectual property to the other "where" concerns, guides the location and its nature at which knowledge can be accessed.

Table 5.2   Guiding Questions to Assist in Deciding on Where to Share Knowledge

1. What is the purpose of sharing?
2. Who is the audience? Where can they be best reached?
3. What venues are legitimate for the purpose?
4. What type of knowledge is to be shared?
5. What is the intended outcome of sharing?
6. How imminent is this knowledge?
7. Whose knowledge is it, and how important is it for the thinker and doer to be identified and protected for attribution?
8. What ethical models should guide sharing?

Consider how these "where" questions that were answered in the TAP project (The "why" or purpose question has been discussed previously so we will not repeat it here):

1. Who is the audience? Where can they be best reached?
   a. No limit was placed on who has access to this knowledge. However, the primary audience for the project comprised individuals with low or no English literacy.
   b. A location that was flexible, readily available to anyone in private or public settings, and an immediate and free environment was the ideal.

2. What venues are legitimate for the purpose?
   a. To attain the purpose of full access, electronic venues with automated literacy translation as well as alternative language and text to speech functionality delimited the venue to a digital format.

3. What type of knowledge is to be shared?
   a. Public health knowledge with no confidential or sensitive content was developed for dissemination.
   b. Evaluation research knowledge about the outcome of the project and for whom complemented the collaborative social work practice information.

4. What was the intended outcome of sharing?
   a. The outcomes identified were contribution to healthy decision making, healthy behaviors, decrease in smoking, and informing social work practice regarding the critical role of Internet access for public health knowledge dissemination.

5. How imminent is this knowledge?
   a. Given the purpose of public health, the knowledge needed to be immediately shared.

6. Whose knowledge was it, and how important was it for the thinker, the doer to be identified and protected for attribution?
   a. As discussed above, the public health knowledge was public and thus fully available and attributable to its original sources. However, the algorithms were kept as proprietary by the programming members of the team and thus were not detailed in any public forum. The overall project was attributed to the social workers who conceptualized and implemented the innovation.

7. What ethical models should guide sharing?
   a. As discussed above, several considerations shaped the response to this question. First, the proprietary nature of the website design had to be

considered. Second, to be considered was the confidentiality of the participants. Both of these factors were subjected to principlism, the ethical model that guides us to do no harm and promote maximum benefit by our actions. Free use of the website was a distributive justice concern proposing that all people should have equal access to information, and particularly that which concerned health decisions and behaviors.

HOW TO SHARE?

Although peer-reviewed publications and presentations in scholarly and professional conferences form the majority of formal knowledge sharing in social work, how these are structured and what contemporary textures are added to these methods are dynamic as virtual technology continues to grow. Sharing structures and methods are way too numerous to detail in this chapter section. However, there are some major points to consider as both professional duty and consistent with the values and aims of social work.

First is the civil right to knowledge. Knowledge access as a right is a complex issue that is becoming increasingly important and convoluted in the digital age. Cerf (2012) asserts that knowledge itself is not well defined and that venues such as the Internet are only "enablers of rights, not rights [themselves]." As clearly demonstrated by the TAP project, how information is crafted, expressed, and exchanged is purposive and frequently complicated by intellectual and other ownership motives. However, in concert with social work's commitment to equality and civil rights, we agree with Hyde (2010) and Mathiesen (2008) who have identified the right to information as fundamental in the twenty-first-century Information Age.

But not all information is of interest or relevant to all audiences. A decision consistent with the principlist ethics of social work (discussed previously and illustrated above) therefore needs to be made regarding what to share with whom. Who has a right to what information should be deliberated with the principle of beneficence in mind for all involved. As an example, sharing public health knowledge is distinct from sharing the details of social work clinical intervention and outcomes and thus different decisions were made regarding how to share each body of knowledge.

Following on the heels of equality of rights is accessibility. Structures that exclude people from relevant information that is both valued and necessary for their flourishing, even without intention, are unacceptable. As demonstrated by the TAP project, exclusion comes in many forms that can be mediated and reversed through thoughtful planning. The TAP project exemplifies "how" to craft knowledge access for the full diversity of communication and knowledge consumption styles.

The Tobacco Access Portal front page is pictured in Figure 5.1.

Figure 5.1   The TAP Entry (Gilson & DePoy, 2007)

TAP is available to anyone free of charge. Because it uses automated literacy translation, the information it contains is both substantive and accessible to low-literacy readers. However, upholding the ethic of beneficence, lower literacy text has additional advantages. As noted above, it can be read accurately by text to speech apps that are now built into operating systems on computers and mobile devices. Low-literacy text can also be translated more accurately than complex narrative into languages other than English on apps such as Google Translate and Babelfish. Both are free and simple to use even for individuals who have little familiarity with these technologies. So regardless of how individuals access information, with few exceptions, the knowledge transmitted on the TAP site about health is available to almost all people.

As demonstrated by the TAP project, careful consideration of the questions in Table 5.2 are necessary to maximize social work activity and outcome.

SUMMARY

In this chapter, the examined practice step of sharing knowledge was discussed. Questions regarding why, how, what, where, and when to share were addressed culminating in the professional obligation to thoughtfully share knowledge with purpose and benefit in mind.

Table 5.3 presents just a partial typology of structures and methods through which knowledge is shared by social workers.

Table 5.3   Summary of Methods of Sharing Examined Practice Knowing

1. Sharing Through Documenting

   Professional papers and online journals

   Mailed and electronic newsletters

   Monographs

   Presentation apps (PowerPoint, Pressie, Keynote, Open Office)

   Books and book chapters

   Technical reports

   Reporting for consumers

   Executive summaries

   Legislative briefs

   Program descriptions

   Online videos

   Virtual world hosting

   Blogs, Vlogs

   Social networking

   Knowledge management systems

   Images

   Databases

   Podcasts

   Mobile hosting

2. Oral Exchanges

   Presentations at scholarly conferences

   Continuing and in-service education

   Presentations at professional meetings

   Presentations at community meetings

   Presentation at legislative sessions

   Online presentations

   Virtual meetings

   Video chats

   Mobile interactions

3. Presentation Through Art and Literature in Image, Text, and Performance

Even this incomplete list of methods to share knowledge is varied and to some extent overwhelming. Purposive selection to accomplish dissemination goals is the key to choosing the most efficacious dissemination methods.

Exchange of knowledge both completes and commences the sequence of steps in examined practice. Knowing the extent to which and how a social work intervention addressed and changed a problem or issue in essence creates new knowledge that in turn redefines the problem.

The main points in this chapter are as follows:

1. Different forms of evidence are credible for different professional and other stakeholder interest groups.

2. Systematic knowing at different stages of research (incomplete through completed) forms the criterion for credible formal social work knowledge to be shared.

3. Answering why, who, what, where, when, and how questions guides the selection of a knowledge exchange strategy.

4. After considering what should be shared, purpose within deontological (duty-based) and principlist social work ethics frame the remaining thinking and action steps.

5. The guiding questions in Table 5.2 are a valuable resource to aid in the selection of methods for purposively sharing social work knowledge.

6. Knowledge exchange both completes and restarts the sequence of steps in the examined practice model.

REFERENCES

Bell, K. (2012). Towards a post-conventional philosophical base for social work. *The British Journal of Social Work, 42*, 408–423.

Booth, A., Purdy, R., Ward, S., & Lindsay, D. (2010). *eLearning: Managing knowledge to improve social care*. Retrieved from http://www.scie.org.uk/publications/elearning/knowledge management/index.asp

Brekke, J. (2012). Shaping a science of social work. *Research on Social Work practice, 22*, 455–464.

Cerf, V. (2012, Jan. 5). Internet access is not a human right. *New York Times*, p. A25.

CSWE. (2015). *Distance education*. Retrieved from http://www.cswe.org/Accreditation/Information/DistanceEducation.aspx

Department of Health, Education, and Welfare. (1979, April 18). *Belmont report*. Retrieved from http://www.hhs.gov/ohrp/humansubjects/guidance/belmont.html

DePoy, E., & Gitlin, L. (2016). *Introduction to research*. St. Louis, MO: Elsevier.

Dissemination. (2015). *Dictionary.com*. Retrieved from http://dictionary.reference.com/browse/dissemination?s=t

Gilson, S., & DePoy, E. (2007). *Tobacco access portal*. Retrieved from http://ccids.umaine.edu/research-projects/completed/tap

Gray, M. (2008). *Knowledge production in social work: The 'gold standard' of mode 2?* Retrieved from www.newcastle.edu.au/The%20Australian%20Institute%20for%20Soc

Greylit.org. (n.d.). *What is grey literature?* Retrieved from http://www.greylit.org/about

Hyde, L. (2010). *Common as air.* New York, NY: Farar, Straus & Giroux.

Jaheil, R. (2012). *First annual conference of the alter: European society of disability research.* Retrieved from http://lettre.ehess.fr/2910?file=1

Lau, F. (2004). Toward a conceptual knowledge management framework in health. *Perspectives in Health Information Management, 1*(8).

Leung, Z. C. (2007). Knowledge management in social work: Towards a conceptual framework. *Journal of Technology in Human Services, 43,* 179–196.

Luoma, B. (2010). An exploration of intuition for social work practice and education. *Social Thought, 18,* 31–45.

Mathiesen, K. (2008, Sept. 7). *Access to information as a human right.* Retrieved from http://ssrn.com/abstract=1264666 or http://dx.doi.org/10.2139/ssrn.1264666

NASW. (2013). *NASW code of ethics.* Retrieved from http://www.socialworkers.org/pubs/code/Default.asp?print=1&

Rasmussen, T. (2011). Knowledge production and social work: Forming knowledge production. *Social Work & Social Sciences Review, 15,* 28–48.

Rose, E. (2013, Sept. 29). *Seniors and fraud: What you can do.* Retrieved from http://socialworkworld.blogspot.com/2013/09/seniors-and-fraud-what-you-can-do.html

Share. (2015). *Dictionary.com.* Retrieved from http://dictionary.reference.com/browse/share

Smith, M. (1996–2011). *The functions of supervision.* Retrieved from http://infed.org/mobi/the-functions-of-supervision

Trevethick, P. (2008). Revisiting the knowledge base of social work: A framework for practice. *The British Journal of Social Work, 38,* 1212–1237.

SECTION II

Chapter 6

TWO DESIGN TRADITIONS AND THEN MIXING THEM

We have completed Section I, in which the model of examined practice was detailed and illustrated. This chapter begins the methodological section of the text with several foci. Recall that in examined practice, knowledge is defined as "belief plus something else." Section II details the "something else" as systematically generated evidence created by one of three traditions of inquiry: experimental type, naturalistic, and mixed methods.

Regardless of the tradition, all types of systematic inquiry contain seven parts defined in Table 6.1. Each is detailed in subsequent chapters. Depending on the step in the examined practice process, the purpose, scope, and resources, the substance and sequence of the parts are varied.

As an example, in needs assessment in known contexts, a specific question and research method testing the viability of an already-tested theory and practice might be chosen, whereas unexamined or new situations might call for a discovery

Table 6.1   Parts of Systematic Inquiry in Examined Practice

The Essential	*Definition*
Identification of a Philosophical Foundation	The ontological and epistemic grounding of systematic inquiry (the branches of philosophy that address what is knowledge, and how can we know it?)
Review Literature and Resources	Critical examination of scholarly literature, practice, and other resources to inform or contribute to an inquiry
Forming Questions, Hypotheses, and Queries	Asking/proposing to specify a research direction
Design the Inquiry	Structure how the study will be conducted to answer the research question or query
Set and Protect Study Boundaries	Delimiting the scope of the study
Obtain Information	Collecting information data
Conduct the Analysis	Make sense of the information collected to answer the question or query

method from naturalistic design. Collecting data within the reflexive intervention step may rely heavily on inquiring about how the social work process unfolded from a naturalistic stance and then answering specific quantitative questions about cost and attainment of objectives. In outcome assessment, if resources allow, the questions may follow a mixed-method tradition such that accountability as well as new discovery can occur and contribute to social work knowledge with a mix of evidence-based practice and new theory.

In this chapter, the philosophical foundations (Section I) along with the language and thinking processes that form the methods and justification for knowing are advanced and illustrated as they fit within the examined practice model.

As introduced in Chapter 1 and then illustrated subsequently, we view systematic thinking and action, the necessary and sufficient conditions for "something else" in examined practice, as divided into the three major research traditions each rooted in a philosophical home (Howell, 2013). Although social workers do not have to be philosophers to engage in systematic investigation and use of knowledge, it is, however, important to begin with a clear understanding of the philosophical foundations and assumptions about how knowledge is developed, justified as credible, and used to characterize and predict human experience. By being aware of these assumptions, the social worker can make well-considered decisions about what type of knowledge is useful for diverse purposes. An understanding of these philosophical foundations is therefore not frivolous or tangential but is fundamental to assure the professional recognizes that "knowledge" just doesn't happen in a vacuum. It is shaped by the methods and strategies used create it (DePoy & Gitlin, 2016).

Waxing historical for just a moment, the questions, "What is reality?" (*ontology*) and "How can reality be known?" (*epistemology*) have been posed by philosophers and scholars from many academic and professional disciplines over the chronology of documented history. In Western cultures, until recently, there have been two basic but often competing categories of knowing: monism (the view that one truth exists) and pluralism (many truths can coexist about the same phenomenon). These two perspectives reflect the basic differences between naturalistic inquiry and experimental-type research. *Logical positivism,* which espouses monism*,* forms the rationale and foundation for experimental-type research. In contrast, a number of pluralistic philosophical perspectives underpin naturalistic inquiry (Audi, 2011). As detailed below, logical positivism, a theory of knowledge as unitary and knowable through a prescribed, specified set of rules, previously has been seen as incompatible with views that suggest multiple or even no discernible realities exist (Howell, 2013). This quagmire, however, was rethought by Tashakkori and Teddlie (2010) building on the philosophical work of Pierce and Mannehim (Letherby, Scott, & Williams, 2013), who suggest pragmatism, a view that proposes thought as a practical application. Teddlie and Tashakkori used this philosophical school of thought to transcend debates about the opposition of monism and pluralism. Rather, they proposed that pragmatism is the philosophical reason for mixing research methods from both traditions. Accordingly, monistic and pluralistic knowledge are considered valuable by themselves but incomplete. In order to meet the challenge of making knowledge most useful and informative about daily human activity, purpose and practicality trump opponent ontologies and unite them under the banner of utility.

Consider the example of the elder device study. Recall the problem of mobility device abandonment by elders. Quantification revealed disappointment with the functionality of these devices (Bateni & Maki, 2005), but without the naturalistic study, the role of device aesthetic would not have been known. Mixing methods provided a well-developed and complete understanding of abandonment to reveal what was needed to engender usage.

With this brief introduction and illustration, we are now prepared to encounter each tradition more fully.

PHILOSOPHICAL FOUNDATION OF EXPERIMENTAL-TYPE RESEARCH

Experimental-type researchers share a common frame of reference, or epistemology, that has been called rationalistic, positivist, reductionist, or logical positivism

(Letherby, Scott, & Williams, 2013). Although theoretical differences exist between these concepts, we use the term *logical positivism* to name the overall perspective on which experimental-type design is based.

Descartes, a seventeenth-century philosopher, is often considered the father of Western philosophy (Kenny, 2010). He proposed dualism, an idea that cleaved the mind and the body into distinct entities. Because of the inaccuracy of embodied senses (hearing, seeing, and so forth), Descartes further proposed logical deduction as the only reliable way to come to know about phenomena (Decartes, 2012). Building on Cartesian dualism, Hume, an eighteenth-century philosopher, was most influential in developing the traditional theory of science, which positioned a separation between individual thoughts and what is real in the universe. That is, traditional theorists of science define knowledge as part of a reality that is separate and independent from individuals and that is legitimately verifiable only through the scientific method (Howell, 2013). These theorists believe the world apart from human ideas and a single truth are real, objectively knowable, and can be discovered through observation and measurement that, if properly conducted, is considered unbiased. This epistemological view is based on the fundamental empiricist assumption that it is possible to know and understand phenomena that reside outside humans. This principle is referred to as objectivity. That is to say, objective knowledge is defined as truth, independent of the mind, opinion, or human bias (Gaukroger, 2012). Objective investigation proposes that knowledge is thus separate from the realm of our subjective ideas and passions (Kenny, 2010). Only through systematic observation and sense data, defined as information obtained through observation, listening, feeling, smelling, and tasting, can we come to know truth and reality (Letherby, Scott, & Williams, 2013).

Philosophers in subsequent centuries further developed, modified, and clarified Hume's basic notion of empiricism to yield what in current vernacular is named logical positivism. Essentially, logical positivists purport a single reality (monism) that can be discovered by theorizing its presence, reducing the theory into its parts, a concept known as reductionism, and then testing the parts to verify or falsify all or part of the theory. The relationship among theoretical elements and the logical, structural principles that guide these linkages can also be discovered and known through the systematic collection and analysis of sense data, finally leading to the ability to predict phenomena from what is already considered to be known. Bertrand Russell, a twentieth-century mathematician and philosopher, was instrumental in promoting the synthesis of mathematical logic with sense data (Kenny, 2010).

Statisticians, such as Quetelet, Fischer, and Pearson, developed numeric theories to reveal "fact" (elements of knowledge considered to be real) logically and objectively through mathematical analysis (DePoy & Gitlin, 2016). The logical positive school of thought therefore provided the foundation for what most laypersons have come to know as "experimental research." In this approach, a theory or set of principles is held as potentially true. Specific areas of inquiry are isolated within that theoretical perspective, and clearly defined hypotheses (expected outcomes of an inquiry that investigate only those phenomena) are posed and tested under carefully controlled conditions. Sense data are then collected, measured, and mathematically analyzed to support or refute hypotheses. Through incremental **deductive reasoning**, which involves theory verification and testing, "reality" can become known.

Another major tenet of logical positivism is that objective inquiry and analysis are possible; that is, the investigator, through the use of prescriptive, standardized thinking and action techniques involving translating sense data into numeric indicators, can eliminate alterative explanations for findings and thus verify theory through objective, quantitative measurement (Audi, 2011; Gaukroger, 2012).

PHILOSOPHICAL FOUNDATION OF NATURALISTIC INQUIRY

Several schools of theorists have argued alternative positions to logical positivism and monism. As reflected in their classic text, Braud and Anderson (1998) highlight the common pluralist underpinnings of the naturalistic tradition of knowledge generation. Followers of this tradition seek to understand multiple realities in which context and influence cannot be extracted from the knowing. Further highlighting pluralism in this tradition, there is a range of perspectives in naturalistic approaches about the stability of ideas, symbols, and the role of language in communicating or even creating ideas and experiences. This broad and diverse scope of ideas shapes and directs naturalistic designs in different ways. Second, naturalistic thinking and action are based on the view of knowledge as subjective ranging from simply influenced to fully created by the knower (Letherby, Scott, & Williams, 2013).

Although research based on pluralism has only recently gained acceptance and advantage similar to experimental-type investigations, many of these philosophical perspectives are not new. Ancient Greek philosophers struggled with the separation of idea and object, and philosophers throughout history have continued this debate (Letherby, Scott, & Williams, 2013). The essential characteristics of what we refer to as pluralistic philosophies are as follows:

1. Human experience is complex, holistic, and cannot be understood by reductionism, that is, by identifying and examining it as the sum of its parts.

2. Meaning in human experience is derived from an understanding of individuals in their social, economic, political, cultural, linguistic, physical, and virtual environments.

3. Multiple realities exist or are created by the knower.

4. Those who have the experiences may be the most knowledgeable about them but in all cases hold a form of knowledge that is credible.

In addition to these common characteristics, pluralistic philosophies encompass a number of principles that guide the selection of particular research designs in this category. For example, *phenomenologists* believe that human meaning can be understood only through experience (Detmer, 2013). Thus, a phenomenological understanding is limited to knowing experience without imposing interpretation from those who do not experience the phenomenon under study. In contrast, interpretive and social "semiotic" *interactionists* assume that human meaning evolves within the context of social interaction (Leeuwen, 2004).

More recent philosophies in the postmodern traditions reject the construct of "reality" altogether, suggesting that is a grand narrative, or cultural story that has "lost . . . credibility" (Sims, 2011, p. 4). The instability of linguistic and imaged signs, and thus research based on that philosophical thought, examine how language and symbol both co-opt and undermine what can be known. These philosophies therefore suggest a continuum of knowledge from multiple realities that can be identified to no reality at all. To the extent possible, coming to know anything requires a research design that investigates phenomena in their natural contexts and seeks to discover complexity, meaning, and in some instances, local interpretation (Sims, 2011).

Consider for example recent research in disability studies that informed the elder mobility device project. From one postmodern perspective, disability has been referred to as a category with no common meanings. Who belongs to the category is theorized differently and investigated through multiple lenses such as linguistic, architectural, art, and literary pathways. Thus, while embodied impairment is not denied, which impairments are disabling is unclear and debated, as is disability itself as a category (DePoy & Gilson, 2011, 2014).

PHILOSOPHICAL FOUNDATION OF MIXED METHODS

The brief discussions about philosophical foundations of experimental-type and naturalistic research traditions illuminate why integrating them in a single study has met with significant skepticism, specifically about how objectivity and subjectivity can simultaneously be claimed when they argue against one another. Yet, mixed methods are gaining in popularity as the approach to create and share comprehensive systematic knowledge in humanities and social and behavioral science fields. Scott (Letherby, Scott, & Williams, 2013) provides some clarity about this phenomenon in his comment, "the first approximation to an objective representation of the world must be based upon a recognition and acceptance of . . . diversity and relativity of subjective experience" (p. 151). He then argues for intellectual synthesis, which Creswell and Plano Clark (2011), Brewer and Hunter (2005), and Tashakkori and Teddlie (2010) seemed to achieve through selecting pragmatism as the philosophical foundation for mixing methods. Although there are many versions of this school of thought, pragmatists privilege purpose over other concerns. Rather than adhering to objectivity or espousing **subjectivity**, pragmatist philosophers look at effectiveness in achieving a goal as the criterion for shaping investigation. Applied to systematic knowing, the most effective way to meet a knowledge generation aim philosophically drives how one comes to know. Thus, as suggested first by Brewer and Hunter (2005) and more recently by Tashakkori and Teddlie (2010), contemporary researchers who adopt integrated or mixed methods are not necessarily proceeding from opposing philosophical bases at all but rather from a single perspective, that of pragmatism.

Foregrounding purpose as the frame for all thinking and action, the examined practice model reflects pragmatism throughout all five elements delimited within a perimeter of systematic knowledge development, use, and sharing.

IMPLICATIONS OF PHILOSOPHICAL DIFFERENCES FOR SYSTEMATIC INQUIRY IN EXAMINED PRACTICE

Although a social worker does not have to take a single position in the ongoing debate between different philosophical schools, fundamental to the examined practice model is the principle that all rigorous systematic activity must be recognized as knowledge generating. How knowledge is explicitly or implicitly defined and created and how the relationship between the knower (researcher) and the known (research outcomes or phenomena of the study) is characterized in large part directs the study effort, from framing a question or query to reporting findings.

Return to the elder mobility abandonment problem. In order to find out why elders did not continue regular use of mobility aids, Bateni and Maki (2005) used experimental-type meta-analysis, a review and analysis of numerous previously conducted studies, all investigating adaptive equipment abandonment from a theoretical point of view that lent itself to measurement (see Chapter 9 for more detail on meta-analysis). Recall that experimental-type research begins with a theory and then delimits what is measured within that theory to verify or falsify it or its parts. Bateni and Maki theorized that device abandonment was a direct result of the user's concern for the device's function and safety. They sought studies that examined their theory, and from their meta-analysis of studies affirming this point of view, Bateni and Maki concluded that the perception on the part of the user (that safety and functionality of walking aids were inadequate) was the reason for non-use. The investigators met their articulated purpose: "to examine the biomechanic principles and related literature about the advantages and the possible disadvantages associated with the most commonly used types of mobility aids" (Bateni & Maki, 2005, p. 134)

However, in their conclusion, Bateni and Maki (2005) acknowledged that the full scope of demands and consequences of using such devices remains unknown and proposed further research to reveal new information. Note that they delimited their focus to biomechanics. "Although many of the functional benefits of cane and walker use appear to be well established, further research is needed to better characterize specific demands and adverse consequences using these devices" (Bateni & Maki, 2005, p. 143).

Now consider an alternative purpose that may have been implied by Bateni and Maki (2005) but was not stated, to enhance safety and function of elders by decreasing abandonment of support devices. This purpose calls for an approach that can examine both expected and unanticipated influences on device use. To meet this purpose, pragmatism comes into play as the purpose is not delimited to a research agenda based on the single theory that identified the biomechanics of mobility devices as the reason for use or refusal to use.

Now, consider the naturalistic part of the needs assessment in which elders were asked why they did not continue to use prescribed walking supports (DePoy & Gilson, 2014). To address the problem of immobility, a systematic, mixed-method needs assessment relying on **survey** and interview was conducted. It was not until device users and abandoners were interviewed that the issue of aesthetics was raised. The needs assessment systematically revealed the unsightly appearance of medical devices as the most critical barrier to overcome in order to promote use of these aids in communities where people live.

THEORY IN EXAMINED PRACTICE

The link between social work theory, research, and practice is affirmed by the Council on Social Work Education (2012), which requires that both accredited undergraduate and graduate curricula contain and link content in all three areas. Examined practice integrates these areas and thus can be used in all three curriculum components as all create or reflect social work knowing. Because theory is an intimate partner of research and practice, we briefly define it here and engage with its role in research and in examined practice before beginning a more detailed voyage into systematic designs and methods.

Kerlinger and Lee (2009), define theory as "a set of interrelated constructs, definitions, and *propositions* that present a systematic view of phenomena by specifying relations among variables, with the purpose of explaining or predicting phenomena." Note that theory is not defined as fact or truth but rather as a set of well-developed, organized ideas that has the potential to explain or predict human experience in an orderly fashion. As further clarified by Brewer and Hunter (2006), "theory plays a dual role in research. On one hand new theories solve research problems by accounting for unexplained phenomena and by superseding questionable old theories. On the other hand, existing theory guides researchers in formulating research problems" (p. 52).

Development of novel theory tends to be the province of naturalistic methods while continued acceptance and use of well-supported theory is the job of logico-deductive (experimental-type) research.

Consistent with their philosophical foundations, naturalistic designs tend to develop theory and thus increase abstract complexity, whereas experimental-type methods follow a "reductionist" logic structure in order to test existing theory. That is to say, experimental-type research reduces abstracts to parts, then further to shared experience, and then to numbers. The term "shared experience" is used by DePoy & Gitlin (2016) to supplant the words *data* or *evidence* as the phrase broadly characterizes a range of sense and experiential information relevant to systematic inquiry. This point creates a segue to language and thinking processes in research.

Figure 6.1   Trajectory of Each Tradition in Theory Development and Testing

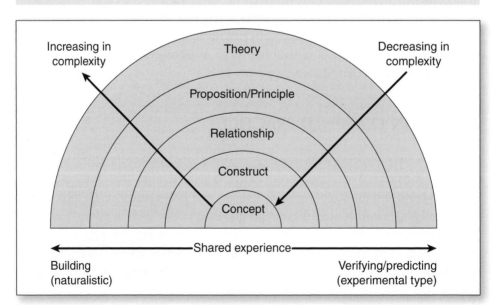

As evidenced even in philosophy, each research tradition uses its own language, its own thinking and action processes, and each poses specific design issues and concerns. We now turn to design terminology and processes in each tradition.

Experimental-Type Research

We begin delving more deeply into design by discussing experimental-type research. Recall that this tradition is anchored in logical positivism and as reflected in Figure 6.1, uses deductive logic to verify or falsify a theorized single reality. This process involves theorizing to describe and/or explain the part of "reality" about which the social worker is concerned, reducing theory to incrementally smaller parts, examining the parts through operationalizing (translating constructs into measurables), and using the numeric findings to determine the degree to which the analysis verifies or falsifies part or all of the theory. These action processes are discussed in more detail in subsequent chapters in this section of the book.

As discussed previously, a second principle of logical positivism is that it is possible and desirable to understand the world objectively. Recall that objectivity refers to eliminating bias, defined within research vernacular as unintended or unanticipated influences on the findings or outcome of an inquiry (Gaukroger, 2012). Note that this definition of bias differs from more popular usages in which bias is defined as inclination or prejudice (Dictionary.com, 2013).

As an example, within this tradition, the social worker begins by defining a topic specific to the purpose of the study. Think back to the TAP project in which the problem statement was framed as "disparities to web-based health information. This statement formed the broad substantive content of social work concern." After narrowing and clarifying a topical area and purpose, supporting theoretical knowledge was obtained by conducting a review of scholarly literature and resources. Note that this process is retrospective in that existing knowledge that has already been developed is reviewed and used as the basis for further inquiry. Thus, the social worker discerns how the problem has already been theoretically and methodologically engaged. With this systematic information critically analyzed, the social worker proposed a specific research question derived from and building on previous scholarship. To answer the research question "objectively" as required in this tradition, a systematic design was crafted that controlled, to the extent possible, factors that could have potentially introduced bias. Action processes for collecting and analyzing data, or what is referred to as "shared experience" in Figure 6.1, and from what sources, were clearly and succinctly specified and followed without deviation. Through analysis of the data, the social worker judged the extent to which findings either confirmed or questioned the "truth value" of the theoretical tenets and their capacity to explain and ultimately predict the slice of "reality" under investigation.

Many designs are anchored in the philosophical foundation of logical positivism. Table 6.2 lists the four major categories of design that form the experimental-type tradition, each of which is discussed in detail in Chapter 9.

Table 6.2   Four Major Categories of Experimental-Type Design

True experimentation: Contains all of the elements (random selection, control, manipulation) necessary to answer cause and effect questions

Quasi-Experimentation: Contains control and manipulation but not random selection

Pre-Experimentation: Contains only one of the true-experimental elements

Non-Experimentation: Structurally does not manipulate designs

Language and Thinking Processes

All designs in each of the four categories in Table 6.2 share a common language and standards for adequacy of design. First, the word *design* in this tradition refers to the plan or blueprint that specifies and structures the action processes of collecting, analyzing, and reporting data to answer a research question. Different from popular usage, the term *structure* specifies the relationships among the variables (constructs lexically defined and measured) of a study and must be fully and clearly articulated in a formal research question. The purpose of experimental-type design is to craft the study prior to the occurrence of any action processes in order to answer the study question. The design therefore serves to restrict or decrease extraneous influences (bias) on the findings such that the claims can be supported by the study. The element of design is a major distinction of research that separates it from the everyday types of observations and thinking and action processes.

Unlike naturalistic thinking and action, experimental-type design follows a rigid sequence. From a critical review of the literature, the theory being tested is articulated, a theory-specific research question is posed, data are collected and analyzed, and conclusions about the accuracy of the theory or part that was tested are then developed based on the analysis.

Of particular note is that the literature review justifies not only the rationale for the study but also the variables included, type of questions that a study can answer, and how. Thus, the social worker proceeding with experimental-type inquiry develops a design that builds on both previously developed and well-supported ideas and the actions that have been conducted in ways that conform to the rules of experimental-type rigor.

Design adequacy is based on how well the design answers the research question that is posed. If it does not answer the research question, then the design, regardless of how complicated or sophisticated it may appear, is not appropriate or valid.

Structure of Experimental-Type Research

Experimental-type research has a well-developed language with clear rules for the adequacy of thinking and action processes. Table 6.3 lists seminal key terms in this tradition.

To illustrate, we use the outcome study of elder abandonment of mobility aids. In this initiative, as a means to address the aesthetic barrier to engaging in fitness activity, a team of social workers and engineers designed a three-wheeled walking device to support weight bearing and balance.

Recall that this project emerged from a needs assessment that created theory about the role of aesthetic preference in the willingness of elders to accept devices for their participation in movement, particularly in public. Thus to study the outcome of the project and to verify theory regarding the importance of aesthetics in functional devices, it was hypothesized that abandonment (construct) of this device

Table 6.3   Definitions of Key Experimental-Type Terms

Term	Definition
Concept	Word or idea that symbolically represents phenomena not directly observable
Construct	Theoretical elements based on observations that cannot be observed directly or indirectly but can only be inferred
Definitions	A *conceptual definition*, or lexical definition, stipulates the meaning of a concept or construct with other concepts or constructs. An *operational definition* stipulates the meaning by specifying how the concept is observed or experienced (primarily through measurement in experimental-type design).
Variable	A concept or construct to which numerical values are assigned. The three basic types of variables are independent, intervening, and dependent. An ***independent variable*** "is the presumed cause of the dependent variable, the presumed effect." Thus, a ***dependent variable*** (also referred to as "outcome" and "criterion") refers to the phenomenon the investigator seeks to understand, explain, or predict. An *intervening variable* (also called a "confounding" or an "extraneous" variable) is a phenomenon that has an effect on the study variables but that may or may not be the object of the study.
Hypothesis	A testable statement that indicates what the researcher expects to find, given the theory and level of knowledge in the literature

(concept) would occur significantly less frequently than the use of typical wheeled walkers with a medical appearance. The jogger was named as the independent variable (measured as present or absent). Abandonment, defined as nonuse and operationalized as frequency of use per week, was compared for both devices.

Plan of Design

The plan of an experimental-type design requires a set of thinking processes in which the five core issues are considered: bias, manipulation, **control**, **validity**, and reliability. Each is defined in Table 6.4.

Return to the jogger outcome study as an example. The experimental-type element of the outcome assessment was designed to answer the following question:

> To what extent do elders abandon an aesthetically designed mobility device compared to a typical "medicalized walker" with equivalent functionality?

Given that the object of the study was abandonment, the design was structured with a comparison rather than a **control** group. A control group would not have been appropriate since the absence of the device would not be an **internally valid** design for answering the research question. One must possess something in order to abandon it!

Elders who had just received hip replacements were selected purposively from a population of such clients in an outpatient rehabilitation practice. To reduce **bias**

Table 6.4   Five Core Issues in Experimental-Type Design

Term	Definition
Bias	The potential unintended or unavoidable effect on study outcomes
Manipulation	The action process of maneuvering the independent variable so that the effect of its presence, absence, or degree on the dependent variable can be observed
Control	Set of action processes that direct or manipulate factors to achieve an outcome
Validity	The extent to which a study answers the research questions and findings are accurate or reflect the underlying purpose of the study
	Internal validity refers to the structure of the design in answering the question, while external validity addresses the capacity of the sampling process to answer the research questions about the population from which the sample was selected.
Reliability	The stability of a research design

related to assignment of elders to one group or the other based on personal prefer-ence, time of day, or so on, each participant was **randomly** assigned to one of two groups and provided with instructions for use of the device. Manipulation occurred in the type of device assigned to each group. Over a month-long period, elders were asked to document their frequency and duration of use of the device on an indoor track. The track was selected to eliminate the influence of extraneous vari-ables such as weather and to enhance **reliability** through creating equivalent and stable testing conditions. Note that the sample was one of convenience, and thus the results of the study were specific to that group only, limiting **external validity** (generalizability). This point is discussed more fully in Chapter 10. While limited generalizability is one of the major criticisms of evaluation research, we suggest that within examined practice, the object of inquiry is typically the social work effort and its success in solving the defined or implied problem. Thus, while the utility of the strategy for groups beyond the participants should be examined in subsequent social work needs assessment, sharing the knowledge gained in a proj-ect even when external validity is limited renders this device, theory, and princi-ples available to the body of social work literature and innovation.

Naturalistic Inquiry

There is great diversity in strategies categorized as naturalistic inquiry. As already introduced, inquiry that fits within this tradition is rooted in diverse philo-sophical and theoretical perspectives, and thus, the language and thinking pro-cesses vary depending on approach. However, all naturalistic thinking and action share some basic commonalities, including pluralism, logical structures of induc-tion or abduction, flexibility and acceptance of shared experience, sometimes including but most frequently more varied than numeric data.

Within the naturalistic tradition, the social worker may vary (1) the extent to which a study involves his other personal "essence," language, experiences, and insights; (2) the extent to which individual "experience" and meaning versus pat-terns of human experience is sought; (3) the extent to which structure is imposed by the social worker on the action processes; and (4) the sequence of the research.

Different from experimental-type thinking and action, in naturalistic study, neither the point of entry into the inquiry nor the sequence of the thinking and action processes is prescribed *a priori*. Thus, a social worker may obtain data even prior to reviewing literature and resources to inform the design, may dynamically change specific action strategies in response to findings throughout the process, and/or revisit steps that have been previously conducted. The term *iterative* describes the repetitive, flexible, and progressive building process of many types of naturalistic inquiry (Audi, 2011).

Although there are many design variations, Table 6.5 lists the major categories of design that comprise the tradition of naturalistic inquiry. Once again, recall the example of abandonment of mobility supports by elders. The naturalistic element of the needs assessment study revealed the role of aesthetics in acceptance or rejection of equipment, a phenomenon that has not been investigated and extensively theorized previously.

In Chapter 9, the designs listed in Table 6.5 will be detailed and illustrated. However, just a glance at the names and nature of each strategy reveals the diversity of naturalistic approaches. Despite their variation, however, naturalistic designs have common denominators in their language and thinking.

Context Specificity

Because of the discovery aims of naturalistic inquiry, systematic investigation in this research tradition is conducted where it naturally occurs, ergo the name naturalistic (DePoy & Gitlin, 2016). Because of the perspective that what can be known about a phenomenon cannot be separated from its context, claims to generalize, referred to as external validity in experimental-type design are not made

Table 6.5 Major Categories of Naturalistic Inquiry

Categories of Design	Brief Description
Endogenous	Conceptualized, designed, and conducted by insiders of the culture, using their own epistemology and their own structure of relevance
Participatory Action Research	Conceptualized, designed, and conducted by a team of investigators and "insiders"
Critical Theory	An approach that uses inquiry for social change
Phenomenology	Explication, narrative presentation, and interpretation of the meaning of lived experiences
Heuristic Research	Investigator experience and attributed meanings as primary data
Ethnography	Immersion to understand the patterns of a culture
Narrative Inquiry	Storytelling as data
Life History	Biography investigating the sequence of all or part of a life
Grounded Theory	Theory discovery through prescribed analytic processes
Naturalistic Meta-Analysis	Aggregation of disparate data sets for analysis

Table 6.6 Common Denominators of Naturalistic Designs

Term	Definition
Context Specificity	Knowledge is embedded in surroundings.
Complexity and Pluralism	Systematic inquiry about social phenomena is a human activity that is both messy because of its humanity and multifaceted because of its interpretive nature.
Transferability of Findings	What is learned can inform similar contexts.
Flexibility	Design deviates from its original plan.
Language and Symbol	This term refers to concern with meaning of linguistic symbols
Emic and Etic Perspectives	The insider/outsider status of the investigator influences the nature of the knowledge derived from the study.

in naturalistic inquiry. Thus, this rigor criterion is not relevant for this research tradition. Rather theory is developed and then may be tested for relevance in future activity.

The elder mobility project illustrates how theory developed in naturalistic needs assessment was then subjected to experimental-type testing in the outcome assessment.

Complexity and Pluralistic Perspective of Reality

Social workers proceeding from the naturalistic tradition propose that systematic thinking and action are complex and pluralistic because they are conducted by different people in natural settings. Moreover, interpretation and focus take varied pathways as a result of the underlying philosophical beliefs and inductive and abductive logic structures. With inductive reasoning, principles emerge from previously unrelated information. Because induction assumes that individual perspective (bias) is part of the logic structure, a single data set can be organized and analyzed differently by each individual who thinks about it. The end result of induction is the development of a complex set of relationships uniting smaller pieces of information (opposite in direction to the reduction of principles to their parts, as in deductive reasoning). It is therefore not only possible but likely that the same information may have different meanings or that there may be differential interpretations by different individuals. This element of naturalistic research is one of its major criticisms by those who espouse the existence of a single, knowable reality.

Transferability of Findings

As noted above, because the findings from naturalistic studies are specific to the research context, the aim to generalize or to achieve external validity is not relevant to this tradition. However, because a primary purpose of naturalistic research is the generation of new theory, a desired outcome of naturalistic design is the development of knowledge that can be thoughtfully transferred to more expansive contexts.

It is because phenomena are context bound and, according to naturalistic principles, cannot be understood apart from the settings in which they occur, that naturalistic inquiry is not concerned with the issue of generalizability or external validity as articulated in experimental-type inquiry. Rather, naturalistic inquiry is directed to understanding the richness and depth in one environment with the capacity to retain unique meanings that are lost when generalization is a goal (Creswell & Clark, 2011). The development of in-depth descriptions (referred to as thick description) and interpretations of different contexts leads to the ability to transfer, not generalize, meanings from one context to another domain (Tracy, 2013). In so doing, the social worker is able to compare contexts and their elements as a means to gain new insights about the specific setting itself and the relevance of findings from another naturalistic study to diverse domains.

Flexibility

Different from experimental design, which requires adherence to the plan of inquiry once it is developed, naturalistic activity is fluid and flexible. An important and expected feature of a naturalistic study is that the procedures and plans for conducting it are apt to change as the work proceeds. Therefore, the social worker may use the results of preliminary findings as guidance for planning or altering subsequent action processes.

Consider Janice as an example. Typical of reflexive intervention in clinical work, even when evidence-based processes are used, is the flexibility of the social worker to change directions on the basis of systematic observation. The first social work encounter did not illustrate this approach and thus was unsuccessful in making changes necessary to facilitate the achievement of Janice's objectives. The approach used by the second social worker was both systematic and naturalistic, not only contributing to Janice's progress, but adding to the formal body of knowledge informing social work with clients who have abrupt changes in functional status.

Language and Symbol

A major shared concern in naturalistic designs is meaning of linguistic and other types of symbols. Even within the same cultural or language context, pluralism of language, imagery, and their diverse meanings is assumed. As mentioned, however, not all investigators concerned with symbol believe that naturalistic inquiry can reveal meaning or even that there is a common meaning assigned by all who share in a communication.

This point is aptly illustrated in the elder mobility device project. The meaning of mobility device (the word *walker*) to Bateni & Maki (2005) is a biomechanical object to aid in function, while to elders who abandon the device, it is a visual artifact creating stigma.

Emic and Etic Perspectives

Design structures vary as to their **emic** or **etic** orientation. An emic perspective refers to the **"insider's"** or member's understanding and interpretation of experience. An etic orientation reflects perspectives from nonmembers of a **culture** or group. A design on the extreme end of the emic continuum is endogenous inquiry in which the investigator relinquishes all control over a study.

To illustrate, we use the naturalistic element of the mobility device design project. As we noted, the needs assessment sought to understand what was necessary to reverse abandonment and thus promote involvement in safe physical activity and movement among elders who needed equipment for active engagement. The explanations in the literature were not productive in resolving the problem. Therefore, we determined that theorizing need beyond what was already proposed was indicated. From the group of elders who were receiving outpatient rehabilitation following hip replacement, we therefore entered as **etic** (outsiders) to seek knowledge from members. Face-to-face open-ended interviews were conducted with consenting "informants," the elders themselves. Participants were each asked to reflect on how the use of a mobility device made them feel, what it meant to them to be using a walker, and how the use of this device affected their lives. Several of the informants noted that using a walker made them feel old, one informant indicated that she did not like the way she looked when she saw her gait with the walker in the mirror, and several others said that they were embarrassed to be using this device. Countering the literature, the device function was a secondary concern to a majority of the informants. More important, the material symbol, the walker, had diverse meanings among the group interviewed because they refused to use the equipment. Illustrating flexibility, this unanticipated knowledge led us to rethink the needs assessment to

Figure 6.2   Mixing Methods

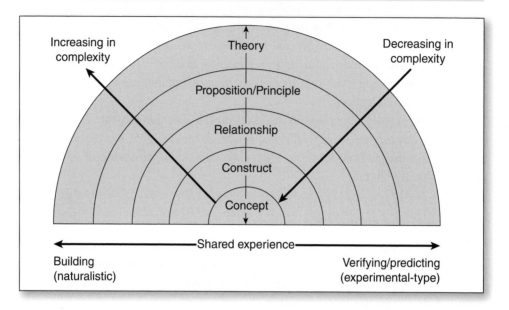

ask about aesthetic preferences and assume diverse responses. When asked, elders had varied preferences for activity and appearance of a mobility device illustrating the multiple meanings of symbol and object meaning (Candlin & Guins, 2009). Further illustrating flexibility of research design, we then convened a group and showed them computer assisted design (CAD) drawings of potential walkers, eliciting pluralistic meanings for the visual symbols. As illustrated in detail in Chapter 12, the narrative data were analyzed to reveal commonalities to guide theory development. From the etic perspective, abandonment was attributed to device function. But knowledge derived from insiders contradicted what was published and thus was invaluable in refining what was needed to resolve a problem that had not been well informed by previous etic knowledge. Moreover, the differential interpretation of the meaning of a single object was evident in the group, thus pointing to the heterogeneity within a group that was distinguished from and thus contrasted to device users in experimental-type inquiry.

INTEGRATING THE TWO RESEARCH TRADITIONS

As discussed, there has been significant and heated debate over which tradition is most useful in advancing an understanding of human experience. Because proponents of experimental-type thinking and action believe that credible evidence can only be generated through implementing "objective" thinking and action processes, they may not value the naturalistic foundations of *pluralism* and "subjectivity." Conversely, social workers who resonate with the naturalistic tradition challenge the extent to which human experience can be reduced to a single, observable, predictive reality, particularly through the process of measurement. As noted above, because of the basic philosophical differences between the traditions, debates on integrating approaches have raged as well. However, as we noted above, mixing methods within the foundation of pragmatism has transcended these debates such that purpose can trump rigid adherence to a single tradition and can therefore rely on the strengths of both to test theory while advancing new understandings.

Within the examined practice sequence, mixed methods used at the needs assessment stage can both test existing theory and reveal unanticipated needs linked to the problem element being addressed. During reflexive intervention, mixing methods can generate accountability statistics as well as narrative description of social work activity. Outcome assessment similarly can benefit from mixed methods to measure objective attainment while uncovering unexpected outcomes for the target and others (Creswell, 2014). Efficacious integration is contingent on the social worker's understanding of the purpose of the research effort and of the strengths and limitations of the thinking and action processes, the design strategies, and the particular methodological approaches of each tradition.

Consider both the TAP and mobility device projects. Note that mixed-methods designs were used in the needs assessment phase of examined practice in the device innovation project and in the outcome assessment in the TAP project. Each mixing strategy differed according to purpose.

Although there are numerous schemes for mixed methods, the three listed in Table 6.7 show variations and frequently used approaches to serve social work knowing.

Table 6.7 Mixed-Method Schemes

Mixing experimental-type sampling with naturalistic data collection
Mixing experimental-type and naturalistic data collection
Following naturalistic inquiry with experimental-type theory testing

SUMMARY

In this chapter, we entered the precise world of systematic thinking and action. Philosophical foundations of each of the three traditions were discussed following which the language, general thinking and action processes, and common denominators within each of the three approaches were presented and illustrated.

The main points in this chapter are as follows:

1. Legitimate examined practice knowledge is generated by one of the three research traditions.

2. Process, the purpose, scope, and resources shape how each tradition is used.

3. Seven essentials comprise all three traditions, albeit in different sequences.

4. Each tradition is underpinned by a set of philosophical tenets that both define knowledge and propose how it can be known (if at all).

5. Aligned with the purposive foundation of examined practice, mixed-method research is based on pragmatism.

6. Theory is central to both inquiry and practice. Naturalistic thinking tends to generate new theory while experimental-type thinking is designed to test and thus verify or falsify theory.

7. Each tradition has its own terminology, thinking, and action processes.

8. Design in research refers to a blueprint or plan for conducting a study. Each tradition treats design differently.

REFERENCES

Audi, R. (2011). *Epistemology* (3rd ed.). New York, NY: Routledge.

Bateni, H., & Maki, B. (2005). Assistive devices for balance and mobility: Benefits, demands, and adverse consequences. *Archives of Physical Medicine and Rehabilitation, 86*, 134–145.

Bias. (2013). *Dictionary.com*. Retrieved from http://dictionary.reference.com/browse/bias

Braud, W., & Anderson, R. (1998). *Transpersonal research for the social sciences*. Thousand Oaks, CA: Sage.

Brewer, J., & Hunter, A. (2006). *Foundations of multimethod research*. Thousand Oaks, CA: Sage.

Candlin, F., & Guins, R. (2009). *The object reader*. London, UK: Routledge.

Council on Social Work Education (CSWE). (2012). *Educational policy and accreditation standards*. Retrieved from http://www.cswe.org/File.aspx?id=13780

Creswell, J. (2014). *Research design*. Thousand Oaks, CA: Sage.

Creswell, J., & Clark, V. P. (2011). *Designing and conducting mixed methods research.* Thousand Oaks, CA: Sage.

Decartes, R. (2012). *A discourse of a method.* Amazon Digital Services.

DePoy, E., & Gilson, S. (2011). *Studying disability.* Los Angeles, CA: Sage.

DePoy, E., & Gilson, S. (2014). *Disability as design.* London, UK: Routledge.

DePoy, E., & Gitlin, L. (2016). *Introduction to research* (5th ed.). St Louis, MO: Elsevier.

Detmer, D. (2013). *Phenomenology explained: From experience to Insight.* Chicago, IL: Carus.

Gaukroger, S. (2012). *Objectivity: A very short introduction.* Oxford, UK: Oxford University Press.

Howell, K. (2013). *An introduction to the philosophy of methodology.* London, UK: Sage.

Kenny, A. (2010). *A new history of Western philosophy.* New York, NY: Oxford University Press.

Kerlinger, F., & Lee, H. (2009). *Foundations of behavioral research.* Belmont, CA: Wadsworth.

Leeuwen, T. V. (2004). Semiotics and iconography. In T. V. Leeuwen & C. Jewitt, *Handbook of visual analysis.* Thousand Oaks, CA: Sage.

Letherby, G., Scott, J., & Williams, M. (2013). *Objectivity and subjectivity in social research.* Thousand Oaks, CA: Sage.

Sims, S. (2011). *Routledge companion to postmodernism.* New York, NY: Routledge.

Tashakkori, A., & Teddlie, C. (2010). *Handbook of mixed methods in social and behavioral research* (2nd ed.). Thousand Oaks, CA: Sage.

Tracy, S. (2013). *Qualitative research methods: Collecting evidence, crafting analysis, communicating impact.* Malden, MA: Wiley-Blackwell.

Chapter 7

THE ROLE OF LITERATURE IN EXAMINED PRACTICE

With the advancement of information technology, sources of knowledge in addition to scholarship appearing in print have been increasingly accepted as part of the **literature review**. In concert with this trend, the term *literature* is pluralistic both in format and venue (Huffine, 2010). Within the examined practice model, however, a major element of social work knowing of course is systematically generated knowledge. However, different from models of evidence-based practice and other research to practice approaches, examined practice knowledge may emerge from broad sources. Still, the knowledge must be transparent, conform to the logic structures of one of the three research traditions, and locate the basis for its claims in the evidence presented. The "how do you know" question therefore must be logically and systematically answerable in order for knowledge to be included as a legitimate addition to social work knowing.

PURPOSES OF LITERATURE
REVIEW IN EXAMINED PRACTICE

In general, social workers review the literature to inform their thinking and action (Kiteley & Stogdan, 2014). Any review of the existing knowledge synthesizes both what is theorized and known and what is missing but needs to be developed in order to understand, respond to, and assess the value of a social work response to a problem or phenomenon. Moreover, areas of theoretical and practice controversy are uncovered in conducting a comprehensive literature review such that the social worker can proceed from a well-rounded knowledge base. Thus, in concert with the purposive underpinning of examined practice, literature review in each of the steps serves multiple aims that the social worker should be able to identify.

At the point of problem identification, systematic knowledge helps to clarify, expand, and document a claim (University of Southern California, n.d.). Refer back to Chapter 2 for a review of problem statements. Recall that a problem begins with an initial value statement. However, contained within this definition of problem is substantive and theoretical concern as well. Literature documents this theory and content and may even serve to support wide agreement with a value position. Therefore, the literature serves to systematically elaborate the nature and magnitude of the circumstance being defined as a problem, the degree to which and how it has been theorized, and may illuminate how others have framed and explained it as a problem or not.

As an example, abandonment of mobility devices by elders as a risk for falling is well documented in the health provider literature, providing evidence that this phenomenon is not local or trivial. However, the causes of abandonment theorized in the literature were incomplete, leading to its continuation even in the presence of efforts to convince device users that they needed walking supports to be safe. Synthesizing both the evidence of abandonment and the failure of theory-based strategies to improve this undesirable situation, questions were raised by the social work team about the extent to which the need statement provided reasonable theoretical and empirical guidance for social work intervention.

The example above points to a second purpose of literature review. Literature is or should be reviewed at the point of determining what is needed to resolve or address the identified problem area. Social workers typically use literature and systematic knowledge sources to understand how others have theoretically approached need and then attempted to meet it. In examined practice, the social worker evaluates the relevance of the literature to understanding need and guiding action. In the example of mobility device abandonment above, the causal theory was obviously missing the mark, as the knowledge derived from research was not productive in shaping responses that met the goal of increasing device use.

Now recall Janice, who was referred to a social worker for depression following the early occurrence of a cerebrovascular accident (CVA). The social worker who initially saw Janice proceeded to organize her goals and intervention from a Jungian theoretical position, a well developed and tested body of literature that theorized depression as a protective response to something awry. Within Jungian literature, brief intervention is not indicated as depression is seen as a signifier that calls for depth of analysis and slow, long-term healing of historical wounds (Wilde, 2011). Over several weeks of social work intervention, Janice became frustrated, not receiving the guidance that she sought on how to resume life following the loss of so much physical function. When the social worker continued to work with Janice through a Jungian theoretical lens, Janice left to obtain help from a new social worker. In this interaction, the social worker asked Janice to state what she saw as the problem, which Janice perceived as her lack of knowledge on how to regain the activity that made her life worth living. Consulting the literature on stroke rehabilitation did not suffice to guide the intervention, and thus, the new social worker turned to literature in progressive disability theory to understand alternatives for redefining the problems of depression and poor adaptation. The literature on disability theorized Janice's problem as a barrier to activity and geographies in which Janice used to engage. The new social worker revised the need away from depression intervention to involving Janice in a centered process in which she identified and learned how to resume her valued activities. She and the new social worker collaborated to find the resources that Janice needed to bypass or eliminate barriers to the parts of life that gave her great joy and maintained health, one of which was outdoor sports activity in cold climates. Because the literature did not contain systematic inquiry on the availability of equipment or methods to aid ambulatory individuals with mobility barriers to engage in cross country skiing, the new social worker proceeded to conduct his own investigation on how Janice might proceed to regain this valued part of her life.

The examples above model how literature is used to determine what is needed to resolve the identified problem. Systematic knowledge and the theory it supports should be critically evaluated for efficacy in informing a direction for intervention. If the literature is not adequate in theory, content, or method, systematic needs assessment should be undertaken within a purposive and resource framework. The Jungian social worker failed to judge the relevance of her own theoretical perspective for understanding what was needed to address Janice's problem and thus traveled down a path that was not meaningful to Janice. The new social worker read widely and critically to obtain guidance for what was needed to address the problem presented by his client, and when he did not find satisfactory substance, he then proceeded to conduct his own research. As we discuss later, this systematic inquiry led to social work innovation.

Goals and objectives are well informed by literature but typically are not articulated in it unless practice manuals form the sources of knowledge. However, even when not articulated, because goals and objectives in examined practice emerge from need and set a direction for outcome, they essentially derive from the literature on need.

At the reflexive intervention stage, social workers use literature in many ways. First, literature informs a theoretical framework to organize social work activity to achieve the articulated goals and objectives. Revisit Dean here. From Dean's initial presentation, it was certainly feasible to look to knowledge of drug use and relevant interventions to guide social work action. However, when Dean's seizures recurred, evidence-based medical knowledge informed the alternative approach that ultimately resolved Dean's medical problem. Thus, in the absence of social work theory to guide intervention, literature from fields outside of social work and its typical canon is extremely valuable as illustrated by Dean's outcome.

Janice's social worker turned to two bodies of literature to guide his action. First, he looked to adaptive sports and kinesiology to find a method to help Janice resume outdoor fitness. What he found was not satisfactory, and thus he consulted knowledge on fabrication of adaptive equipment. Informed by preliminary reflexive intervention literature detailing the social work project on elder mobility device usage, and because this work was not in his knowledge and skill domain, the social worker engaged with an engineering department at his local university to champion opportunities for fitness through working with students who could design adaptive sports equipment.

Outcome assessment method and substance are significantly informed by literature as well. How to best assess the extent to which goals and objectives were met by the social work intervention is part and parcel of evaluation and research methodological literature as reflected in Chapter 4 of this text. What methods to select and how to conduct them form the corpus of many research courses in schools of social work. In addition to method, the literature identifies instruments and substantive content that have been successfully (or unsuccessfully) used to examine outcome.

Dean's social worker used well-documented outcome assessment tools to examine his goal attainment in substance abuse intervention. When the empirical findings did not correlate with absence of seizures, it became clear that the problem had not been accurately identified.

Finally, at the stage of sharing knowledge, literature is the primary outlet. Janice's social worker wrote a scholarly article on social work collaboration with mechanical engineering, contributing innovative reflexive intervention to the knowledge base of social work and detailing cooperative work with a field that is not typically involved in providing social work services but should be.

Thus, an important purpose of reviewing the literature is to sharpen the focus of social work theory, concern, and activity. Discovering what others know, how they have theorized their universe, how they come to know it, and what is missing in social work knowledge are essential functions of the review and should be conducted throughout the examined practice sequence.

As discussed in more detail later in the book, a literature review may be used not only to inform but also to serve as a source of data itself. Using some forms of naturalistic inquiry, literature and other sources are brought in at different points of the examined practice process to emphasize, elaborate, or reveal emergent themes. Consider how a careful analysis of the ADA and ADAAA policies might have revealed why Elton's employer was reluctant to maintain his employment and proceeded to invoke the financial hardship clause rather than looking for other alternatives.

A systematic literature review may also be used as data in experimental-type thinking. Literature used as data expands the universe of systematically created evidence for re-analysis and application. Returning to Elton, examining the outcomes of employer education as a strategy to maintain employment for people who develop the need for workplace accommodations while on the job could be expanded to test theory and inform practice beyond local practice.

HOW TO CONDUCT A LITERATURE SEARCH

For us, conducting a literature search and preparing a literature review are exciting and creative processes. However, there may be so much literature and other resources in the area of interest that the review process can initially seem daunting. The following six steps provide guidance for the thinking and action processes of searching the literature, organizing the sources, and extracting information to be used in a comprehensive critical review.

Table 7.1 below lists each of the six major thinking and action processes necessary to conduct a comprehensive and purposive literature review.

Table 7.1   Six Steps to Conducting a Literature Review

Step 1: Determine when to conduct a search

Step 2: Delimit what is searched

Step 3: Access databases for periodicals, books, images, and other important sources

Step 4: Organize the information

Step 5: Critically evaluate the literature

Step 6: Formally prepare the literature review

Step 1: Determine When to Conduct a Search

The first step in a literature review is the determination of when a review should be done. The initial decision on timing involves planning when to formally approach the literature. This point was addressed in the previous section specific to how literature and other sources are used in each stage of the examined practice model. In this section, we refer to the timing of literature review within the conduct of formal systematic inquiry in all stages of examined practice.

For the social worker developing knowledge through the experimental-type research tradition, a literature review always precedes both the final formulation of a research question and the implementation of the study. In the experimental-type tradition, definitions of all variables studied and the level of theoretical complexity underpinning a study must be presented for the research to be sound and rigorous (Fink, 2014). (We discuss rigor in greater detail in subsequent chapters.)

Consider the Tobacco Access Portal (TAP) project here as an example. At the point of outcome assessment, the team specifically examined the **frequency** of use of the TAP website. Thus "use" was named as the outcome variable. However, in order to define and then determine how "use" has been successfully measured, the social worker and team members turned to the research literature on website use. From the literature, they found many definitions of use, including simply viewing, to spending time, to engaging in interactive functions. They chose to define use as both viewing and time spent (Krug, 2014). The literature further pointed to automated strategies that could be integrated into the website design to obtain data on both measures of the use variable. Given that web design was outside of the social workers' knowledge and skill, once again the programming team member was called upon to create the functionality that would accomplish the outcome assessment measurement aim.

In the tradition of naturalistic inquiry, the literature may be reviewed at different points throughout the project. Although defining variables and instrumentation is not relevant and thus a function of literature review in the naturalistic tradition, examining information serves multiple purposes (Creswell, 2013). For example, as discussed immediately above, the literature may be used as an additional source of data and included as part of the information-gathering process that is subsequently analyzed and interpreted. Another purpose of the literature review in naturalistic inquiry is to inform the direction of data collection once the social worker has already entered the examined practice sequence with a client or client group. As discoveries occur in data collection, the investigator may turn to the literature for guidance about how to interpret emergent themes and identify other queries that should be posed in the field (Fortune, Reid, & Miller, 2013; Patton, 2012).

Returning to the TAP example, the unanticipated use of the website by immigrants who spoke English as a second language prompted a new literature review to inform the social work team in methods to meet the smoking prevention and cessation information needs of this subpopulation group. Another example is provided by the elder mobility device example. As noted previously, one direction for the literature review in equipment abandonment might have led to conducting an experimental-type study on barriers to use created by device functionality and ease of use. However, by conducting open-ended individual and group interviews, the social worker and team found that the appearance of supportive and adaptive mobility aids was perceived as stigmatizing and was the primary barrier to full participation in outdoor sports. Looking to literature on device redesign informed the innovative direction for this project. And recall that this team contributed to the literature, inciting Janice's social worker to engage in collaborative thinking and action to meet his client's needs.

Within some forms of naturalistic research, no literature is reviewed before or during fieldwork. The purpose of avoiding literature is to foster creativity that cannot occur if one seeks to rationalize social work activity with what was done (Creswell, 2013). Typically, however, working in the naturalistic-type tradition includes review of the literature before conducting research to confirm the need for a naturalistic study. If, for example, improving the functionality of mobility devices was successful for other groups, the social worker may have considered that route and tested it in practice.

Step 2: Delimit What Is Searched: Research, Theory, Practice Literature, Virtual Sources

Once a decision about when to conduct a formal literature review is made, the next step involves setting limits to define the scope of the search; after all, it is not feasible or reasonable to review every topic that is "somewhat related" to the defined problem. Delimiting the search, or setting boundaries around the search, is an important but difficult step. The boundaries must ensure a review that is comprehensive but still practical and not overwhelming (Kiteley & Stogdan, 2014). An important point to be made here is about the need for current sources. Unless there is a purpose for using historical sources, contemporary, context-relevant work should be used to inform all steps in examined practice (University of Southern California, n.d.).

One useful strategy across all elements of examined practice and systematic traditions is basing a search on the core concepts of concern. Determining the primary concepts provides a path to begin a search through keywords (words or phrases that are used in online searches to identify and categorize work that contains these specific concepts). The selection of precise keywords is a skill that should be mastered in order to obtain a targeted yet comprehensive review of sources (Mertens, 2014). Consider these comparative examples from Dean. Entering the key terms, "delusions of grandeur" and "drug use" into the Google search engine brings up the first entry titled *What is Delusion?* (Hartney, 2012). This short web page then discusses delusion as a well-known, unpredictable problem often precipitated by drug abuse. The next four sources all contain information pointing to mental illness diagnoses including bipolar disorder, schizoaffective disorder, and substance abuse. From this literature review, it therefore would make sense to proceed in the direction of mental health and substance abuse intervention with Dean. However, entering "nonmental health causes of delusions" brings up references to neurological causes of such experiences that may better have informed accuracy of intervention for Dean (Frith, 2005).

Precision of language and thought is the key to a useful, expansive, yet manageable literature review (Kiteley & Stogdan, 2014). If one does not possess these skills, assistance from those who do helps streamline and improve the creative mining of viable social work knowledge sources.

Step 3: Access Databases for Diverse Sources

For us, the excitement of searching and finding nuggets of literature and other sources is a great gift. But we are often faced with the dilemma of how to proceed to access diverse sources when time is limited. Fortunately, the internet creates a tool not only for accessing formal print materials but for access to any type of resource that can be imaged and beyond even from one's home. The disadvantage of web-based sources is their enormity and their variability in quality. Given that so many libraries and search engines provide opportunities for human interaction and guidance, the overwhelming and uncertain nature of information can be tamed. Of course, we are not suggesting that entering and working within the physical space of a library is not valued. To the contrary, the library and other collections often contain the only sources to inform examined practice. The screen shot in Photo 7.1 on page 130 presents all of the options for working with a librarian at our university.

Return to the mobility equipment abandonment project as an example. The extent to which and how the design of objects has influenced use over time was one area of great importance to consider in this project. The social worker, in a comprehensive literature review, was led to the theoretical and methodological work on **"object reading"** (Berger, 2009; Candlin & Guins, 2009; Bennett, 2010), a body of literature from material culture that seems to answer the questions about how objects create personal and public identity. But the theory further suggested systematic methods on how objects are "read" in order to inform relevant and innovative social work practice that would promote safe use of mobility support. In order to obtain further understanding, the social worker went onsite to view

Photo 7.1   Fogler Library Ask a Librarian Service

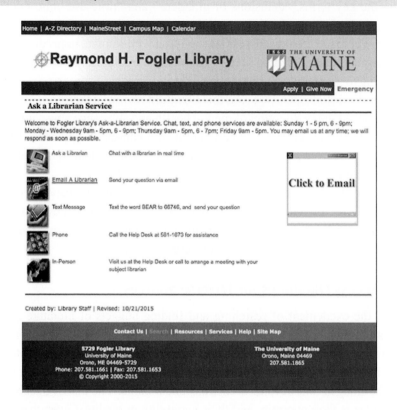

exhibits in two repositories of current and historical mobility objects and their social/emotive interpretations, a medical library and the Library of Congress. Without this knowledge, a large part of the thinking work for promoting adoption of mobility support would have been omitted.

Thus, there are many choices about where and how to begin a search. One can access literature through public online databases, formal library search engines, or through other means such as museum collections, seminar listings, and so forth. For example, for this book, we consulted many papers found through an electronic newsletter that contained a link to an evaluation conference held yearly (Morariu & Pankaj, 2015). One can browse hard copies of journals, peruse museum exhibits and online sites relevant to the social work domain of concern, lurk on **listserves**, or actively participate in dialogue to direct a search and obtain sources. In examined practice, as long as sources are systematically developed and supported, they meet the professional criterion for social work knowledge and can foster innovation and creative thinking and action. However, the social worker should always frame the search within a purposive aim. As an example, evidence-based practice relies primarily on prefiltered sources. As stated by Schlosse (2006), "Pre-filtered evidence is established when someone with expertise in a substantive area has reviewed and presented the methodologically strongest data in the field."

Knowledge conforming to this definition can be found in four primary locations: books, online and paper journal articles, online resources such as collections of papers and scholarly blogs, and government documents (Schlosse, 2006). Although not most desirable for evidence-based practice, newspapers, news websites, and newsletters may be useful for social work knowing, especially if they originate or are affirmed by professional social work associations. A fruitful place to find respected work is the reference section of scholarly work. Not only can references inform the reader about the previous work upon which the authors build, but it can point to authors previously unknown to the reader. A word of caution is indicated here, however. Depending heavily on references from other scholarship is both retrospective and limited in that these sources represent what the author has considered as important (DePoy & Gilson, 2009).

Searching Formal Literature: Books, Online and Paper Journal Articles, Online Resources Such as Collections

One can typically access formal sources through entering subjects, authors, or titles of works into a library or online database. To illustrate the range of options, Photo 7.2 on page 132 presents a screen capture of the website home page into Fogler Library at the University of Maine. Note the multiple methods of obtaining information listed on this single web page. The user can conduct a single search (One Search) which accesses all databases simultaneously, can select from diverse search sources, and can even chat with a reference librarian online.

To illustrate the range of databases, we chose the term *social work* in the drop down menu "select subject." Eleven were suggested initially, and over 60 databases were listed on a secondary page. At the end of 2015, the Fogler Library website, not including e-journals and reserves, lists over 90 databases for finding sources of knowledge. Listed are references along with many full text and image sources that can be accessed by these databases. As an example, the Sage Research Methods database was searched by the social worker to obtain methodological guidance on conducting an "object reading" study used to inform the need for mobility equipment that was not only functional but nonstigmatizing in its appearance.

One of our favorite databases is Project Muse (Project Muse, 2015). As reflected in the narrative excerpted from its description, Project Muse is particularly productive and for finding legitimate full text and image books, articles, collections, and other resources relevant to all phases of examined practice. Note the criteria of peer review and high quality scholarship in the excerpt.

Photo 7.2   Fogler Library Home Page

Project MUSE is a leading provider of digital humanities and social sciences content; since 1995, its electronic journal collections have supported a wide array of research needs at academic, public, special, and school libraries worldwide. MUSE books and journals, from leading university presses and scholarly societies, are fully integrated for search and discovery.

An additional way of finding scholarship is to insert a quote into a search engine such as Google, Yahoo, Bing, or others. This method will often lead the social worker to the work in which the quote appeared.

A Full Range of Search Options for Formal and Informal Sources

Informal sources are also called grey literature.

Grey literature stands for manifold document types produced on all levels of government, academics, business and industry in print and electronic formats that are protected by intellectual property rights, of sufficient quality to be collected and preserved by libraries and institutional repositories, but not controlled by commercial publishers; i.e. where publishing is not the primary activity of the producing body. (Bengtson, 2013)

Grey literature may embody quality and peer review, but once again, we emphasize that systematically developed thinking and action form the criteria for legitimate knowledge in examined practice. Thus, while pluralistic in method and nature of evidence, social work knowledge must be developed using systematic methods from one of the three traditions of inquiry. The challenge in seeking knowledge outside of scholarly publication outlets lies in the huge volume of information available. With this caution in mind, we now discuss productive options for seeking and uncovering knowledge of great value to social work.

The internet provides a kaleidoscope of options for social work. Because there are so many options, this chapter only samples this growing population. First discussed are the well-known search engines, Google, Yahoo, Chrome, Safari, and so forth. As an example, Google contains a host of knowledge sleuthing tools, including Google Books, Google Image, and Google Scholar. Entering keywords, authors, titles, images, and even broad topical queries into the search engine produces thousands of resources, some useful and some not. We searched our names in Google and obtained 11,700 entries in 0.57 seconds. Using Google Images, we then searched using a photo and immediately found the identical photo on the web. The lesson here is to be creative but precise and meticulous in your search and evaluation of the sources that emerge. Several other search engines are worth considering. BASE is a browser devoted to open source scholarship (Bielefeld University Library, 2004–2015). To access the deep web, hidden sources or those not always indexed and accessible on more commonly used search engines, deep web browsers are extremely valuable. Deep web search engines such as TOR allow anonymous searching as well.

Another important feature of the Internet is that one can now access knowledge presented in languages in which the reader's literacy is low. Google Translate, Babelfish, and other automated translation tools, although not perfected for full accuracy, open a global universe of sources to the knowledge seeker.

A final set of internet browsing sources worth noting is the host of academic and scholarly open source repositories such as Digital Commons, Researchgate, Academia.edu, and so forth. These sites provide open access to work posted by the author. The advantages of such tools include immediate and open access to full text documents and even works in progress. One can also contact the author to ask for additional information beyond what is posted. Remember, however, that careful scrutiny and evaluation are warranted, given that peer review is not a requisite criterion for this material.

Some Unconventional Gems

In addition to the known and identified search engines and browsers discussed above, there are some unconventional methods through which knowledge can be sought. One of our favorite ways to sample book material is Amazon's "Look Inside" feature. Using this tool, the social worker can often access introductory chapters and search for keywords in order to decide if a purchase is warranted. Publishers' websites allow a range of browsing from sampling excerpts to examining the table of contents of their book collections.

Blogging, vlogging, and social media should be considered cautiously but not eliminated. These sources can provide both well-developed knowledge as well as data for research and inquiry. As an example, three Facebook sites, Woman of Advanced Style, Age and Beauty (Women of Advanced Age Style and Beauty), Opulent Mobility (A. Laura Brody), and Disability Arts (DisabilityArts), were used as data sources by the social worker in informing the need for nonstigmatizing mobility equipment for elders.

Finally, we discuss Wikipedia, the online encyclopedia that can be edited by anyone (Wikipedia.org, n.d.). Similar to any repository, Wikipedia entries need to be evaluated by the reader for the rigor. However, to some extent, Wikipedia has a built-in evaluation of its own sources. The social worker, in searching for knowledge to inform the problem of elder abandonment of mobility devices, encountered this message:

> This article **needs additional citations for** *verification*. Please help *improve this article* by *adding citations to reliable sources*. Unsourced material may be challenged and removed. (Wikipedia, n.d.)

WikiPedia is an encyclopedia, and thus, if used purposively and critically, provides an efficient source for brief summaries of topical areas.

The Search Process

A search typically begins by identifying the major concepts of concern. As noted above, images can now be used as well. In examined practice, the problem statement delimits the topical area, but the social worker may also be seeking guidance on practice or methodological techniques and thus refines the search to move in those directions. Lexical definitions (definitions in words) of the constructs of interest are then translated into keywords or even images, which are used to identify sources that contain or refer to the named concepts. Because of the exponential increase in the sheer volume of information, most search engines are configured for "smart searching" or computer-assisted searching with functions that do not necessarily require the user to spell correctly or even type keywords into a browser. As an example, Firefox offers the following assisted function: "Right-click on a word or group of selected words, and from the popup menu, select a website. SmartSearch will perform a search as though you had gone to that website and entered the selected words" (Mozilla Firefox, n.d.).

Most formal scholarly and professional journals and book publishers that form a major part of the knowledge repository in social work, in addition to the title, author, and abstract required by most articles, ask authors to specify and list keywords that reflect the content of their work. This content allows the quick identification of literature and resources in a search.

For example, Table 7.2 presents part of the title pages of two studies used by the social worker in early formulation of the problem statement on elder mobility device abandonment (Cornman & Freedman, 2008). The words, "elder, abandonment, and mobility device" were used as search terms. The article by Cornman and Freedman (2008) was quickly identified in the first search because the keywords used by the authors closely matched those entered by the social worker. Note that the term *elder* was not used in the keyword list in the publication of Jutai, Coulson, Fuhrer, Demers, and DeRuyter (2008) and thus did not appear in an initial search on elder abandonment. Yet this study did emerge in a smart search in which the search engine browsed for individual search terms entered by the social worker.

This example illustrates the value of keywords both in precision of searching as well as in the author's potential to have his or her work found and used.

Because of their expertise and formal study in information management, seeking, and use, reference librarians are excellent resources for assisting in the development of accurate and exacting keywords. A thesaurus can serve as a worthwhile tool to find synonymous terms, if the words initially selected are not productive.

Table 7.2 Article Entries

Article #1	*Article #2*
Journal of Gerontology: Social Sciences	Archives of Physical Medicine and Rehabilitation
Copyright 2008 by The Gerontological Society of America	Volume 89, Issue 10, October 2008, Page e2
2008, Vol. 63B, No. 1, S34–S41	Predicting Assistive Technology Device Continuance and Abandonment
Racial and Ethnic Disparities in Mobility Device Use in Late Life	Jeffrey Jutai, Sherry Coulson, Marcus Fuhrer, Louise Demers, Frank DeRuyter
Jennifer C. Cornman and Vicki A. Freedman	Keywords: Assistive devices; Rehabilitation
Keywords: Race and ethnicity; Mobility device use; Older adults; Disparities	

Given the overwhelming amount of information available, a purposive, parsimonious, and well thought out search is always indicated. There are numerous ways to approach searching in a practical manner, however. The social worker can limit a search by selecting a targeted database such as Social Work Abstracts. Or if a broader scope is relevant and needed, once key terms and images are identified, searches can be delimited by selecting one or more of many options within search engines themselves. As an example, One Search at Fogler Library identifies the advanced search options displayed in Photo 7.3.

Some search engines, such as Google Scholar, retain a search history and recommend additional sources on the basis of previously reviewed work. Most social workers become familiar with the most important authors, studies, and knowledge sources in their topic area, but when new to an area or if in need of clarification, direct contact with other knowledgeable professionals and individuals makes sense to add to individual searching, reading, and viewing.

Step 4: Organize Information

Organizing is a critical step in being able to apply what is learned from a review of the literature. We usually begin by reading abstracts of journal articles, online excerpts from books or their reviews, and descriptions of curated collections and images to determine their value. On the basis of the abstracts, excerpts, and summaries, the extent to which a source is productive is predictable. Sources can then be accessed by the strategies above and organized by topic, year, step

Photo 7.3   One Search Refinement Options—Fogler Library (One Search, n.d.)

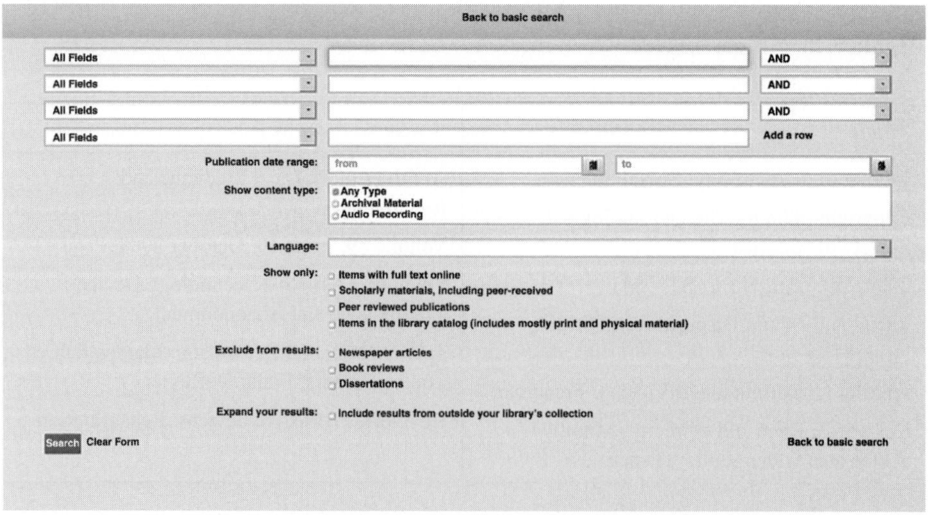

in the examined practice sequence or another framework that is purposive and useful for social work thinking and knowing.

Although it is not necessary to complete searching before accessing sources, we suggest that an efficient way of seeing a broad landscape of knowledge is through creating a list or a taxonomy before more in-depth exploration of single sources. This task can be accomplished manually or digitally. We find that "tagging" a source is useful and quick in identifying it as part of a body of content. Tagging is a digital step through which a file is placed in a larger category by name or color. Digital databases located on local or cloud repositories provide simple though sophisticated organizing tools as well.

Recall in Chapter 2 that problem mapping and force field analysis were presented as steps in the process of problem clarification. This framework may also be used to organize literature manually or through other automated processes. The initial problem statement is bolded in Table 7.3 on page 138. The two rows above the initial problem are causal, and those below are consequential. The sources are just several that illustrate how the problem map can be used to organize literature.

Note that the problem areas, dates, sources, or other categories can function as tags for automated organization.

Because it is not possible to remember all the important information presented in reading, documenting the type of information, the content, and critical relevance of each source is the major part of organizing and preparing sources for use and sharing. Similar to organizing citations and sources, there are many schemes for documenting. Some may prefer manually taking notes on index cards because they can be shuffled and reordered to fit into an outline. However, we prefer to take notes electronically. As an example, apps such as Index Card (DenVog, 2015) are invaluable for those who prefer note cards that can be automated and used to prepare a report. But if paper-and-pen note writing is preferred, scanning tools with optical character recognition can import notes into a computer or tablet so that they can be aggregated and shared. Writing notes directly on a tablet screen is also an option in apps such as Notetaker (Software Garden, 2015) and Microsoft One Note. Systems that both annotate and allow note taking are increasing in number and popularity. As an example, Refworks (Refworks, 2009) is offered in many university libraries. This powerful tool not only automates referencing but also provides the option for notations as well as sharing. References can be imported into formal reports and maintained in a cumulative searchable, manipulatable database. To use this tool, an active Internet connection has to be maintained. However, there are other apps and software that can be used offline. In general, your notes should reflect a synopsis of the content, the conceptual framework for the work, the method, and a brief review of the findings. Whatever method you use, always be sure to cite the full reference. We have all had the miserable experience of losing the volume, page number, or URL of a critical source and then spending hours trying to find it later.

Table 7.3   Framework for Organization of Literature

Problem area	Sources	Examined Practice Element
Device appearance	Berger, A. (2009). *What objects mean.* Walnut Creek, CA: Left Coast.	Reflexive intervention, outcome assessment
	Candlin, Fiona, & Raiford Guins. (2009). *The object reader.* London, UK: Routledge.	Problem and need identification, goals and objectives, reflexive intervention
	Conrad, Peter. (2007). *The medicalization of society: On the transformation of human conditions into treatable disorders.* Baltimore, MD: Johns Hopkins.	Problem and need identification
	Garland-Thomson, R. (2009). *Staring: How we look.* New York, NY: Oxford University Press.	Problem and need identification, reflexive intervention, goals and objectives, outcome assessment
	Laughlin, L. (2011, May 4). *Tennis balls for walkers: A sorry way to help disabled people get around easier.* Retrieved from View from The Handicapped Space.	Problem and need identification
	Turkle, S. (2011). *Evocative objects.* Boston, MA: MIT Press.	Problem and need identification, goals and objectives, outcome assessment
Functionality	Architect Design Forum. (2011). *Accessibility v. universal design.*	Problem and need identification
Elders abandon prescribed walking devices	Cornman, J., & Freedman, V. (2008). Racial and ethnic disparities in mobility device use in late life. *Journal of Gerontology, 63B,* 34–41	Problem and need identification
	Jutai, J., Coulson, S., Fuhrer, M., Demers, L., & DeRuyter, F. (2008). Predicting assistive technology device continuance and abandonment. *Archives of Physical Medicine and Rehabilitation, 89,* 2	
Sedentary lifestyles	Cornman, J., & Freedman, V. (2008). Racial and ethnic disparities in mobility device use in late life. *Journal of Gerontology, 63B,* 34–41	
	Jutai, J., Coulson, S., Fuhrer, M., Demers, L., & DeRuyter, F. (2008). Predicting assistive technology device continuance and abandonment. *Archives of Physical Medicine and Rehabilitation, 89,* 2	

Problem area	Sources	Examined Practice Element
Negative consequences of inactivity	Cornman, J., & Freedman, V. (2008) Racial and ethnic disparities in mobility device use in late life. *Journal of Gerontology, 63B,* 34–41	
	Jutai, J., Coulson, S., Fuhrer, M., Demers, L., & DeRuyter, F. (2008). Predicting assistive technology device continuance and abandonment. *Archives of Physical Medicine and Rehabilitation, 89,* 2.	

Step 5: Critically Evaluate the Literature

This step is the most important for social workers using and generating knowledge to inform the profession. By *critical*, we do not simply mean determining what is deficient about sources. Rather, we refer to an evaluation, analysis, interpretation, synthesis, and purposive use over repetition or decimation of existing sources (Bressler, 2011). Table 7.4 contains general questions to guide this critical process.

Table 7.4 Questions to Guide Critical Evaluation of Knowledge

1. What is the specific problem or part of the problem the source addresses?
2. What is the purpose of this review, and how does this source fit? How does it inform theory?
3. How does this source inform needs assessment, intervention, reflexive intervention, and outcome assessment?
4. What is the scope of the review? What types of sources are used (e.g., journals, books, government documents, popular media, images, etc.)?
5. What fields of study? (e.g., social work, psychology, gerontology, technology, disability studies)
6. What was the scope of the search? How and why was it delimited in the way chosen?
7. What knowledge can be summarized from this source?
8. If relevant, how are the claims and presentations observable and supported? What systematic procedures were used to create and support the source?
9. What are the strengths and weaknesses of this source?
10. What competing knowledge is available, and why is this approach fitting?
11. What knowledge is needed but not available? Not developed?

To guide a critical analysis of research literature, Table 7.5 contains questions to provide a framework for complete evaluation of each source. Table 7.6 contains questions to structure a critical review of nonresearch literature. We make the distinction here as research literature is not only systematic in its generation but as discussed, follows specific rules of logic to support, refute, or generate theory with evidence. Nonresearch literature, if critically examined and systematically integrated into social work thinking, is a rich source of data as well but does not adhere to the rules of logic and evidentiary criteria of research.

Table 7.5 Evaluating Research Knowledge

Was the study presented in a clear, unambiguous, and internally consistent manner? If not, what were the limitations?

What is (are) the research question(s)? Queries? Are they clearly and adequately stated?

What is the purpose of the study?

How does the purpose influence the design and the conclusions?

Describe the theory that guides the study and the conceptual framework for the project. Are they clearly presented and relevant to the study?

What are the key constructs identified in the literature review?

What level of theory is suggested in the literature review of the study? Is it consistent with the selected research strategy?

What is the rationale for the design found/implied in the literature review? Is it sound?

Does the design of the project fit the level of theory? Is relevant knowledge presented in the literature review?

How would you describe the design?

Does the design answer the research question(s)? Respond to queries? Why, or why not?

What are the boundaries of the study? How are the boundaries selected?

What efforts did the investigator make to ensure rigor?

What techniques were used to collect evidence and information to answer the questions and queries? Is the rationale for these techniques specified in the literature review or in the methods section?

How does information collection approach fit with the study purpose and study question? Query?

How are the data analyzed? Does the analysis plan make sense for the study? How does the analysis plan fit with the study purpose and study question? Query?

Are the conclusions supported by the study?

What are the strengths of the study?

What level of knowledge is generated?

What use does this knowledge have for examined practice and in what steps?

Are there ethical dilemmas presented in this article? What are they? Did the author(s) resolve the dilemmas in a reasonable and ethical manner?

Table 7.6 Guiding Questions for Evaluating Nonresearch Sources

1. What way of knowing and level of knowledge are presented?
2. Was the source presented clearly, unambiguously, and consistently?
3. Is the source credible?
4. What is the purpose of the work? Is the purpose implicit? Is it stated? How does the purpose influence the knowledge discussed in the work?
5. What is the scope and application of the work?
6. What is the purposive use of this knowledge in examined practice?
7. What debates, new ideas, and trends are presented in the work?
8. What are the strengths and weaknesses of the work?

Step 6: Preparing the Review

Once searched, obtained, read, and organized, the actual review is next. A sound review is purposive, relevant to the steps of examined practice, and presents a critical discussion and use of the relevant work. There is no recipe for preparing a narrative literature review. Consistent with the principles of examined practice, the preparation of a review is purposive. In Chapter 13, we provide examples of structures and uses of knowledge reviews, so consult that chapter for illustration.

SUMMARY

This chapter focused on the uses and conduct of literature review. We first expanded the definition of literature beyond the written text to include diverse sources such as image, object, and so forth. The purposes and roles of literature within each step of examined practice were presented and then followed by the mechanics of access, review, organization, summary, and criticism of knowledge.

The main points in this chapter are as follows:

1. Credible sources of social work knowledge must be systematically generated.

2. Literature in the problem identification element helps to clarify, expand, and document a claim.

3. Literature should be reviewed in the needs assessment phase to determine how others framed need statements and formed an evidentiary basis.

4. Goals and objectives are not typically directly informed through review of literature as they are based on need.

5. In reflexive intervention, literature is used to frame action and to specify strategies that have been successful.

6. Methodological literature provides a direction for systematically assessing outcomes.

7. Literature is a primary venue for sharing knowledge.

8. Literature review comprises six steps. Timing and purpose are tradition dependent.

9. Libraries and librarians are invaluable resources in organizing and conducting a literature review.

10. Electronic sources are widespread and should be carefully evaluated for quality.

11. A host of Internet search engines can access literature through keywords, titles, authors, and even images.

12. Searching begins broadly and is then focused by purpose, resources, methodological tradition, and step in examined practice.

13. Problem mapping and force field analysis provide useful frameworks for organizing literature.

14. All literature should be critically analyzed.

15. A sound review is purposive, relevant to the steps of examined practice, and presents a critical discussion and use of the relevant work.

REFERENCES

Bengtson, J. (2013). *Grey literature 101*. Retrieved from http://libguides.health.unm.edu/content.php?pid=200149

Bennett, J. (2010). *Vibrant matter.* Durham, NC: Duke University Press.

Berger, A. (2009). *What objects mean.* Walnut Creek, CA: Left Coast.

Bielefeld University Library. (2004–2015). *BASE*. Retrieved http://www.base-search.net

Bressler, C. (2011). *Literary criticism: An introduction to theory and practice* (5th ed.). New York, NY: Longman.

Candlin, F., & Guins, R. (2009). *The object reader.* London, UK: Routledge.

Cornman, J., & Freedman, V. (2008). Racial and ethnic disparities in mobility device use in later life. *Journal of Gerontology, 63*(1), S34–S41.

Creswell, J. (2013). *Qualitative inquiry and research design: Choosing among five approaches* (3rd ed.). Thousand Oaks, CA: Sage.

DenVog. (2015). *Index card.* Retrieved from https://itunes.apple.com/us/app/index-card/id389358786

DePoy, E., & Gilson, S. (2009). *Evaluation practice.* New York, NY: Routledge.

Disability Arts. (n.d.). Retrieved from https://www.facebook.com/Opulent-Mobility-178272499023481/?fref=ts

Fink, A. (2014). *Conducting research literature reviews: From the Internet to paper* (3rd ed.). Thousand Oaks, CA: Sage.

Fortune, A., Reid, W., & Miller, R. (2013). *Qualitative research in social work.* New York, NY: Columbia University Press.

Frith, C. (2005). The neural basis of hallucinations and delusions. *Biologies, 328,* 169–175.

Hartney, E. (2012, Feb 12). *What is delusion?* Retrieved from http://addictions.about.com/od/designerdrugs/g/What-Is-Delusion.htm

Huffine, R. (2010, June 15). *Value of grey literature to scholarly research in the digital age.* Retrieved from http://cdn.elsevier.com/assets/pdf_file/0014/110543/2010RichardHuffine.pdf

Jutai, J., Coulson, S., Fuhrer, M., Demers, L., & DeRuyter, F. (2008). Predicting assistive technology device continuance and abandonment. *Archives of Physical Medicine and Rehabilitation, 89* (10), e2.

Kiteley, R., & Stogdan, C. (2014). *Literature reviews in social work.* Thousand Oaks, CA: Sage.

Krug, S. (2014). *Don't make me think, revisited: A common sense approach to web usability.* New York, NY: Pearson.

Mertens, D. M. (2014). *Research and evaluation in education and psychology.* Thousand Oaks, CA: Sage.

Morariu, J., & Pankaj, V. (2015, October). *Advocacy evaluation, coalition assessment, and graphic recording.* Retrieved from file:///private/var/folders/b9/9lz0dddd7vz537_vss1rp0780000gn/T/TemporaryItems/fcctemp/Attach0.html

Mozilla Firefox. (n.d.). *Smart search.* Retrieved https://addons.mozilla.org/en-US/firefox/addon/smartsearch

Opulent Mobility. (n.d.). Retrieved from https://www.facebook.com/Opulent-Mobility-178272499023481/?fref=ts

Patton, M. Q. (2012). *Essentials of utilization-focused evaluation.* Thousand Oaks, CA: Sage.

Project Muse. (2015). *Project Muse.* Retrieved from http://muse.jhu.edu

Refworks. (2009). *Refworks.* Retrieved from http://www.refworks.com

Schlosse, R. W. (2006). *The role of systematic reviews in evidence-based practice, research, and development.* Retrieved from http://www.ktdrr.org/ktlibrary/articles_pubs/ncddrwork/focus/focus15/Focus15.pdf

Software Garden. (2015). *Note Taker HD.* Retrieved from https://itunes.apple.com/us/app/note-taker-hd/id366572045?mt=8

University of Southern California. (n.d.). *Organizing your social sciences research paper.* Retrieved from http://libguides.usc.edu/content.php?pid=83009&sid=618412

Wikipedia. (n.d.). *Disability studies.* Retrieved from https://en.m.wikipedia.org/wiki/Disability_studies

Wikipedia.org. (n.d.). *Wikipedia.* Retrieved from http://en.wikipedia.org/wiki/Main_Page

Wilde, D. (2011). *Jung's personality theory quantified.* New York, NY: Springer.

Women of Advanced Age Style and Beauty. (n.d.). Retrieved from https://www.facebook.com/pages/The-Women-Of-Advanced-Style-Age-and-Beauty/266717366687346

Chapter 8

QUESTIONS, HYPOTHESES, AND QUERIES: THE BASIS FOR RIGOR ASSESSMENT

The quality of our thinking is given in the quality of our questions. Thinking within disciplines is driven not by answers but by essential questions. (Elder & Paul, 2010)

This chapter is about asking questions and posing queries. At first blush, the task of questioning may seem simple. However, questioning is a skill that, once honed, provides a valuable tool not only in research and systematic knowledge generation but in all phases of examined practice as well as throughout life.

Within examined practice, questions posed are those that can be answered by systematic processes in the three research traditions. Although questions form the expansive method for problem identification and mapping, the formal questioning discussed in this chapter comprises the specific set of processes and skills necessary to guide a study that begins at the point of ascertaining need. Recall that problem statements are value statements and thus are evaluative rather than empirical. Therefore, questions at the problem identification stage ask for opinion rather than evidence and do not require formal structures used in systematic inquiry. That is not to say that the magnitude or strength of opinion cannot be subjected to research questioning, but at that point, the social worker is really asking about what problems are most frequently perceived as needing to be addressed before the boundary from problem to need is crossed.

The essential action process of questioning represents the first formal point of entry into a systematic study. Consistent with the three traditions that were presented in previous chapters, we make the distinction between questions and queries. Different from popular vernacular, questions in the world of systematic inquiry refer to those asked in experimental-type traditions, while queries are naturalistic in nature. Both represent precisely what an investigator and/or social worker wants to know. Consider this example: A social work faculty was revising prerequisites for their graduate generalist curriculum. In order to inform the rationale and choices of prerequisite content and skill, the faculty decided to study the prerequisite courses required by MSW programs at other universities. They proceeded to develop a survey that asked respondents three questions:

What prerequisite course content do you require?

At what level of study must these courses be taken?

When do they need to be completed?

The faculty were surprised when the responses did not generate the knowledge that they needed. Several errors occurred in the questioning, however, that resulted in the acquisition of inadequate knowledge. First, the faculty neglected to include questions on the academic rationale for the prerequisites. Thus, and reasonably so, only a list of content was provided by respondents. Second, the level of study was unclear. Were they asking simply about undergraduate or graduate levels of study, or more precisely, what years within those divisions? Finally, the third question was vague as well, and thus did not get at the rationale for timing of the courses in preceding core MSW content. This simple example reveals that well-intended questions are not always precise, and without clarity, answers that are sought may never be obtained.

RESEARCH QUESTIONS IN EXPERIMENTAL-TYPE KNOWING

In experimental-type knowing, entry into an investigation requires the formulation of a very specific question with a prescribed set of content and structure. That is, from a broad topic of interest, a specific question is articulated that will guide subsequent thinking and action processes and determine the extent to which those processes were adequate for answering the question. As we discuss later, the extent to which a research question is answered by a design is called validity.

A question must be concise and narrow, establishing the boundaries or limits for the concepts, individuals, or phenomena to be examined. Because it becomes the foundation or basis from which all subsequent action processes are developed and implemented, and on which the rigor of the design is determined, the question must be posed *a priori*, or before engaging in the investigation process. Research questions are developed deductively from the theoretical principles presented in the literature. Their purpose is to identify the constructs that will be examined and how and to specify to whom or what the findings apply. Thus each research question must have three essential elements: (1) constructs, (2) population, and (3) level of questioning.

Constructs

In Chapter 7, we detailed review of literature. Although there are numerous purposes for review of the literature, a primary aim is to identify and detail the constructs to be extracted from theory and investigated in the study. Selected constructs form the focus of measurement necessary to test the accuracy of part or all of the chosen theory. As a reminder, recall that theory comprises increasing levels of abstraction, with constructs functioning as single order abstracts. Moving outward from constructs to increasingly abstract conceptualizations, associations relate two or more constructs and then locate them within a set of principles that coalesce to form a theory. Moving in the opposite direction to more concrete, constructs can be lexically defined (in words) and subjected to operationalization (their definition as measured).

In the previous chapter, within the Tobacco Access Portal (TAP) example, we referred to the construct of website use, extracted from theory, suggesting that immediate availability and linguistic access would increase website visitation sufficient for transmitting health information. Reflexive intervention was therefore conceptualized as website development and piloting, with outcome assessment focusing in part on website use. In the literature, use had been defined in multiple ways and the social work team settled on use as defined by Krug (2014). The research question therefore had to contain use as the dependent or outcome variable.

Figure 8.1 Moving From Theory to Construct

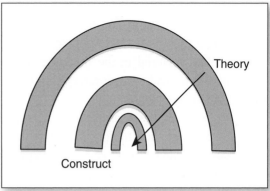

Level of Questioning

Within the experimental-type tradition, different structures reflect a particular level of knowledge and theory development concerning the topic of interest. Questions that seek to describe a phenomenon, referred to as Level 1 questions, are asked when little to nothing is known about the topic. Level 2 questions explore relationships among phenomena and are asked when descriptive knowledge is known and presented in the literature, but relationships are not yet supported by evidence. Level 3 questions test existing theory or models, predict, and are asked when a substantial body of well-developed knowledge is presented in the literature review.

In examined practice at the need phase, descriptive questions guide an examination of what is necessary to resolve a problem in the absence of acceptance or of prior knowledge to that effect. If the social worker accepts a well-developed need statement as relevant for guiding social action, Level 3 questioning to test the theoretical fit of previously determined need would be warranted. Reflexive intervention most often lends itself to Level 1 questions or naturalistic query. Level 1 questions simply quantify what was done, while naturalistic query would examine the nature of practice as we discuss later. Similarly, if predicting the outcome as a result of the intervention was not possible or the aim of this phase, once again, descriptive, noncausal questioning would occur. However, if it were possible or desirable to set up an outcome assessment study to verify a causal relationship between intervention and tested result, Level 3 would be warranted. In many cases in social work, it is not possible to develop a study to answer Level 3 questions, so the social worker would ask a Level 2 question about the association between reflexive intervention and outcome.

LEVEL 1: QUESTIONS THAT
SEEK TO DESCRIBE PHENOMENA

Level 1 questions are *descriptive questions* designed to study descriptions of a single topic or a single population about which there is some theoretical or conceptual material in the literature but little or no empirical knowledge. Level 1 questions lead to exploratory action processes with the intent to describe an identified phenomenon.

Consider the example of elders and equipment abandonment. In the needs assessment, description answered the "how much" question, the magnitude of device abandonment. As we noted previously, the first step in understanding what was needed to resolve the abandonment problem was the conduct of a comprehensive literature review. As we noted previously, keywords such as *abandonment*, *elder*, *assistive*, and *mobility* were entered into search engines. Because the literature review revealed that despite a significant body of research, abandonment remained constant, a mixed-method study employing Level 1 questioning in the experimental-type part was undertaken to describe patterns of abandonment. The Level 1 research question was:

What are the articulated reasons for nonuse of mobility equipment among elders?

To answer this question, elders were interviewed and their responses were coded and then counted for frequency. The question contained the (1) construct to be described, "reasons for abandonment," and (2) the population, elders. As stated, the question asks simply for description by its use of the term *what*, and thus the focus of a Level 1 question is on "the what" and "how many times."

Level 1 questions focus on the description of one concept, construct, or variable in a population. A variable is defined as a characteristic or phenomenon that has more than one value. As briefly discussed above in the example of the TAP literature, to describe a variable, a definition of the concept is extrapolated from the literature and then operationalized (defined by how it will be measured). However, the measurement strategy is not contained in the question itself.

One can recognize a Level 1 question by its structure and wording. These types of questions frequently use the stem of "what are" or "what is" and refer to a single population. As shown in the example, only one population is identified, such as elders, since including another would be seeking group differences and would therefore be adding a comparison variable and complexity beyond the scope of Level 1 questioning.

In the TAP outcome assessment, several questions were asked. The Level 1 question examining the "use" outcome was phrased as:

To what degree do Internet browsers use the TAP website?

Level 1 questions describe the parts of a whole. Because the underlying logical structure of experimental-type research is deductive, learning about a broad topic by reducing complexity to its parts, examining each through measurement, and then determining the extent to which the theory, reduced to its smaller elements, is in part verified or falsified by the study is the aim. If the TAP website use were measured as very low, the theory about availability and literacy access would not be supported. Thus, Level 1 questioning serves as the foundation for clarifying the parts of theory and measuring their specific magnitude.

Level 1 questions lead to the development of descriptive designs, such as surveys, exploratory studies, trend designs, feasibility studies, needs assessments, and case studies. In the example of the elder study, interviewing was used with responses numerically coded for frequency. For the TAP outcome assessment, the variable of use was measured by an automated web counter.

LEVEL 2: QUESTIONS THAT EXPLORE RELATIONSHIPS AMONG PHENOMENA

The Level 2 *relational questions* build on and refine the results of Level 1 studies. Once a "part" of a phenomenon is described and there is existing knowledge about it in the context of a particular population, the social worker using experimental-type methods may pose questions that are relational. The key purpose of Level 2 type of questioning is to explore relationships among phenomena that have already been identified and described through Level 1 study. Here, the stem question asks, "What is the relationship?" or a variation of this (e.g., "association"), and the topic contains two or more concepts or variables.

Consider the needs assessment in the elder study. A Level 2 question was asked:

What is the relationship between age of user and abandonment of mobility device?

In this case, the two identified variables that are measured are abandonment and age. The specific population is elders.

This Level 2 question would lead to measurement of the association between two variables, age and abandonment frequency. If an association was found, directions for practice specific to age might be warranted. Suppose, for example, that the younger respondents were more likely to abandon mobility devices than their older counterparts. Further study about why this was the case might be indicated to then shape strategies to promote safety for the younger group and concentrate later on the older cohort of elders who are found to accept mobility devices.

From the Level 2 question above, the roots of the Level 1 question on abandonment can be seen. Because Level 2 questions address relationships between variables, studying this level of questioning represents the next level of complexity above Level 1 questions.

Level 2 questions continue to build on knowledge in the experimental-type tradition by examining relationships between and among concepts and constructs that have been measured and supported in previous inquiry. As an example, in the first study of abandonment, the magnitude of this phenomenon was identified. Given the large age range of elders, further refining which age groups tend to abandon equipment more than others would be a logical next step to inform social work practice providing that there was theory in the literature to support age as a potential influence to be tested.

LEVEL 3: QUESTIONS THAT TEST KNOWLEDGE

Level 3 questioning, or predictive inquiry, builds on the knowledge generated from answering Level 1 and Level 2 questions. A Level 3 question asks about a cause-and-effect relationship among two or more variables, with the specific purpose of testing knowledge or the theory underpinning the knowledge (Grinnell & Unrau, 2011). As an example, in the elder needs assessment study, it would have been important to know not only if device function was associated with abandonment but also if functional disappointment caused it. Suppose that increasing level of physical impairment was the cause both for functional disappointment and abandonment? Assuming that the function of a device itself was causal of nonuse would lead the social worker in the wrong direction. Building on the knowledge already generated, in the needs assessment phase, we would ask the following question: "To what extent does limited functionality and difficulty of use cause abandonment?" Given that abandonment did not change over time despite efforts to improve ease of use and to make devices more functional, it made sense to ask what else was causing elders to reject devices even at the risk of falling. (We discuss the query below about the nature of device appearance as informing the needs assessment.)

To study outcome, a Level 3 question was posed:

To what extent do contemporary designs result in acceptance (decreased abandonment) of mobility devices for elders?

Note the structure of this question. It contains concepts (acceptance and design) and the population (elders), and it articulates the causal nature of the question in the word *result*.

The inquiry to answer this question tests the theory that proposes appearance as a major factor in acceptance of mobility devices. At this level of questioning, the purpose is to predict what will happen and provide a theory to explain the reason(s). On the basis of a Level 3 question, specific *predictive hypotheses*, statements predicting the outcome of one variable on the basis of knowing another, are formulated. Thus, the redesign of the device is theorized to predict improvement in use in the population being tested. As we indicated in Chapter 6, structuring a research design to answer this question is not simple within the scope of social work action. However, as we discuss in subsequent chapters, prediction was studied in multiple ways in each research tradition. For the most part, however, experimental-type researchers assert that Level 3 questions should only be answered by true experimentation or statistical manipulation in the absence of the capacity to mechanically structure a true experiment. Moreover, unlike examined practice in which acceptable knowledge is broader than that created by true experimentation, evidence-based practice holds Level 3 research as the primary credible form of knowledge.

In order to conduct a study answering a Level 3 question, the literature should contain knowledge that already establishes a relationship between the constructs subjected to predictive inquiry. Level 3 is the most complex of experimental-type questioning. Once the foundation questions formulated at Levels 1 and 2 are answered, Level 3 questions can be posed and answered to develop knowledge— not only of parts and their relationships but also how and why these parts interact to cause a particular outcome (Alvesson & Sandberg, 2013).

So far, we have discussed levels of questions in experimental-type design specific to groups. So what about social work practice with individuals? Because of the nature of experimental-type investigation and its purpose in looking for within-group commonalities and between-group differences, similar levels of questioning are relevant for individuals, but most experimental-type designs to answer these questions are not. Case study designs and single subject approaches focus on one unit as holistic or as a single entity with multiple parts. These designs are most relevant to examine description, association, and prediction for individual clients in social work practice. Case studies are classified as mixed-method because they typically integrate multiple forms of data collection and analysis about one unit of study and thus do not conform to the basic experimental-type principles and language (Yin, 2014).

Question formulation for experimental-type research is relatively straightforward. Table 8.1 presents basic guidelines for developing questions at each of the three levels.

HYPOTHESES

Although a social worker might have a hunch or hypothesis about description, formal hypothesis development in research is reserved for questioning at Levels 2 and 3. Restricting hypothesis to the upper two levels of questions presupposes that descriptive questions are asked when little is known about a single variable, and thus an educated guess would not be based in theory or systematic thinking when one has insufficient information on which to make a judgment (DePoy & Gitlin, 2016).

A classic definition of hypothesis is "a proposition to be tested or a tentative statement of a relationship between two variables" (DePoy & Gitlin 2016).

Hypotheses serve important purposes in experimental-type inquiry. First, they form an important link between the question and the design of the study. In essence, hypotheses rephrase the research question and turn it into a testable or measurable statement. Second, hypotheses may, but are not required to, identify the anticipated direction of the proposed relationship between stated variables. Therefore, hypotheses can be *directional* or *nondirectional*. Information regarding directionality of a relationship between variables is usually not contained in the actual research question. So if a purpose of a systematic inquiry is to verify a theory-based hunch, hypothesis testing is warranted.

A nondirectional hypothesis proceeding from the Level 3 question about elders might state,

Contemporary designs will result in changes in acceptance of mobility devices for elders.

Table 8.1 Developing Experimental-Type Research Questions

Level	Stem
1	What is . . .? What are . . .?
2	What is the relationship . . .?
3	Why . . .?

A directional hypotheses might look like,

Contemporary designs will increase acceptance of mobility devices for elders.

A third and critical purpose of hypotheses is that these purposefully constructed statements set the stage for the type of data analysis that will be used. We discuss these logical thinking processes and actions later in the book.

RESEARCH QUERIES IN NATURALISTIC INQUIRY

Now we turn to a completely different approach to formulating systematic inquiry. In naturalistic research, formal entry into a study requires the initial development of a broad query. Although various philosophical perspectives underpin naturalistic research, as previously discussed, and although the tasks of framing the problem and query are somewhat different among varied approaches, there is some underlying similarity to query development among variations in this tradition.

The naturalistic research process generally begins by identifying a topic and a broad problem area or specifying a particular phenomenon from which a query is pursued. As noted above, the term *query* rather than *question* is used as it refers to a curious statement that identifies the phenomenon or natural field of interest rather than a structured question about variables or their relationships within a population.

Characteristic of naturalistic inquiry, the environment and/or context in which the phenomenon of interest occurs forms the basis for discovery from which more specific and limited questions evolve in the course of conducting the study. Environments may be physical or conceptual spaces or even a group of interest (DePoy & Gitlin, 2016). Thus, the initial entry into the natural environment is based on a query statement that identifies the subject of interest and locus of concern (Agar, 2006). Once the field of inquiry has been entered, new insights and meanings can be obtained and may even call for reformulation of a study.

As an example, consider Dean to understand the process of clarifying new insights and issues that emerge after the initial entry into a study. The social worker was interested in how Dean was experiencing his participation in substance abuse intervention. From this interest query, the next process involved formulating narrower, more concise subquestions to elicit specific responses from Dean that would be relevant to his experience in the intervention. These questions are contextual; that is, they are derived from the context of the study and are rooted in the social worker's ongoing efforts to understand the broad problem area in depth. In turn, each subsequent question that is posed may lead to a different methodological approach. This interactive questioning-data, gathering-analyzing-reformulating of the questions and initial query represents a critical and core action process of naturalistic inquiry.

Dean's social worker in the reflexive intervention stage of examined practice posed the following broad query:

What is the nature of Dean's participation in the substance abuse intervention?

Dissimilar to experimental-type questioning that precisely counted the frequency of Dean's attendance, this query does not specify a measurable phenomenon within an intervention. Rather, the wording reflects a broad focus on participation that provides an entrée into the reflexive intervention field of study. In this example, the social worker is thus guided to collect sufficient descriptive information to capture the process and nature of intervention and Dean's interactions and activities within it.

So far, we have discussed query in general. Now, we turn to queries as they appear in different naturalistic designs.

Ethnography

As the primary research approach in anthropology, ethnography is concerned with describing and interpreting cultural patterns of groups and understanding the cultural meanings people use to organize and interpret their experiences (Agar, 2006) and more recently has included consumption and response to images within visual culture (Harper, 2012). The investigator assumes the learning role as an active way to interpret and experience different cultural settings, objects, and images. After the ethnographer has identified a phenomenon and cultural setting, a query is pursued. There is always a strong descriptive element in ethnography, so the ethnographic query must denote what the ethnographer is to describe. An ethnographic query is not complete until the focus of the study is clear.

If time and resources allow, the luxury of such broad queries as "What is going on here?" can be the researcher's entry into the study.

If practical and fitting within the time frame of the project, ethnography would have been ideal for depth of understanding of the "cultures of mobility impairment and stigma of rehabilitation equipment users." However, ethnography is time intensive, often requiring the social worker to be immersed in the study over a long period of time. Thus, in examined practice, ethnographic queries are perhaps best used when a social worker is already engaged or is emic. For example, Dean's social worker, who was already onsite because of conducting the substance abuse intervention, might have posed a query such as "What is happening here?" to understand the nature of Dean's involvement in this "culture." Or in examining the meaning of a mobility device object to elders, a query may have been posed such as "How is this object 'read' by elders for whom a mobility support has been prescribed?"

As the processes of data gathering and analysis proceed in tandem, specific questions emerge and are pursued. These questions surface in the cultural context as a consequence of what Agar (2006) classically labeled as *breakdowns,* or disjunctions, a concept that we still find useful and central to ethnographic inquiry. A breakdown represents the difference between what the investigator observes and what he or she expects to observe. These inconsistencies stimulate a series of questioning and further investigation. Each subquestion is related to the broader query and is investigated to resolve the breakdown, thereby developing an increasingly comprehensive understanding of the phenomenon under study. An ethnographic query therefore establishes the phenomenon, the setting of interest, or both.

Social workers have used ethnographic methods, such as interviewing and participant observation (discussed more fully in subsequent chapters), to examine cultures in a broad sense. Different from classical ethnographers who saw culture as the shared meanings, beliefs, and traditions of a geographically bounded group, contemporary ethnographers aim to develop depth of understanding of groups that are formed by varied methods. As an example, Murthy (2008) proposed virtual "cultures" as ripe for ethnographic inquiry. Haight, Kayama, and Korang-Okrah (2013) suggest that in social work, ethnographic queries can accompany practice and thus can be used within the daily work of the social worker.

Phenomenology

The purpose of the phenomenological line of inquiry is to uncover the meaning of a human experience or phenomenon typically of more than one individual, through the description of those experiences as they are explained by those who live them. Phemonenology

> emphasizes studying empirical phenomena directly, as they are perceived by the senses . . . and thus does not call for interpretation by the investigator. The entry into the context to be studied from this perspective is the identification of the phenomenon of interest. (Bakker, 2010, p. 674)

For example, delusions of grandeur (in the case of Dean), loss of function (Janice), abandonment of mobility devices, and so forth, may be phenomena in our examples that are relevant to the social worker. From the articulation of the phenomenon, research queries could be generated, such as the following:

How are delusions of grandeur experienced by those who have them?

What is the meaning of loss of function for women who experience strokes in midlife?

What is the reading of mobility device objects for elders whose providers have prescribed them?

This approach is distinct from ethnography in that rather than seeking to interpret cultural identifiers, phenomenological queries focus on particular experiences (e.g., delusions, functional loss, mobility device stigma) from the perspective of the individuals who experience them. However, similar to ethnography, the inquiry begins with a broad query and then proceeds with subquestions to further inform the query.

Grounded Theory

Grounded theory is a method in naturalistic research that is used primarily to generate theory (Bryant & Charmaz, 2007). The social worker begins with a broad query in a particular topic area and then collects relevant information about the topic. As the action processes of data collection continue, each piece of information is reviewed and compared with other information and with the organizational structure emerging from data already. From this constant comparison process, commonalities and dissimilarities among categories of information become clear, and ultimately a theory that explains observations is developed. Thus, queries that will be answered through grounded theory do not relate to specific domains but rather to the structure of how findings are organized (Wertz et al., 2011).

If grounded theory were used to examine the relevance of current psychoanalytic theory to clients such as Janice, the following grounded theory query might be posed:

How can the current Jungian theory be expanded or modified to explain functional loss in middle-aged women who experience strokes?

The query itself indicates the aim to reveal theoretical principles about the phenomenon under study.

Narrative

Although there is no single definition of narrative, all have two common elements, storytelling and meaning making (Squire, 2013). In general, narrative methods are interpretive strategies used in diverse disciplines and fields but are particularly popular in postmodern studies such as women's studies and disability studies. Synthesizing the multiple definitions, DePoy & Gitlin (2016) define narrative as a naturalistic method in which stories are told and analyzed for meaning. Stories can be generated by an individual or group in response to a query or can already exist in the form of text or even image. However, regardless of the form, the data must tell a story that can be interpreted. According to Andrews, Squire, and Tamboukou (2013), narrative queries are particularly useful when knowledge is not known or is insufficient to describe a phenomenon. Squire (2013) also suggests that narrative queries may serve to illuminate difficult phenomena or those not easily discussed.

If, for example, delusions of grandeur were the broad topic, a query such as "tell me about your life" might be posed to Dean about his life history. Subquestions would then be used to guide the inquiry so that the social worker could generate knowledge about the experience of such delusions, the perceived causes, the consequences, and their effect on Dean's life as it has unfolded over time.

DEVELOPING NATURALISTIC RESEARCH QUERIES

Ethnography, phenomenology, and grounded theory reflect distinct approaches in naturalistic inquiry. Queries developed within each methodology reflect a different purpose and a way of knowing. Moreover, consistent with examined practice, purpose and resources available to the social worker ultimately factor into the queries that can be posed and answered. Nevertheless, underlying each of these approaches is an essential iterative process of query-subquestion-reformulation central to knowledge generation in naturalistic inquiry.

INTEGRATING RESEARCH APPROACHES

As discussed earlier in this book, integrated designs combine different research traditions and approaches and, by their nature, may be complex. These designs may rely on the formulation of a query, a question, or both, and each may be ordered in diverse ways to accomplish the overall research purpose.

Consider the following examples to highlight the differences in approach among the experimental-type and naturalistic research traditions and an integrated design.

In determining the extent to which and how the design of a mobility device resolved the problem of abandonment, we conducted a mixed-method outcome assessment guided by the following questions and queries:

1. To what extent do elders abandon an aesthetically designed mobility device compared to a typical "medicalized walker" with equivalent functionality?

2. What meanings are perceived by elders regarding the aesthetic design of mobility devices?

Question #1 reflects the structure of an experimental-type Level 2 question. Note that it asks for association between abandonment frequency and design by crafting a comparison group approach to inquiry. Question #2 seeks meaning of object, or what we have introduced as object reading (Candlin & Guins, 2009).

An integrated study may pose both a concise question and a query, and the studies may be conducted sequentially or simultaneously. The elder outcome assessment answered both questions within the same time frame.

As shown, integrated designs can be complex. Therefore, it is important for the social worker to clearly articulate the specific questions and queries that are posed jointly and to delineate how each contributes to the other. In the elder intervention, the advantage of a mixed-method study was its capacity not only to understand use but also to delve into the visual world and meanings that prevent elders from following safety practices.

We introduced single subject and case study design above. Briefly, these methods focus on a single unit of analysis that may be studied as holistic (as single entity) or embedded (as multiple parts of a single entity) (Yin, 2014). Single subject and case study research methods are particularly useful throughout the examined practice sequence in that they are designed to generate findings as well as theory through collecting and analyzing data through more than one approach. Moreover, because single subject design refers to one phenomenon and does not aim to examine groups and subpopulations within groups (unless a group is framed as a single entity) these mixed-method designs are feasible and robust within the daily context of social work practice. Single subject design is particularly useful in clinical practice. Consider Janice, for example. Both questions and queries may be posed in single subject schemes. As an example, the social worker might pose the following reflexive intervention study:

> What progress does Janice feel she is making (query), and how is it exhibited in her mood assessment (Level 1 type question)?

> These two inquiries illustrate unstructured and structured questioning, respectively characteristic of single subject thinking and action.

SUMMARY

Each approach to problem formulation and query or question development differs within the three traditions of inquiry. In experimental-type approaches, the question drives each subsequent research step. Refinement of a research question occurs before any further action processes can be implemented. Conciseness and precision of language are critical to the conduct of the study and are the hallmarks of what makes the experimental-type research question rigorous, meaningful, and appropriate. Experimental-type questions are definitive, structured, and derived from the theory presented in the literature review before the social worker engages in specified actions. These questions must contain three elements: variables, level of questioning, and the population to be studied.

In naturalistic inquiry, the query establishes the initial entrance and boundaries for the study but may be continuously revised in the actual process of collecting and analyzing data. The social worker proceeding in this tradition fully expects and prepares for new queries and subquestions to emerge during the course of the study. That is, refinement of query and question emerges from the action of conducting the inquiry itself. Unlike experimental-type questioning, querying is a dynamic and flexible process. Integrated or mixed-method thinking and action use the strengths of both experimental-type and naturalistic traditions to pose questions and queries that can reveal, describe, relate, or predict need and outcome.

Table 8.2 summarizes the form and purposes of questions and queries across the three traditions.

The main points in this chapter are as follows:

1. Formal questioning begins at the needs assessment stage.

2. Naming and structuring research questions are tradition dependent.

3. In experimental-type design, determining validity is dependent on the presence of a properly structured, complete research question.

4. Experimental-type questioning occurs at three levels: description, relation, and prediction.

5. Naturalistic queries, while varied according to design type, hold the commonality of broad entrance into a study. Each design approach then has its own version and processes through which queries and probing questions are posed.

6. Mixed methods use questions from both experimental-type and naturalistic traditions as they examine single entities framed as holistic or embedded with more than one part.

Table 8.2   Form and Purposes of Questions and Queries

	Experimental-Type	*Naturalistic Inquiry*	*Integrated Design*
Form	Focused, carefully structured question	Broad query	Both or either
Purpose	Define variables, population, and level of inquiry	Identify and bound phenomena of interest and context, identify an entry point, respond to the unfolding of an inquiry	Both or either

REFERENCES

Agar, M. (2006). *An ethnography by any other name.* Retrieved from http://www.qualitative-research.net/index.php/fqs/article/view/177/395

Alvesson, M., & Sandberg, J. (2013). *Constructing research questions: Doing interesting research.* Thousand Oaks, CA: Sage.

Andrews, M., Squire, C., & Tamboukou, M. (2013). *Doing narrative research* (2nd ed.). Thousand Oaks, CA: Sage.

Bakker, H. (2010). Phenomenology. In A. J. Mills, G. Durepos, & E. Wiebe, *Handbook of case study research* (pp. 674–678). Thousand Oaks, CA: Sage.

Bryant, N., & Charmaz, K. (2007). *The SAGE handbook of grounded theory.* Thousand Oaks, CA: Sage.

Candlin, F., & Guins, R. (2009). *The object reader.* London, UK: Routledge.

DePoy, E., & Gitlin, L. (2016). *Introduction to research* (5th ed.). St Louis, MO: Elsevier.

Elder, L., & Paul, R. (2010). *The art of asking essential questions.* Tomales, CA: Foundation for Critical Thinking Press.

Grinnell, R., & Unrau, Y. (2011). *Social work research and evaluation* (5th ed.). Oxford, UK: Oxford University Press

Haight, W., Kayama, M., & Korang-Okrah, R. (2013). Ethnography in social work practice and policy. *Qualitative Social Work*, 1–17.

Harper, D. (2012). *Visual sociology.* New York, NY: Routledge.

Krug, S. (2014). *Don't make me think, revisited: A common sense approach to web usability.* Pearson.

Murthy, D. (2008). Digital ethnography. *Sociology, 42*(5), 837–855.

Squire, C. (2013). *Narrative research: An interview with Corrine Squire.* Thousand Oaks, CA: Sage.

Wertz, F. J., Charmaz, K., McMullen, L. M., Josselson, R., Anderson, R., & McSpadden, E. (2011). *Five ways of doing qualitative analysis: Phenomenological psychology, grounded theory, discourse analysis, narrative research, and intuitive inquiry.* New York, NY: Guilford Press.

Yin, R. (2014). *Case study research: Design and methods.* Thousand Oaks, CA: Sage.

Chapter 9

DESIGN IN BOTH TRADITIONS

This chapter examines and then applies the characteristics of designs in each of the traditions to examined practice. Recall that experimental-type designs are **"nomothetic,"** or rely on group trends, to generate knowledge. Thus, these approaches are most relevant to understanding group need and outcome as well as differences among and between groups. **Idiographic** designs are best suited for analyzing local uniqueness and assessing contextual outcomes.

SPECIFIC EXPERIMENTAL-TYPE DESIGNS

Experimental-type designs have traditionally been classified as true-experimental, quasi-experimental, pre-experimental, and non-experimental. Because the primary aim and structure of this tradition are ultimately designed to test cause and effect relationships, the true experiment is the criterion by which all other experimental-type methodological approaches are judged. As discussed previously, the true experiment and its variations form the gold standard for evidence-based practice. Although the true-experimental design is continually upheld as the most objective and true scientific approach, every design in the experimental-type tradition has merit and value providing that the research questions being posed are appropriate for the design structure. The experimental-type approach should be chosen purposively because it fits the intention of the study, the question, level of theory development, and setting or environment.

True-Experimental

To express the structural relationships of true-experimental designs, we use Campbell and Stanley's (1963) classic, widely adopted simple notation system to diagram a design: X represents the **independent variable**, O the **dependent variable**, and R denotes random sample selection as follows:

$$\frac{ROXO}{RO\ \ O}$$

The solid line denotes that experimental (above the line) and control groups (below the line) are being used. DePoy and Gitlin (2016) added the symbol r to refer to **random group assignment** in the absence of **random sample** selection. We use both notations because in examined practice, at the stages of needs and outcomes when experimental-type inquiry would be most useful, it is often difficult and frequently inappropriate or unethical for social workers to select a sample from a larger, predefined population based on random selection (R). More typically, subjects enter social work investigations on a volunteer basis or as naturally occurring groups (Grashaw, 2011). In these samples of convenience *r* denotes random assignment rather than random selection from a population. Designs in which samples are not randomly selected but are randomly assigned still meet the randomization criterion for true experimentation but are limited in their external validity, or the degree to which the sample represents the population from which it was selected (see Chapter 6).

Regardless of randomization of assignment, true-experimental design refers to the classic two-group design or its variations in which subjects are randomly selected or assigned (R, r) to either an experimental or control group condition. Before the experimental condition, all subjects are pretested or observed on a dependent measure (O). In the experimental group, the independent variable or experimental condition is imposed (X), and it is withheld in the control group. After the experimental condition, all subjects are posttested or observed on the dependent variable (O).

Recall in Chapter 4 that the Tobacco Access Portal (TAP) project used true experimentation. Consistent with the notation from DePoy and Gitlin (2016), the social worker structured the inquiry by randomly assigning an existing group to one of two groups: the experimental group that received the independent variable (the website) or the control group (the waiting list without access to the website). Both groups were tested on the dependent variable, positive attitude toward smoking cessation, prior to and then after the experimental group was exposed to the independent variable.

$$\frac{rOXO}{rO\ \ O}$$

r = random group assignment, *X* = website exposure, *O* = positive attitude toward smoking cessation

In this design, the social worker expects to observe no difference between the experimental and control groups on the dependent measure at pretest. In other words, subjects are chosen randomly from a larger pool of potential subjects and then assigned to a group on a chance-determined basis; therefore, subjects in both groups are expected to perform similarly in both groups as none have been exposed to a variable that others could not theoretically encounter. In the example, we would expect that subjects in experimental and control group conditions would have a similar range of attitude scores on pretest and hypothesize that differences will occur between experimental and control group subjects on the posttest scores as a result of the experimental group being exposed to a condition not available to the control group. This expectation is expressed as a null hypothesis, which states that no difference is expected. In a true-experimental design, the investigator always states a null hypothesis that forms the basis for statistical testing. Usually in sharing this knowledge, the alternative (working) hypothesis is stated (i.e., an expected difference). If the data analytical procedures reveal a significant difference (one that does not occur by chance) between experimental and control group scores at post-test, the null hypothesis fails to be accepted within a reasonable degree of certainty. In failing to accept the null hypothesis, the working hypothesis can be accepted with a certain level of confidence. That is to say, the social worker can conclude that the independent variable or experimental condition (X) caused the outcome observed at posttest time in the experimental group. In other words, the investigator infers that the difference at posttest time is not the result of chance but is caused by participation in the experimental condition.

Three major characteristics of the true-experimental design allow this causal claim to be made: randomization, control, and manipulation (DePoy & Gitlin, 2016).

Randomization occurs at the sample selection phase, the group assignment phase, or both. It is a technique that increases control and eliminates bias by theoretically neutralizing the effects of extraneous influences, or bias, on the outcome of a study that may occur from purposive selection. In principle, enacting randomization (see Chapter 10 for more detail on the processes) assures equal chance of each subject to group assignment (r) or participation in the study (R). If random selection (R) does not occur, external validity (the extent to which the knowledge learned from a study can be generalized with a degree of assuredness to the population from which the sample was selected) cannot be supported. So while random sample selection is often not possible or appropriate, random assignment of subjects to groups provides a high degree of assurance that subjects in both experimental and control conditions will be comparable at pretest on the initial, baseline measure (Alferes, 2012). The reasoning then proceeds to suggest that any influence on one group can similarly affect the other group as well. In the absence of any other differences that could influence outcome, an observed change in the experimental group at posttest then can be attributed with a reasonable degree of certainty to the experimental condition.

The concept of control introduced in Chapter 6, in true-experimental design, refers to the inclusion of a control group in a study. The control group allows the social worker to determine what the sample will be without the influence of the experimental condition or independent variable. The logic holds that a control group theoretically performs or remains the same relative to the independent variable at pretest and posttest, since the control group has not had the chance of being exposed to the experimental (or planned change) condition. Therefore, the control group represents the characteristics of the experimental group before being changed by participation in the experimental condition (DePoy & Gitlin, 2016).

In true-experimental design, manipulation refers to the presence or absence of the experimental or independent variable.

VARIATIONS OF EXPERIMENTAL-TYPE DESIGN

Many design variations of the true experiment have been developed to enhance its internal validity (the rigor of the design structure in answering the research question). Each has been developed to contain the three criteria for true-experimentation and to account for possible alternative explanations that may occur as a result of unwanted influences. For example, experience with a pretest may provide the opportunity for learning on the posttest, and thus one variation involves a third group that is simply posttested without pretest or exposure to the experimental condition. (Martin & Bridgmon, 2012). The third group is referred to as a "silent control group" because its members have no knowledge of their own participation. Thus, this structure may be used to eliminate any change in a group as a result of knowledge that an experiment is being conducted. To learn more about these design structures, we refer you to the many excellent methodological texts that already detail them. (We have cited many in the references).

Unless substantial financial support is available, it is not likely that complex designs will be used by social workers within daily social work practice (Grinell & Unrau, 2013). We introduce these approaches for awareness and to acknowledge their importance in the development of evidence-based practice knowledge. Regardless of how many variations are used, all conform to the logic of true-experimentation discussed above. In Chapter 13, the outcome assessment study examining the attitudes of web users is fully detailed. Note that the claim of attitude change as a result of social work intervention can be supported because a true-experimental design was used.

Quasi-Experimental

Quasi-experimental studies contain two of the three true-experimental elements: control group and manipulation (Beyman, 2014). Because random assignment is absent in quasi-experimentation, causal claims may be made while acknowledging potential alternative explanations for findings, or causal inferences may simply be avoided if they are unjustified by the purpose, design, or practice context (DePoy & Gilson, 2009). As we have indicated throughout this book, in social work, true experimentation is often not feasible, ethical, or even relevant to the knowledge being sought. Therefore, within the experimental-type tradition, other design options are extremely useful in generating systematic social work knowing, even though the language of the experimental-type tradition implies that designs other than true-experimentation are "missing something."

Two basic design types fit the criteria for quasi-experimentation: nonequivalent control group designs and time series approaches (Rubin & Babbie, 2016).

Nonequivalent control group designs contain at least two comparison groups, but subjects are not randomly assigned to these groups. Using Campbell and Stanley (1963), the basic design is structured as presented below:

$$\frac{\text{O X O}}{\text{O \quad O}}$$

It is also possible to add additional comparison groups or to alter the testing sequence. This design can answer the basic question, "What changed after being exposed to the experimental condition compared to nonexposure?"

Consider the mobility device abandonment initiative. In the outcome assessment, the social worker asked the question:

> Compared to the group that did not undergo the experimental condition (aesthetically designed mobility device), what changes in abandonment occurred in the group that participated in this program?

Because the groups were not randomly assigned to experimental and control conditions, it would not be possible to isolate the experimental variable (the equipment design) and examine its effect on change in usage. However, comparative change can be compelling in suggesting a desired outcome. Accompanied by naturalistic design, mixing methods can attribute change to the social work effort, as illustrated below and detailed in Chapter 13.

Interrupted time series designs involve repeated measurement of the dependent variable both before and after the introduction of the independent variable (Rubin & Babbie, 2016). There is no control or comparison group in this design. The multiple measures before the independent variable allow the social worker to examine change over time with the added strength of looking at patterns of change before and after the introduction of the experimental condition. A design diagram might look like the following:

OOO X OOO

This type of approach would be warranted to determine the extent to which abandonment of mobility devices decreased over time after a nonstigmatizing design was provided.

Just to summarize, quasi-experimental designs are characterized by the presence of some type of comparison group and manipulation, but they do not contain random group assignment. Although there is no control group in time series and single-subject designs, control is exercised through multiple observations of the same variable both before and after the introduction of the experimental condition. In nonequivalent group designs, the control is built in through the use of one or more comparison groups.

Quasi-experimentation is most valuable when the investigator is attempting to search for change over time or when a comparison between groups and the constraints of the health or human service environment are such that random assignment is not appropriate, ethical, or feasible (DePoy & Gilson, 2009).

Pre-Experimental

In pre-experimental designs, two of the three criteria for true experimentation are absent. Thus, when using these designs, it is possible to describe phenomena or relationships but not to attribute cause to the intervention. Pre-experimental designs therefore can answer descriptive Level 1 questions, Level 2 relational questions, or generate pilot, exploratory evidence. We discuss several frequently used designs below.

In the one-shot case study (Campbell & Stanley, 1963), the independent variable is introduced, following which the dependent variable is measured in only one group, as follows:

XO

Without a pretest or a comparison group, the social worker can answer the question, "How did the group score on the dependent variable after the intervention?" (DePoy & Gitlin, 2016). This design is familiar to many students who have taken a class in which a final exam was given to test knowledge. Although the implication of learning reflected in a test score is most often attributed to learning as a result of the class, this claim cannot be justified using a one-shot case study. So care in interpretation is important for social workers who employ this thinking and action process. If knowing the source of or reason for an outcome is not important, this approach is ideal. But if there is a need to know if the intervention produced the outcome, an alternative or additional study should be undertaken.

The pretest–posttest design (OXO) provides information, the pretest, such that change following a social work action can be measured. Consider the TAP initiative. Testing knowledge of smoking risk before and following the use of the website would provide information on change but not on its cause.

A static group comparison is diagrammed as follows:

$$\frac{XO}{O}$$

This design, as in other pre-experimental structures, can answer descriptive questions about phenomena or relationships but is not considered a desirable choice for causal studies (DePoy & Gilson, 2009). Its power lies in comparing the difference of presence and absence of the independent variable on the dependent variable. If this structure were used in the TAP project, the group exposed to the website would be compared on posttest to a group without exposure. While the design itself does not allow for causal inference, the comparison group adds credibility to hunches about the value of the website in attaining its outcome.

To briefly summarize, pre-experimental design structures are frequently used by social workers to examine what happened after an intervention or what changed following an intervention. A control group can even be added to create an additional source of evidence. These designs are often used in social work contexts when research and evaluation occur as part of practice. As an example, it may not be reasonable to pretest an entire group of clients on a smoking attitude scale before the social worker even knows who the clients will be. Given typical conditions of daily social work practice, the use of experimental-type traditions, particularly in outcome assessment, may be limited to approaches that by themselves cannot support cause and effect between social work action and outcome but can provide evidence to suggest a successful outcome. Moreover, as we discuss throughout, mixing methods may be just the strategy for causal understandings.

Non-Experimental

Within experimental-type approaches, there is a way to create true-experimental conditions without manipulating the actual mechanics of an inquiry. **Non-experimental designs** (Kent, 2015) that rely on statistical manipulation of data rather than mechanical manipulation and sequencing are excellent choices for creating social work knowing that meets the criteria necessary for attributing outcome to intervention. By definition, non-experimental designs are those in which none of the three criteria for true experimentation exist in the structure of sample selection, exposure to an experimental condition, or data collection, but they can be created through numeric and statistical manipulation (Rubin & Babbie, 2016).

Survey designs are a prime example of methods frequently used by social workers to determine what is needed to resolve a problem and to assess outcome attainment. While surveys are often conducted with large samples, they may also suffice to answer research questions about smaller groups such as clients served by an agency or single social work program. Questions are posed either through online or mailed questionnaires (albeit less frequently not only for conservation but for ease of data analysis as discussed in Chapter 12). Surveys may also be conducted through telecommunications or face-to-face interaction (Fowler, 2014).

Consider Elton as an example. While a survey for a single subject (Elton's employer) would not have been warranted given the nomothetic nature of experimental-type design, the social worker who resolved Elton's immediate problem used the knowledge learned from this social work activity to reframe the problem statement, looking more broadly to prevent unnecessary unemployment under similar circumstances. The part of the problem that was being addressed was negative employer attitudes toward advancing workplace accessibility. Looking to the literature to inform the thinking and action process of needs assessment, the social worker then sought to quantify the magnitude and nature of need for a social work response and to identify the direction for setting goals and objectives. The needs assessment question was framed as,

> To what extent do attitudes expressed by small business owners create barriers to workplace accessibility?

The Affective Reactions Scale (Copeland, Chan, Beyzak, & Fraser, 2010) was used by the social worker to obtain data to verify need and refine its direction. Note that this Level 3 question examines attitudes as causal, but the design is not structured as a true experiment. The statistical analysis accomplishes this part.

Another non-experimental alternative is the **passive observation design** (DePoy & Gitlin, 2016). This approach is particularly well suited to the practice context as it measures naturally occurring phenomena. Designs in this category are capable of discerning association as well as causal relationships between two or more variables. As in the survey, variables are not manipulated but are measured and then statistically examined for relationships and patterns of prediction. Passive observation can occur with current or past (*ex post facto*) phenomena.

Return to the example above. If observation and coding of employer attitudes were substituted for the survey developed by Copeland et al. (2010), the design used to assess need would be classified as passive observation. Note that nothing in the study is structurally manipulated, allowing for a systematic study to be carried out during reflexive intervention.

An example of ***ex post facto* design** can be illustrated by the elder mobility device work. The mobility impairment has already occurred and thus cannot be created. It is therefore an *ex post facto* condition that can be related to device abandonment.

Comparing survey and passive observation examples reveals the strengths and limitations of each for answering the social work question of need. Surveys can be expansive while observation requires more person hours for data collection. However, surveys may not yield as large of a percentage of response as onsite systematic observation. Both are discussed in more detail in Chapter 11 on obtaining information.

To briefly summarize, non-experimental designs have a wide range of uses. The value in these designs lies in their ability to examine and quantify naturally occurring phenomena so that statistical analysis can be accomplished. Therefore, the social worker can use these systematic strategies within the context of daily practice. It is because of these systematic strategies and others that will be discussed, that we claim practice wisdom can be equivalent systematic knowledge developed in any part of social work. Note that social workers always have the tools to conduct systematic thinking and action within all parts of social work and to further contribute knowledge from the field to the repository of social work knowing.

Before leaving experimental-type designs, two additional approaches to systematic knowledge, experimental meta-analysis and geographic techniques, are mentioned because of their value to social work. For more detailed discussion on each, we refer you to the excellent texts listed in the reference section of this chapter.

Meta-analysis involves the review, collection, and analysis of information that has already been generated in other studies. While review of the literature is the core action process in meta-analysis (see Chapter 7, and recall that literature is defined broadly in terms of its sources), what distinguishes this approach from review is the systematic process of statistical analysis of combined data sets. Meta-analysis allows the social worker to amalgamate and thus expand the application of small studies to social work thinking and action without having to collect data at all (Rubin & Babbie, 2016). Over the past decade, data sharing has become almost expected. Look at the policy recently promulgated by the National Institutes of Health:

> Once a researcher has published the results of an experiment, it is generally expected that all the information about that experiment, including the final data, should be freely available for other researchers to check and use. Some journals formally require that the data published in articles be available to other researchers upon request or stored in public databases. In the specific case of federally funded research that is used in setting policies that have the effect of law, research data must be made available in response to Freedom of Information Act (FOIA) requests (OMB, Circular A-110). There is, in other words, considerable support for sharing data with other researchers and the public unless there are compelling reasons for confidentiality. (U.S. Department of Health and Human Services, 2013)

The increasing access to data already generated by investigators allows social workers to obtain sources at no charge and without adding more work intensity to the daily action processes of the social work context. Customary sharing of information is relevant and valued at any part of the examined practice sequence. As an example, to inform the direction for smoking cessation strategies for low-literacy populations in the TAP project, the social work team accessed and analyzed existing data to answer the question on the association between reading level and smoking attitudes.

GEOGRAPHIC ANALYSIS

Geographic analysis is a relatively recent set of techniques in which data are geographically referenced. Although geography has always been used as an important variable in social work research (e.g., rural v. urban need), geographic analysis through geographic information systems (**GIS**) is a sophisticated set of strategies that relies on computer software to quantify and visually present the attributes of a geographic region. Thus, geographic methods are not a specific design but rather a set of specialized techniques that use visual-spatial locations as delimiters of information and analysis (Harder, Ormsby, & Balstrom, 2013).

Consider how geographic analysis might be used to add another layer to the TAP project. Because GIS has the capacity to represent multiple data layers on a single map, the ability to analyze complex relationships is one of its most powerful functions. Applied to smoking prevention, in addition to the website, a next step to preventing smoking among youth might be examining the density or location of cigarette sales outlets, the availability of money to youth within a geographic locale to purchase cigarettes, and the freedom to do so without parental interference. These variables could be visualized on a map so that prevention strategies could be tailored to individual neighborhoods.

Geographic analysis is a powerful tool in itself, but when coupled with statistical analysis, it can be an even more powerful strategy for association and prediction. Both tell the same story but through different means, and thus the strength of multiple communication formats and sets of evidence can be brought to bear on social work sharing to diverse audiences.

CRITERIA FOR SELECTING APPROPRIATE AND ADEQUATE EXPERIMENTAL-TYPE DESIGNS

As previously discussed, some researchers believe that the true-experimental design represents the only structure that is appropriate and adequate for creating professional knowledge. However, each design in the experimental-type tradition has its strengths and limitations. The true experiment is the best design for testing theory about groups, making causal statements, and determining the average efficacy of treatments. If causality is not the intended purpose, however, or if the design structure does not fit the particular environment in which the research is to be conducted, true-experimental design is not an appropriate or adequate choice.

As noted previously, it is often difficult to apply strict experimental conditions to a field setting. For example, although subjects may be randomly assigned to a group, it may not be possible to obtain the initial list of subjects needed for a random sampling process, or it may be unethical to withhold a type of treatment (or experimental intervention) from a client in a service setting. Although clinical drug trials or tests of new technologies present the degree of control necessary for true-experimental conditions, research on the social and psychological dimensions of health and human service work often pose a different set of issues and challenges for the researcher (Grinell & Unrau, 2013). These challenges make it essential for the investigator to be flexible in the use of design so that a research strategy appropriate to the question and to the level of theory, purpose, and practical constraints can be selected and rigorously applied.

SUMMARY OF EXPERIMENTAL-TYPE DESIGN

Experimental-type research designs range from true-experimental to non-experimental, and each design varies in its level of control, randomization, and manipulation of variables (Table 9.1). Field conditions, purpose, and other practicalities influence the choice and use of any type of design. The basic elements of design structure in the experimental-type tradition have many variations, and new applications of experimental designs such as those that use geographic modeling are being developed. Table 9.1 provides a brief comparative summary of the design categories in the experimental-type tradition.

Table 9.1 Summary of Design Characteristics in Experimental-Type Research

	True-Experimental	Quasi-Experimental	Pre-Experimental	Non-Experimental
Randomization	Yes	No	No	No
Manipulation	Yes	Maybe	No	No
Control	Yes	Maybe	No	No

NATURALISTIC INQUIRY DESIGNS

We now turn to the naturalistic tradition. As noted, while there are numerous philosophical and inquiry approaches under this umbrella, in this chapter, we discuss methods which we suggest best serve social work throughout the examined practice sequence.

First, recall knowledge from previous chapters that laid the foundation for naturalistic methods of knowing. A fundamental principle of all naturalistic designs is that phenomena occur or are embedded in a context, natural setting, or field. Moreover, foundational to naturalistic thinking are inductive and abductive logic structures that build in level of abstraction. As such, systematic processes are implemented and unfold in the identified context through the course of obtaining and analyzing information. Unlike experimental-type thinking and action, which is executed sequentially as planned, naturalistic designs are dynamic and fluid and thus can change as new data are obtained and interpreted. Moreover, while counting may occur in naturalistic design, narrative, imagery, unstructured observation, and nonnumeric sources form the typical sources of data that are subjected to analysis in this tradition (Creswell, 2014).

This chapter provides the basic framework of the designs that we believe have greatest value for examined practice: endogenous, participatory action, critical theory, phenomenology, heuristic, ethnography, narrative, life history, object reading, grounded theory, and meta-analysis.

Endogenous Inquiry

This type of design represents the most open-ended approach in the naturalistic tradition (DePoy & Gitlin, 2016). This research is conceptualized, designed, and conducted by researchers who are emic or considered members of a group or culture. What is unique about this infrequently used design is the relinquishment of all parts of knowledge generation on the part of the social worker. Thus, the subjects do not simply respond to interviews or become the subjects for observation but design an inquiry themselves in a manner which they believe will generate knowledge about their own group. Thus, in this type of systematic process, the subjects are truly leaders in the process.

Endogenous research can be organized in a variety of ways and may include the use of any strategy and technique in the naturalistic or experimental-type tradition or an integrated design. What makes endogenous inquiry naturalistic is not its investigative structure but rather its assumptions about the nature of knowledge; that is, the investigator views knowledge as emerging from individuals who know the best way to obtain it. Endogenous design is consistent with the contemporary notion of "emancipatory research," a relatively recent approach to investigations of the needs of marginalized and oppressed groups who do not often get a chance to reflect their perspectives outside of knowledge driven by professionals (Torres & Reyes, 2011). This strategy is also consistent with community-based participatory research and participatory action research (Chevalier & Buckles, 2013), described later, which emphasize the importance of involving members in the community of interest in each step of examined practice, from query formulation, to data collection and analysis in needs assessment, through outcome and even sharing.

The endogenous approach is based on a classic proposition developed by the social psychologist Kurt Lewin (1951), as Argyris and Schon (1991) explained:

> Causal inferences about the behavior of human beings are more likely to be valid and enactable when the human beings in question participate in building and testing them. Hence it aims at creating an environment in which participants give and get valid information, make free and informed choices (including the choice to participate), and generate internal commitment to the results of their inquiry. (p. 433)

Different from any other structure in any of the traditions, this design gives "knowing power" exclusively to the persons who are the participants of the inquiry. Also, because the social worker's involvement in the knowledge generation enterprise is determined by the individuals who are the "subjects" of the investigation, the social worker may participate as an equal partner, or not at all, or somewhere between these two levels.

Because endogenous research was not used at all in any of the examples provided, we turn back the clock to Maruyama (1981) who conducted a classic study. We have chosen this example to illustrate the power of this design in revealing knowledge about need without influence from social work in any way with the exception of asking for the knowledge at the outset. Maruyama was interested in understanding the nature of violence among prison inmates. He therefore entered the prison environment as a collaborator and participant observer rather than as leader, an important characteristic of endogenous research. As a collaborator, Maruyama deferred to the subjects of the investigation to determine the degree of investigator involvement. Two teams, composed of prisoners who had no formal education in research methods, held a series of group meetings and created purposes and plans of action that were important and meaningful to each group. Maruyama described the research in this way:

> A team of endogenous researchers was formed in each of the two prisons. The overall objective of the project was to study interpersonal physical violence (fights) in the prison culture, with as little contamination as possible from academic theories and methodologies. The details of the research were left to be developed by the inmate researchers. (Maruyama, 1981, p. 270)

The inmates themselves chose both experimental-type interview techniques and a form of qualitative data analysis to characterize the violence in the environments in which they were insiders. Even without any formal education in research methods, the inmates were able not only to collect extensive and meaningful data but also to conduct sophisticated conceptual analyses of their data. As illustrated in this classic example, the findings from a study owned and conducted by insiders, particularly in sensitive or potentially punitive circumstances, are likely to yield very different results from knowledge developed by a researcher who enters the environment as a stranger. From Maruyama's study, violence was explicated in the language of the inmates, and the findings clearly displayed the cultural nature of violence in each prison. Consider how different the findings may have been if an investigator went to a group of inmates and asked questions about the reasons prison violence occurs. The endogenous methodology not only gave the inmates a voice, but it also revealed insights that may not have been revealed by techniques in which the investigator would have taken an authoritative position in the project.

The major thinking and action processes in the endogenous research design use social work skills in building and working with a team such that control over process and outcome is owned by the subjects (DePoy & Gilson, 2009). If this approach had been used in investigating small business owner attitudes toward expanding workplace accessibility as the basis for formulating what is needed to resolve the problem of high unemployment rates among groups with mobility impairments, it is not only feasible but likely that results would be different from findings from a survey or even an open-ended interview controlled by an etic researcher.

We would not suggest that endogenous inquiry be enacted unless the social worker is assured that he or she can use the findings to craft social action or to add to the repository of social work knowledge. Consider Janice, for example. The first social worker asked about her needs but limited her clinical intervention to a strategy that did not serve Janice and thus failed to provide any help or useful outcome. More structured types of participatory action would be warranted if there is a limited repertoire of responses or a defined purpose beyond knowledge generation.

Participatory Action Research

The term *participatory action research* broadly refers to a variety of approaches that all share two features: (1) a commitment to active participation from subjects or "informants" in generating knowledge grounded in experience, and (2) the acceptance of the principle that those who experience a phenomenon are among the most qualified to examine and share knowledge about themselves (Chevalier & Buckles, 2013). Different from endogenous methods, however, participatory action typically is led from outside the emic group.

The purpose of action research is to generate knowledge to inform responsive action, with the emphasis on *responsive*. Social workers using a participatory framework usually work with groups or communities at the needs assessment phase and in the reflexive intervention element to understand client experiences with social work practice (Fortune, Reid, & Miller, 2013).

The concept of action research was first developed in the 1940s by Lewin (1951), who blended experimental-type approaches into research with programs that addressed social problems. Consistent with the mission of social work, social problems served as the basis for formulating the purpose, questions, and methodology. Therefore, each step in classical participatory inquiry was connected to or involved with the particular organization, social group, or community affected in some way by the identified problem or issue. More recently, others have expanded this approach. The action research design is now used in planning and implementing solutions to community problems and service dilemmas (Hatch, 2013).

Action research is based on four principles or values: democracy, equity, liberation, and life enhancement. *Democracy* refers to action research as participatory, involving all individuals who are identified as stakeholders in a problem or issue and its resolution. *Equity* proposes that all participants are equally valued in the research process, regardless of previous experience in research. *Liberation* suggests that action research is aimed at giving knowing power to participants themselves, decreasing oppression, exclusion, or discrimination. *Life enhancement* positions action research as a systematic strategy to promote growth, development, and fulfillment of participants of the process and the community they represent.

Participatory action research uses thinking and action processes from the experimental-type or naturalistic tradition or an integration of the two. Similar to endogenous design, there is no prescribed or uniform design strategy. Nevertheless, action research is consistent with naturalistic forms of inquiry in that all research occurs within its natural context (Chevalier & Buckles, 2013).

Consider Janice as an example. The second social worker asked Janice to be a full participant in the development of knowledge not only about her own needs but more broadly about the experience of losing functional capacity such that theory to guide responsive social work action for similar clients could be generated. In seeking this knowledge, the social worker discarded evidence-based practice built on theories of grieving after functional loss. He looked to Janice to characterize need as well as to guide intervention and desired outcomes. Janice's lived experiences were obtained through life history methods, as discussed below, using open-ended interview, systematically documented through audio recording and subsequent transcription, subjecting the data to thematic analysis (discussed in Chapter 12) and then sharing newly developed social work theory.

Participatory action research is now used for many purposes, often involving advocacy for marginalized groups. Unfortunately, we often find that action research is named but controlled by etic researchers. In examined practice, characterizing a design approach incorrectly, even if politically purposive, does not qualify for legitimate knowledge. Therefore, if a study is controlled primarily by etic researchers with minimal participation in the study design by the objects of inquiry, it belongs in other categories of mixed methods, but not in participatory action research.

Critical Theory

This type of design is another social change–oriented part of naturalistic thinking and action. By itself, the theory is not a research method but forms "pluralistic worldviews." We use the term *pluralistic worldviews* to characterize critical theory as inspired by political action-oriented schools of thought, including those informed by Marx, Hegel, Kant, Foucault, Derrida, and Kristeva. In essence, critical theory is a response to post-Enlightenment philosophies and positivism in particular, which rejects the principle of a unitary truth knowable by objective observation. Rather, critical theory represents a complex set of strategies that are united by the commonality of sociopolitical purpose (Denzin & Lincoln, 2011).

Critical theorists seek to understand human experience as a means to change the world. The common purpose of social workers who approach investigation through critical theory is to come to know about social justice and human experience as a way to promote local through global social change, and thus even before the turn of the twenty-first century, social workers were proposing critical theory as relevant for knowledge (Rodwell, 1998).

Critical theory is consistent with fundamental principles that underpin naturalistic strategies, such as a view of informant as knower, the dynamic and qualitative nature of knowing, complexity, and pluralism. Furthermore, critical theorists suggest that inquiry crosses disciplinary boundaries and challenges current knowledge generated by experimental-type methods. Because of the radical view of critical theorists, the essential step of literature review in the research process is primarily used to understand the status quo of social institutions (Willink & Suzette, 2012). Thus, the action process of literature review may occur before the research, but the theory derived is criticized and taken apart to expose its core assumptions. The hallmark of critical theory, however, is its purpose of social change and empowerment of marginalized and oppressed groups. Critical theory relies heavily on interview and observation as methods through which data are collected. Strategies of qualitative data analysis are the primary analytical tools used in critical research agendas (as discussed in Chapter 12). Consistent with tenets of examined practice, Mackinnon (2009) proposed that social work should proceed from an intellectual foundation in which systematically and publicly shared knowledge developed from practice, and community knowledge should guide social work in its commitment to social change and elimination of oppression.

> If we neglect to take our work a step further and share our knowledge with those who have been the focus of our research, we can miss an important pedagogical opportunity that could contribute to empowerment, emancipation and social change. (MacKinnon, 2009, p. 7).

Phenomenology

The specific focus of phenomenology is the narrative presentation of lived experiences (Howell, 2013). Phenomenology differs from other forms of naturalistic inquiry in that phenomenologists hold the extreme perspective that only those who have an experience can understand and explain it. Phenomenologists do not impose an interpretive framework on data but rather look for it to emerge from the information they obtain from their informants. Phenomenological inquiry is further anchored on the principle that the methods by which experience is shared and communicated are limited. "The phenomenon we study is ostensibly the presence of the other, but it can only be the way in which the experience of the other is made available to us" (Darroch, 1982, p. 4).

The primary data collection strategy used in this design is the telling of a biographical story or narrative with emphasis on eliciting experience as it relates to time, body, and physical and virtual space, as well as to other persons. For example, the social worker interested in facilitating Janice's goals would not structure an initial interview at all but rather would prompt her to discuss her experiences to some extent extemporaneously. The initial query might be something like "What is it like for you to have had a stroke? In phenomenology, the informant interjects the primary interpretation and analysis of experience into the interview rather than, as in life history or other more investigator-structured approaches, the inquirer. The use of literature may illustrate the constraints of understanding of human experience or corroborate the communication of the other.

In phenomenological research, involvement by the investigator is limited to life experiences and hearing and reporting the narrative perspective of the informant. Active interpretive involvement during data collection is not typically part of the investigator's role. The use of phenomenological inquiry in reflexive intervention to understand the experiences of clients who are involved in social services is a valuable application of this method. Remember that the choice of systematic strategy is purposive. Thus, if the experiences of an individual cannot be used or are not relevant to inform the nature of practice in the direction desired by the client, phenomenology is not indicated other than for sharing and thus generating knowledge for use by a broader audience. If feasible, once engaged in services, phenomenology is particularly powerful in the reflexive intervention phase, in that it decreases or eliminates the interpretations of social workers such that client experience is not filtered by a provider lens.

Heuristic Research

Another important design in the naturalistic tradition is heuristic research. According to Moustakas (1981) in his classical work, heuristic design involves the researcher's experience as data, thereby promoting knowledge as well as self-discovery.

The heuristic design strategy involves complete immersion of the social worker into the phenomenon of interest, including the use of investigator personal experiences as primary data. The investigator engages in intensive observation of and listening to individuals who have experienced the phenomenon of interest, recording their individual experiences. The investigator then interprets and reports the meanings of these experiences.

Similar to phenomenology, the premise of the heuristic approach is that knowledge emerges from personal experience and is revealed or known through experience of the phenomenon (Moustakas, 1990). Thus, social work involvement in heuristic design is extensive and pervades all areas of inquiry, from the formulation of the query to the collection of data from the investigator as an informant.

The elder mobility device project provides an example. The impetus for this project emerged from the personal experience of the social worker who herself had contracted encephalitis, resulting in balance and motor planning difficulties. When confronted with the need to use a walker, the social worker did so in the hospital but abandoned it upon discharge. Her experience of using a stigmatized medical device was the knowledge that initiated the problem statement discussed earlier.

This example illustrates how heuristic research is conducted by an individual for the purpose of discovery and understanding of the meaning of human experience including that of the social worker. Experience and the information derived from a literature review are considered primary and critical sources of data.

Ethnography

A primary method used in the discipline of anthropology, ethnography is a systematic approach to understanding the beliefs, rituals, patterns, and institutions that define a culture. Recall that classic ethnography was conducted by etic (outsider) researchers in previously unexplored remote geographies of the globe with the aim of using knowledge of isolated cultures to reveal the universal commonalities of all cultures (Salkind, 2010).

As introduced previously, there are numerous definitions of culture. Fundamental to all is the set of patterns that characterize and thus define a group and its membership (DePoy & Gilson, 2012). Ethnography is the accepted method for coming to understand culture. Classic systematic ethnographic methods relied on the investigator immersing him or herself in a distant culture for extended periods of time, during which observation, interview, and artifact review were conducted as methods to obtain information for subsequent analysis. The term *informant* emerged from this systematic approach. Informant refers to membership in the culture under study and the belief that insider status was necessary for expert and legitimate knowledge of the culture.

Contemporary ethnography retains some of the basics and practices of classical methods but is enacted in diverse groups no longer only defined by geographic boundaries. Given the ubiquity of the Internet and virtual worlds, it is not surprising that many investigators activate ethnographic methods to discover the nature of electronic, social media, and gaming cultures among others located online (Kozinets, 2010).

Ethnographic methods begin by using a range of techniques to gain access to a context or cultural group. Initial research activity involves observation to characterize the context and to begin describing a culture. Equipped with this understanding, the social worker uses participant and nonparticipant observation, interview, and examination of materials, texts, or artifacts to obtain data. Recording may occur in varied narrative, text, voice, and video formats. Analysis of the data is concurrent with their collection, and thus is continuous, moving from description to explanation. The knowledge generated therefore begins with description and then expands to meaning and theory.

To assure rigor, specific methods are used to verify that interpretive analysis and thus the theory derived is endorsed as accurate by those emic to the group. Reflexive analysis, or the analysis of the extent to which the researcher influences the results of the study, is one of the most important rigor strategies, which involves the researcher examining the influence of his or her thinking and action on the knowledge generated. This systematic process forms the foundation for the examined practice step of reflexive intervention, given its focus on self-examination. These rigor processes are described in more detail in Chapter 12.

Ethnography falls under the rubric of naturalistic design because of its reliance on qualitative data collection and analysis, the assumption that the investigator is not the knower, and the absence of *a priori* theory, or imposed theory. However, the classic ethnographer has a high degree of investigator involvement and control given that he or she makes the decisions regarding the "who, what, when, and where" of each observation and interview experience. Moreover, classical ethnography upheld the belief that through reflexivity, the investigator could remove personal bias from any interpretation and thus characterize the reality of a culture. More contemporary forms of ethnography challenge some of the basic assumptions held by classic ethnographers such as investigator objectivity and the presence of an objective social setting apart from its ongoing construction and reinvention by the people who inhabit and view it (Salkind, 2010). Current use of ethnography aims to represent the participants' own perspectives and their ways of explaining their lives, which may be in flux. The focus is on the interpretive practices of group members themselves, or how people make sense of their lives in context as reflected in their own words, stories, objects, and narratives. These concerns are similar to those of the phenomenological and life history approaches.

Ethnography has changed from its classic roots in other ways as well. Recall the discussion of critical theory above. Within this segment of ethnographic thought, the purposes and action processes of contemporary ethnography are becoming much more diverse, in contrast to classic ethnography. Nevertheless, one key element continues to "bound" all forms of ethnography: the examination of cultural and social groups and underlying patterns and ways of experiencing context.

Ethnography might be used in reflexive intervention in each of the examples to understand the context in which the social work intervention takes place or to characterize the culture of the social work agency or domain of concern. Consider Elton, for example. The social worker might use ethnographic methods to discover the culture of small business owners with specific focus on the social worker's influence on beliefs and practices about accessibility.

NARRATIVE INQUIRY

The many definitions of and approaches to narrative inquiry all have the common element of "storytelling" (Salkind, 2010). The storytelling may be autobiographical, biographical, testimonial, or in another form. As an example, narrative may be spoken, written, signed, acted, imaged, oral, electronic, and so forth. Narrative can also be interactive and immediate in response to a query or be present as in memoirs. Thus, narrative can be shared in various formats, serves multiple purposes, and can be approached in diverse analytical and interpretive ways (Denzin & Lincoln, 2011). Narrative inquiry is frequently used to hear the voices and experiences of marginalized or excluded populations and individuals, although this is not its only purpose. Because of the complexity and extensive detail, narrative data provide rich description and reveal meanings embedded not only in the content of the story but also in the words, acts, and images (symbols) used to tell the story (Silverman, 2013).

Because of its flexibility and potential to elicit pluralistic local knowledge, narrative has become one of the most popular contemporary research methods. The view of language as a dynamic, embedded human phenomenon drives the analysis of multiple and reciprocal meanings that can be understood through examining the symbolic, nonneutral nature of the data. (Andrews, Squire, & Tamboukou 2013). Narrative has also been used for clinical social work purposes, such as therapeutic use of autobiography and biography. The power of story in healing has been highlighted in numerous scholarly works (Freeman, 2011; Baldwin, 2013).

There are many methods to obtain narrative data. Interviewing and recording (audio or video) are among the information-gathering strategies used most frequently in social work to collect narrative data. Photography (Tinkler, 2013; Helle, 2011), drawing, painting (Rose, 2012), creative nonfiction, autobiography, and coconstructed narrative (Gubrium, Holstein, Marvasti, & McKinney, 2012) are other methods used to tell and present the story. Selecting the methods for collecting information is first purposive and then practical in nature.

Consider how narrative was used with Janice. The second social worker asked her to construct a life history so that he could systematically elicit what was meaningful to her throughout her life. From the narrative, it was clear that Janice valued physical activity and intellectual involvement throughout her life, and thus the social worker used this information to find relevant literature and then craft goals and objectives as well as intervention strategies. Throughout the social work intervention, Janice was asked to document her experience, once again in narrative form. These data served as evidence to guide reflexive intervention as well as for part of the outcome assessment. Moreover, the social worker sought permission to publish his practice knowledge, and thus this rich understanding joined the social work literature to inform others who might encounter similar clients and needs.

In Chapter 12, we discuss the basic analytical action processes used in the naturalistic tradition. These same strategies are used for narrative analysis (Denzin & Lincoln, 2011). From a data set, inductive analysis is used to reveal the themes, patterns, and meanings that emerge from storytelling. Although narrative can ultimately generate theory (Denzin & Lincoln, 2008) we suggest that its primary purpose is the illumination of how meaning is made and experienced locally.

Life History

This type of narrative, illustrated above by Janice, is an important design in naturalistic inquiry. What distinguishes life history from other forms of narrative is its focus on the unfolding of all or part of a life over time. Life history can be an integral part of other forms of naturalistic research, such as ethnography, or it may simply stand on its own as revealed in the multiple memoirs of social work clients and social workers. The life history approach is a part of the naturalistic tradition because of its contextual, interpretive nature. Similar to other designs such as phenomenology, the investigator is primarily concerned with eliciting life experiences and with how individuals themselves interpret and attribute meanings to these experiences.

The purpose of life history is to "generat[e] . . . and interpret . . . the stories or narratives of individuals' lives" (Schwandt, 2007).

Life history research involves a particular methodological approach in which the sequence of life events is elicited and the meaning of those events examined from the perspective of the informant within a particular sociopolitical and historical context (Goodwin, 2012). In this approach, the social worker seeks to uncover and characterize marker events, or "turnings," defined as specific occurrences that shape and guide the direction of individual lives (Verd & López, 2011). Typically, life history relies heavily on unstructured interviewing techniques, although no direct interaction may occur in order to reveal the sequence of a life or part of it. An interview may begin with asking an informant to describe the sequence of life events from childhood to adulthood. On the basis of a timeline of events, the social worker may ask questions to uncover the meanings of these events (Gubrium et al., 2012). Observation may also be combined with interview to examine meanings and understand how life is experienced.

A good example of observation is raised by the elder mobility device work. The presence of a device tells a story about a current experience. If elongated in time, the "turning" of the acquisition of a mobility device could be uncovered and its meaning explored.

A recent work by MacGregor (2011) used visual object reading to tell the "life history" of the world on 100 objects. Although life history may rely mostly on the person who tells his or her story or the objects examined and used to craft a longitudinal narrative, the social worker shapes the story in part by the types of questions asked or observations enacted.

Object Reading

This research design is a relatively contemporary approach within naturalistic inquiry. Although artifacts have been considered to be the domain of archeology over several centuries, the recent emergence of the field of material culture has brought life, interactivity, intertextuality, and interpretation to objects. *Object* refers primarily to tangible artifacts but may also include visual, text, or oral images. *Reading* refers to the interpretation of meaning of an object, similar to the analysis of narrative in which texts are inductively analyzed not only for their description but for meanings embedded within them (Berger, 2009). Object reading involves both **denotative** and **connotative** elements. Denotative elements describe the object, while connotative properties refer to the rich interpretive meanings attached to objects (Barthes, 1988). MacGregor (2011) combined object reading with life history to create a timeline of the world inscribed in objects.

Return to the mobility device intervention. Recall that medicalized mobility devices were abandoned in large part because of their stigmatizing appearance. The social work team used object reading in part to study the meaning (connotative element) of typical mobility objects to elders whose providers prescribed them, as the basis for understanding what was needed to resolve the abandonment problem and its consequences. The systematic inquiry involved interviewing elders about the meaning (connotation) of these objects to them. To analyze meanings for observers and prescribers, photos (denotative elements) were taken of typical walkers, crutches, and canes. These photos were then shown to informants who were asked to tell a story about people who might be likely to be seen using the objects represented. The technique of elicitation, or presenting a visual image or actual object to informants to stimulate discussion of meaning, is one method that is frequently used in object reading inquiry. The timing and role of literature review in this method is variable and depends on purpose.

Grounded Theory

This strategy is defined as "the systematic discovery of theory from the data of social research" (Geertz, 1973). It is a more structured strategy than the previously discussed naturalistic designs. Developed by Glaser & Strauss (1967), grounded theory represents the integration of quantitative and qualitative perspectives in thinking and action processes. The primary purpose of this strategy is to develop and "ground" a theory in the context in which the phenomenon under study occurs. The theory that emerges is intimately linked to each datum of daily life experience that it seeks to explain.

This strategy is similar to other naturalistic designs in its use of an inductive process to derive concepts, constructs, relationships, and principles to understand and explain a phenomenon. However, grounded theory is distinguished from other naturalistic designs by its use of a structured data-gathering and analytical process called the constant comparative method (Creswell, 2014). In this approach, each datum is compared with others to determine similarities and differences. Elaborate schemes have been developed to **code**, analyze, recode, and produce a theory from narratives obtained through a range of data collection strategies.

Consider the mobility device intervention. The social worker attempting to develop a theory of the relationship between appearance, stigma, and use of adaptive devices might find this method extremely valuable, providing he or she had the time and resources to enact it. Using this method, data would be collected through object reading, narrative, open-ended interview, elicitation, or another method discussed in more detail in Chapter 11. The data would be combined, read, and reread multiple times to look for themes repeated throughout the data. Following the initial development of categories from themes, the social worker would return to the transcripts to analyze each datum (an experience, articulation, or observation) and compare it with the data in the existing categories to determine similarities and differences between new data and previous information. If a datum did fit within one or more categories, it would be coded with an existing code. If it did not fit, a new category or subcategory would be developed and used as a basis for comparing new data.

The purpose of the constant comparative method is not only to reveal categories but also to explore the diversity of experience within categories and to identify links among categories. Because of these processes, grounded-theory can also be used to generate and verify both new and existing theory (Glaser & Strauss, 1967).

Naturalistic Meta-Analysis

This strategy seeks to aggregate and analyze data sets that have already been generated and shared from earlier research studies (Flick, 2013). As discussed above in the section on experimental-type designs, meta-analysis is a systematic process in which multiple independently conducted studies are combined and analyzed as a single data set to answer a research question or query. Naturalistic meta-analysis is the application of naturalistic methods to the analysis of many studies. Interestingly, naturalistic meta-analysis is not restricted to the analysis of naturalistic studies. Rather, this approach to meta-analysis is characterized by the philosophical perspective that underpins naturalistic inquiry and the use of inductive methods of analysis applied to multiple studies, literature, and theory.

A social worker interested in understanding the themes in attitudes of small business owners regarding workplace accessibility could collect written literature and look for themes throughout narratives, theory, and even experimental-type studies that focus on the particular population and conceptual scope.

There are many purposes of naturalistic meta-analysis. Similar to experimental-type meta-analysis, some naturalistic meta-analyses seek to identify and summarize a universe of studies on a particular topic. In anthropology, however, meta-ethnography has been used to reveal global themes and patterns (Denzin & Lincoln, 2011).

The thinking and action processes of naturalistic meta-analysis follow the processes used in any naturalistic study. The difference, however, is that the data set comprises data from studies already conducted and existing sources of literature, theory, and other data sources. Thus, this technique involves collecting and conducting a secondary analysis of existing knowledge from the perspective of naturalistic inquiry.

Naturalistic meta-analysis can be an extremely valuable methodology for social workers. This approach provides the tools to reveal consensus among competing bodies of social work knowledge, to arrive at agreed upon definitions of complex constructs, and to illuminate important themes and patterns across large bodies of literature.

MIXED-METHOD DESIGNS

There are numerous ways to design studies with methods from both experimental-type and naturalistic research. Chapter 13 illustrates how mixed methods were used in our examples. One frequent approach is to generate theory with one or more of the naturalistic designs discussed above and then to test the theory with experimental-type research methods. Another well-used design involves integrating experimental-type boundary setting discussed in the next chapter with naturalistic data collection. The elder needs assessment illustrates this approach given that the population was known, but the meanings of the appearance of mobility devices had not been theorized or tested.

Case study design is one of the most frequently used mixed-method research approaches in social work. The following two-part definition is derived from the work of Yin (2014).

Case study is an empirical inquiry that:

1. investigates a contemporary phenomenon within its real life context; especially when the boundaries between phenomenon and context are not clearly evident, and

2. copes with the technically distinctive situation in which there will be many more variables of interest than data points, and as one result, relies on multiple sources of evidence, with data needing to converge in a triangulating fashion, and as another result, benefits from the prior development of theoretical propositions to guide data collection and analysis. (Yin, 2014)

Yin's definition clarifies why case study design is classified as mixed-method. Case study is particularly useful when it is not possible or desirable to randomize, when it is not possible or desirable to study a particular population as a group with similar characteristics, when it is desirable to assess social work outcomes or change in a single unit of analysis, and when it is desirable to obtain pilot information in a cost-efficient way. Moreover, case study is an excellent theory-generating tool because the findings of a single case can be theoretically explained and then tested through other types of design strategies.

Case studies can be treated as holistic or embedded. Holistic studies are those that investigate a unit as a single entity while embedded approaches treat a single unit as a sum of its parts (Yin, 2014). Consider Elton, for example. If the social worker treated the work environment as holistic, the needs assessment would have focused on what was needed to resolve access problems for the institution. However, from an embedded design approach, the workplace would be considered as the sum of its parts, including but not limited to Elton, his employer, policy, and other variables. In an embedded case study, each would be investigated as part of a whole.

A second design consideration in case study is the determination of the number of cases to be included in the research. In a **single-case design**, only one study of a single unit of analysis is conducted. In a multiple-case design, more than one study of single units of analysis are conducted. It logically follows, therefore, that the holistic single-case study is conducted only once on one global case. The holistic multiple-case study examines several global units of analysis more than once. An embedded single-case study focuses on multiple parts of a single case using only one case, whereas an embedded multiple-case study examines more than one case in which each case contains many subparts (Yin, 2014).

The decision to conduct a single-case or multiple-case study depends on several considerations. First, the purpose of the design selection must fit the context. If the social worker is only providing social work services for one employer, multiple-case study designs are not feasible or appropriate.

Because the methods for boundary setting in case study design are not consistent with experimental-type boundary setting, using multiple studies to comprise a sample or a population is not appropriate or acceptable. The purpose of selecting a multiple-case study design instead of a more traditional group design lies in the definition of case study designs. Case study, whether single or multiple, is ideal for social workers who are describing a single unit in depth throughout the sequence of examined practice. Janice's second social worker provides illustration as he selected a single holistic approach throughout his work with her.

SUMMARY

In this chapter, research designs in experimental-type, naturalistic, and mixed methods were discussed and illustrated. The range of design approaches available to the social worker throughout the examined practice sequence is broad and varied. Table 9.2 presents an overview of the designs discussed, their purpose sequence, and degree of social work investigator involvement. The next chapters discuss strategies to conduct these designs to build social work knowledge.

The main points in this chapter are as follows:

1. Experimental-type designs are used to foster understanding of group need and outcome as well as to understand differences among and between groups. Naturalistic designs are best suited for analyzing local uniqueness and assessing contextual outcomes.

Table 9.2   Basic Framework of Designs in Naturalistic Inquiry

Design Approach	Purpose	Sequence	Social Work Investigator Involvement
Endogenous	To yield insider perspective through involvement of subject as researcher	Variable	Determined by subjects/informants
Participatory action	To generate knowledge to inform action	Variable	Inclusive team of investigators and participants
Critical theory	To understand experiences for social change	Variable	Investigator directed
Phenomenology	To discover meaning of lived experience	Narrative	Listener/reporter
Heuristic	To reveal personal and lived experience	Variable	Investigator and informant
Ethnography	To understand culture	Prescribed	Investigator directed
Narrative	To understand stories of marginalized individuals	Can be embedded in other designs; analytical strategy	Investigator directed
Life history	To yield biographical experience	Narrative	Investigator directed
Grounded theory	To generate theory	Prescribed	Investigator directed
Meta-Analysis	To synthesize body of knowledge	Prescribed	Investigator directed

2. Experimental-type designs range from true to non-experimental, each with a different purpose but all intended to incrementally build predictive knowledge.

3. Geographic analysis provides information about local context that is useful for tailoring interventions to specific locations.

4. Choice of experimental-type approach is dependent on purpose and field constraints.

5. Within the naturalistic tradition, designs differ according to degree of investigator control and philosophical foundation. Commonalities include informant as knower, inductive or abductive logic to structure most designs, and flexibility in structure and process.

6. Mixed-method designs use multiple strategies from both naturalistic and experimental-type design traditions.

7. Case study is one of the most valuable mixed-method designs for examined practice.

REFERENCES

Alferes, V. (2012). *Methods of randomization in experimental design.* Thousand Oaks, CA: Sage.

Andrews, M., Squire, C., & Tamboukou, M. (2013). *Doing narrative research.* Thousand Oaks, CA: Sage.

Argyris, C., & Schon, D. (1991). Participatory action research and action science compared: A commentary. In William Whyte (Ed.), *Participatory action research.* Newbury Park, CA: Sage.

Baldwin, C. (2013). *Narrative social work.* Chicago, IL: University of Chicago Press.

Barthes, R. (1988). *Image, music, text* (S. Heath, Trans.). New York, NY: Hill and Wang.

Berger, A. (2009). *What objects mean.* Walnut Creek, CA: Left Coast.

Beyman, A. (2014). Social research methods (4th ed.) Oxford, UK: Oxford University Press.

Campbell, D. T., & Stanley, J. (1963). *Experimental and quasi-experimental designs for research.* Belmont, CA: Cenage.

Chevalier, J. M., & Buckles, D. J. (2013). *Participatory action research: Theory and methods for engaged inquiry.* London, UK: Routledge.

Copeland, J., Chan, F., Bezyak, J., & Fraser, R. T. (2010). Assessing cognitive and affective reactions of employers toward people with disabilities in the workplace. *Journal of Occupational Rehabilitation 20*(4), 427–434.

Creswell, J. (2014). *Research design.* Thousand Oaks, CA: Sage.

Darroch, S. R. J. (1982). *Interpretive human studies: An introduction to phenomenological research.* Washington, DC: University Press of America.

Denzin, N., & Lincoln, Y. (2008). *Collecting and interpreting qualitative materials.* Thousand Oaks, CA: Sage.

Denzin, N. K., & Lincoln, Y. S. (2011). *SAGE handbook of qualitative research* (4th ed.). Thousand Oaks, CA: Sage.

DePoy, E, & Gilson, S. (2009). *Evaluation practice.* New York, NY: Routledge.

DePoy, E., & Gilson, S. F. (2012). *Human behavior theory and applications.* Thousand Oaks, CA: Sage.

DePoy, E., & Gitlin, L. (2011). *Introduction to research.* (4th ed.). St Louis, MO: Elsevier.

DePoy, E, & Gitlin, L. (2016). *Introduction to research* (5th ed.). St Louis, MO: Elsevier.

Flick, U. (2013). *The SAGE handbook of qualitative data analysis.* Thousand Oaks, CA: Sage.

Fortune, A. E., Reid, W. J., & Miller, R. L. (2013). *Qualitative research in social work* (2nd ed.). New York, NY: Columbia University Press.

Fowler, F. (2014). *Survey research.* Los Angeles, CA: Sage.

Freeman, E. (2011). *Narrative approaches in social work practice: A life span, culturally centered, strengths perspective.* Springfield, IL: Charles C. Thomas.

Geertz, C. (1973). *The interpretation of cultures: Selected essays.* New York, NY: Basic Books.

Glaser, B., & Strauss, A. (1967). *The discovery of grounded theory: Strategies for qualitative research.* New York, NY: Aldine.

Goodwin, J. (2012). *SAGE biographical research.* Thousand Oaks, CA: Sage.

Grashaw, K. (2011). When might a quasi-experimental design be chosen over an experimental design? What considerations must a researcher make when deciding which approach to take? *Amazon Digital Services.* Retrieved from http://www.amazon.com/quasi-experimental-experimental -considerations-researcher-deciding-ebook/dp/B006AXT9TO/ref=sr_1_6?s=books&ie=UTF8 &qid=1387470428&sr=1-6&keywords=quasi+experimental+design

Grinell, R., & Unrau, Y. (2013). *Social work research and evaluation.* New York, NY: Oxford.

Gubrium, J. F., Holstein, J. A., Marvasti, A. B., & McKinney, K. D. (2012). *SAGE handbook of interview research.* Thousand Oaks, CA: Sage.

Harder, C., Ormsby, T., & Balstrom, T. (2013). *Understanding GIS: An ArcGIS project workbook.* Redlands, CA: ESRI Press.

Hatch, M. J. (2013). *Organization theory: Modern, symbolic, and postmodern perspectives* (3rd ed.). Oxford, UK: Oxford University Press.

Helle, A. (2011). When the photography speaks: Photo analysis in narrative medicine. *Literature and Medicine 29*(2), 297–324.

Howell, K. E. (2013). *An introduction to the philosophy of methodology.* Thousand Oaks, CA: Sage.

Kent, R. A. (2015). *Analyzing quantitative data.* Thousand Oaks, CA: Sage.

Kozinets, R. (2010). *Netnography: Doing ethnographic research online.* Thousand Oaks, CA: Sage.

Lewin, K. (1951). *Field theory in social science.* New York, NY: Harper and Row.

MacGregor, N. (2011). *A history of the world in 100 objects.* New York, NY: Viking.

MacKinnon, S.T. (2009). Social work intellectuals in the twenty-first century: Critical social theory, critical social work and public engagement. *Social Work Education 28*(5), 512–527.

Martin, W. E., & Bridgmon, K. D. (2012). *Quantitative and statistical research methods: From hypothesis to results.* San Francisco, CA: Jossey-Bass.

Maruyama, M. (1981). Endogenous research: The prison project. In P. Reason & J. Rowan (Eds.), *Human inquiry: A sourcebook of new paradigm research.* New York, NY: Wiley & Sons.

Moustakas, C. (1981). Heuristic research. In P. Reason & J. Rowan (Eds.), *Human inquiry: A sourcebook of new paradigm research* (pp.). New York, NY: Wiley & Sons.

Moustakas, C. (1990). *Heuristic research.* Thousand Oaks, CA: Sage.

Rodwell, M. (1998). *Social work constructivist research.* New York, NY: Garland.

Rose, G. (2012). *Visual methodologies: An introduction to researching with visual materials.* Thousand Oaks, CA: Sage.

Rubin, A., & Babbie, E. (2016). *Empowerment series: Essential research methods for social work.* Boston, MA: Cenage.

Salkind, N. (2010). *Encyclopedia of research design.* Thousand Oaks, CA, Sage.

Schwandt, T. A. (2007). *The SAGE dictionary of qualitative inquiry.* Thousand Oaks, CA: Sage.

Silverman, D. (2013). *Doing qualitative research* (4th ed). Thousand Oaks, CA: Sage.

Tinkler, P. (2013). *Using photographs in social and historical research.* Thousand Oaks, CA: Sage.

Torres, M. N., & Reyes, L. V. (2011). *Research as praxis: Democratizing education epistemologies.* New York, NY: Peter Lang.

Verd, J. M., & López, M. (2011). *The rewards of a qualitative approach to life-course research.* Retrieved from http://nbn-resolving.de/urn:nbn:de:0114-fqs1103152

U.S. Department of Health and Human Services. (2013). *Data sharing.* Retrieved from http://ori.hhs.gov/Chapter-6-Data-Management-Practices-Data-sharing

Willink, K. G., & Suzette, J. (2012). Taking theories of cultural dialogue from the classroom to the street corner. *Critical Methodologies 12*(3), 197–212.

Yin, R. (2014). *Case study research: Design and methods.* Thousand Oaks, CA: Sage.

Chapter 10

SETTING AND PROTECTING THE BOUNDARIES OF A STUDY

Setting limits or boundaries to delimit what and who will be included in the scope of an inquiry is an action that occurs in every type of design, whether in the experimental-type, naturalistic tradition, or mixed-method traditions. To set the foundation for the more detailed discussion of boundary-setting techniques, the first part of the chapter provides an introduction and definition of terms. We then address protection of boundaries, specifically referring to humans. The last part of the chapter specifies multiple strategies of setting boundaries in each of the traditions and exemplifies their use throughout examined practice.

DePoy and Gitlin (2016) use the term *setting boundaries* to refer to methods that delimit the scope of a systematic inquiry to a specified group of individuals, phenomena, data collection strategies, geography, or a set of conceptual dimensions. In examined practice, boundary setting is purposive and influenced by the resources available as well as constraints. As an example, the ability to access members of a population would be an important practical consideration in structuring boundaries to assess needs in vulnerable or hard-to-reach groups.

In the experimental-type tradition, consistent with its *a priori* (established before any action occurs) structure, boundary setting is an action process occurring at the design phase before beginning an inquiry. Boundaries are set in three ways: (1) specifying the concepts that will subjected to measurement, (2) establishing inclusion and exclusion criteria (who or what will be part of the study and who or what will be omitted) that define the population of focus, and (3) developing a structured plan to obtain a sample from the population that both answers the question and makes purposive and practical sense (Thompson, 2012).

Different from experimental-type design, naturalistic boundary setting is a dynamic process which begins with an initial action process and unfolds in response to the knowledge generated throughout the inquiry. Who sets the boundaries and how are they dependent on the design and purpose (Denzin & Lincoln, 2011)?

As an example, in the classic study of inmate violence introduced in Chapter 9, Maruyama (1981) set the initial boundaries of the study by defining the topic of interest as interpersonal violence, the setting in prisons, and the informants as inmates. However, as the study proceeded, the inmates decided who would be included and what was to be asked of participants. That process differed from the life history needs assessment conducted by the second social worker who worked with Janice. The boundaries of that needs assessment involved a single informant, Janice, and an elongated timeline, the duration of her life.

In examined practice, what can ultimately be concluded (or not) about need, reflexive intervention, or outcome and then applied to whom or what is one of the most important considerations. Thus, in addition to using systematic processes consistent with a chosen design, bounding a social work study is a purposeful and practical action process in that the inclusion or exclusion of people, concepts, events, or other phenomena has considerable implications for social work knowledge development and use.

GENERAL GUIDELINES
FOR BOUNDING STUDIES

There is nothing inherently superior about one boundary-setting approach over another. The strengths and limitations of a technique depend on its *appropriateness* and *adequacy* in how well it fits the context, purpose, and constraints within each part of examined practice. *Appropriateness* is defined as fit of the boundary-setting strategy with the overall purpose of the inquiry and the steps in the examined practice sequence. For example, it would be inappropriate to use a random sampling technique when the purpose of a study is to understand how individuals interpret the appearance of mobility devices. In this case, the purposive selection of individuals who can articulate meaning and its impact on behavior may provide greater insight than the inclusion of a sample selected randomly from a population with predetermined characteristics. Purposeful selection within this phase facilitates understanding of the need to structure social work action, which is the aim of needs assessment in the examined practice sequence.

Adequacy is defined as the capacity of the boundary-setting method to yield sufficient data to answer the question or query. In experimental-type designs, adequacy is determined by sample size and composition (Thompson, 2012). In naturalistic approaches, adequacy is determined by the quality and completeness of the information and the understanding obtained in the selected domain. **Saturation** is defined as reaching a point in the inquiry at which no new information is obtained (Saumure & Given, 2008). Thus, appropriateness and adequacy are two criteria that can be applied to selecting boundary-setting decisions.

SUBJECTS, RESPONDENTS, INFORMANTS, PARTICIPANTS, LOCATIONS, CONCEPTUAL BOUNDARIES, VIRTUAL BOUNDARIES

There are many names for participants in an inquiry, be they persons or other sources that provide data for analysis. Recall that some of the designs obtain information from people, while others derive data from objects, images, narrative, and so forth. *Subjects*, *respondents*, *informants*, and *participants* are words used to refer to humans or the individuals who agree to become part of a study. Although there is overlap and no consensus on a single designation, each term reflects a different type of participation. Locations, concepts, and virtual spaces are viable boundaries as well, used to delimit studies in experimental-type, naturalistic, and mixed-method approaches.

First, we discuss the distinction among the four terms that describe human roles in inquiry. In experimental-type research, individuals are usually referred to as subjects, a term that denotes their passive role in framing the study method (DePoy & Gitlin, 2016). For example, the social worker examining the attitudinal outcome of exposure to the Tobacco Access Portal (TAP) website would refer to those who participate in the outcome analysis as subjects because they are the object of inquiry and uninvolved in how the testing conditions were conceptualized and conducted. In survey research, individuals are often referred to as respondents because they are asked to respond to very specific questions (Fowler, 2014). So the social worker might also refer to web users who answer the attitudinal survey as respondents. In this example, both terms are correct and explanatory.

In naturalistic inquiry, individuals are often referred to as informants, a term that reflects the active role of informing an investigator about what is being studied (Denzin & Lincoln, 2008). The word *participants* is a broader term and may name individuals who enter and fill varied roles from active engagement in the design of an inquiry to acting as an informant.

Locations, *conceptual boundaries*, and *virtual boundaries* all are terms that are used to denote nonhuman delimiters of a study. Similar to descriptors of humans in a study, these terms overlap as well. Although it was not a part of the needs assessment or outcome for the TAP project, a previous set of usability studies informing the website design used color and placement preference as boundaries (Krug, 2014).

Although there are no specific rules to guide the use of these terms, selecting boundaries reflects one's preferred way of knowing and the role that individuals or concepts play in the study design.

PROTECTING BOUNDARIES

Protection of boundaries is an action process used when humans are involved in a systematic inquiry that is considered to fall under the definition of research. Because of the separation among research, evaluation, and practice set forth in federal policy (National Commission for the Protection of Human Subjects of Biomedical and Behavioral Research, 1979), it is not unusual for practice evaluations to be exempt from review boards who approve and monitor research ethics. The Belmont Report, the major watershed document detailing federal policy on the protection of human subjects in research, was penned in the late 1970s when the methodological literature identified clear distinctions between research and evaluation. Over the years, these divisions have been challenged (see Chapter 1), and thus we suggest that in examined practice, all systematic inquiry involving humans be scrutinized for ethical treatment of subjects, informants, and/or participants. That is not to say that all social work practice should be treated as systematic inquiry. However, because of its emphasis on knowledge generation from all phases of examined practice, social workers following the model should carefully consider the professional actions that warrant review. As an example, the important knowledge derived from working with Janice, despite the emphasis on clinical intervention, if shared more broadly, should be reviewed to uphold ethical research practices and human subject protections according to the Belmont Report (National Commission for the Protection of Human Subjects of Biomedical and Behavioral Research, 1979).

Involving humans in systematic inquiry raises important ethical considerations and signals legally binding actions. The basic ethical decisions that underlie protection of humans in boundary setting across traditions are anchored on principlism, which seeks to maximize knowledge benefit while decreasing harm to those involved in its creation. Although sometimes it is difficult to see how any harm might occur (e.g., from taking a survey anonymously), all systematic inquiry in which people are directly involved has potential risks to its participants, even if minimal. According to federal law (National Commission for the Protection of Human Subjects of Biomedical and Behavioral Research, 1979), social workers and all people who are involved in the conduct of inquiry must submit a plan to an approved board to assure that ethical principles are upheld. This board is mandated to assess (1) the level of risk posed to participants and ratio of risk to potential benefits when used for broader purposes; (2) the adequacy of the plan to provide participants with the necessary knowledge about procedures, risks, and benefits, referred to as "full disclosure"; (3) the plan for ensuring that participation and all procedures are voluntary; and (4) the plan for ensuring confidentiality.

WHAT IS AN IRB, AND WHEN MUST IT BE INVOLVED?

Large institutions such as hospitals and universities have formal committees, typically called *institutional review boards* (IRBs) (U.S. Department of Health and Human Services, n.d.). These groups review and guide adherence to the four ethical mandates listed in the paragraph above. Depending on the population, the nature of the inquiry, and the scope of dissemination, the board determines if one review (expedited) or more prolonged monitoring is appropriate. We have always found IRB review helpful in that other "eyes" look at a plan and provide feedback. In smaller social work agencies, review boards may be ad hoc committees (with a particular purpose) or may not exist at all. We suggest, however, that even in the absence of a review board, protection should be verified. It therefore may be beneficial to seek review from an established IRB when an agency or social work setting does not have a formal review committee. Collaborating with a local university is often allowable, particularly if the agency is accepting social work field students.

PRINCIPLES FOR PROTECTING HUMAN SUBJECTS

As noted above, principlist ethics form the basis for protecting humans. Three primary principles guide all decision-making and systematic behavior: full disclosure, confidentiality, and voluntary participation.

FULL DISCLOSURE

Any person who participates in an inquiry, whether participatory action research, single subject design, or randomized trial, has the absolute right to full disclosure of the purpose and procedures of the study and the intended use of knowledge derived from it. *Full disclosure* means that the social worker must clearly share with the informant, subject, or participant the types and content of data collection methods that will occur, as well as the scope and nature of the person's involvement. Full disclosure also means that any risk to a subject, even if the potential is rare or minimal, must be clearly identified and a plan for remediation offered for each risk to every person. For example, in order for the social worker to disseminate the reflexive intervention and outcome assessment with Janice beyond clinical notes, disclosure of this intent to Janice was required along with her informed consent (see below for discussion on informed consent). Although confidentiality and deidentificaiton (removal of any information that could potentially reveal individual identity) would have to be part of the dissemination, risks might include discomfort.

Because all experimental-type procedures are planned and articulated prior to conducting any activity, identifying and sharing specific study procedures tend to be straightforward in this tradition. However, because the process of naturalistic designs unfolds as the inquiry proceeds, disclosure is not as clear. Social workers relying on this tradition must solve this dilemma in creative, thoughtful, and ongoing ways. Help from a review board is therefore of great benefit when one is stymied by the application of principlist ethics to naturalistic inquiry.

CONFIDENTIALITY

Consistent with social work ethics (National Association of Social Workers, 2014), social workers ensure that all information shared by or about a respondent in the course of examined practice inquiry is kept confidential. *Confidentiality* means that (1) no person other than those specified and agreed upon by the participant (or proxy if the participant is a minor or member of a group considered vulnerable) can have access to the respondent's information, and (2) the information provided by or about a respondent cannot be linked to the person's identity. This second consideration, although relevant to all systematic processes involving human subjects, is especially important in studies that focus on sensitive topics so frequently encountered by social workers.

Confidentiality can be assured in several ways. The name of the respondent may be removed from the actual information that is obtained. This procedure ensures that the identity of respondents is protected and that the information about them will not be linked to their names in the future. One typical way to protect a study participant's identity is the replacement of a name with an identification number. However, as noted above, this action process may present some difficulty when observation or interview is the principal data collection effort. Also, ensuring confidentiality can be difficult when using audio and video recordings as sources of data. In these instances, recorded names can be omitted from transcriptions and dissemination efforts (Comstock, 2013). In the course of daily social work practice, while client names cannot be removed from service documentation, sharing research information may require an alternative set of procedures for coding and storing digital data.

Confidentiality may also be protected during the sharing phase of examined practice by deidentificaiton introduced above. This process involves removing names of individuals and modifying information so that the knowledge is shared without any direct link back to the client. Most experimental-type studies report findings that reflect group scores or outcomes, which makes ensuring confidentiality less challenging in this tradition than in naturalistic inquiry (Comstock, 2013).

VOLUNTARY PARTICIPATION

When humans are involved in research processes designed to generate and disseminate knowledge, their participation must be voluntary. People have the right to choose to participate or not. Also, an individual who initially agrees to participate has the right to withdraw at any point as well as the right to refuse to answer a particular question or participate in a particular set of procedures, even when continuing in the systematic activity. Thus, the voluntary quality of participation must be protected at three points: initial involvement, continuation, and right to refuse to answer specific questions or engage in a particular procedure. To ensure *voluntary participation* at each of these points, investigators must develop approaches to recruiting participants that are not coercive and that provide full disclosure of all procedures (Comstock, 2013).

THE BELMONT REPORT

We briefly introduced the watershed document, the Belmont Report, previously. The ethical issues inherent in research have not always been a focus of national concern. It was not until 1974 that the National Research Act created a commission to delineate the ethical issues and guidelines for the involvement of humans in behavioral and biomedical research in the United States. This act and its subsequent activities arose from revelations of the Nuremberg war crime trials about the devastating human experiments conducted by medical scientists during the Holocaust. Other tragic abuses of human subjects had occurred in the United States as well. Most notable were the Tuskegee experiments in which, in order to observe the natural course of the disease process, treatment was withheld from poor rural Black men diagnosed with syphilis. The resulting Belmont Commission issued a report in 1979 that outlined the three basic ethical principles presented above. The Belmont Report is a brief document that is required reading by all those involved in human subject research. The first ethical principle is the importance of distinguishing between research and practice. Recall the discussion above regarding the difficulty of establishing this difference. When knowledge generation and sharing are planned or considered, the principles of the Belmont report should be heeded (Claremont Graduate University, 2014).

The second principle in the Belmont Report advances principlist ethics: respect for persons, beneficence, and justice. *Respect* refers to upholding the autonomy of individuals who are capable of personal choice and self-determination. A related mandate is that individuals who are not autonomous or who are vulnerable, such as children, active substance abusers, and so forth, must be protected, most frequently by a proxy decision maker. *Beneficence* specifies that the process and outcomes of an inquiry will "do no harm" and will "maximize" benefits. *Justice* refers to treating people equitably (Claremont Graduate University, 2014).

INFORMED CONSENT PROCESS

The principles outlined in the Belmont Report are applied to all research endeavors. *Informed consent* is the process through which potential participants are provided with information about an inquiry, its purpose, procedures, uses of knowledge derived, and all particulars to comply with principlist ethics. It is not unusual for a printed or online form to be provided and signed by participants. Or, if approved by the review board, participation itself may constitute consent. If an individual is not capable of or eligible for giving informed consent, the proxy enters here (Comstock, 2013). As an example, a minor child must have a legal guardian as signatory. More

Table 10.1   Six Areas That Must Be Addressed in an Institutional Review Board Proposal

1. Describe the characteristics of the humans who will participate in the study.
2. Describe any potential risks and benefits of study participation.
3. Describe procedures to ensure confidentiality.
4. Describe data collection sources and procedures.
5. Describe plans for subject/informant recruitment and procedures for obtaining informed consent.
6. Describe procedures for protecting against or minimizing potential risks.

detail and updates on informed consent can typically be obtained from university websites. The University of Maine (n.d.) provides guidance for us and for its social work faculty and students, so we refer you to that resource for detail. Table 10.1 summarizes the areas to be addressed in an IRB application and review

With this introduction, we are now ready to move onto specific boundary-setting techniques. We begin with the experimental-type tradition.

BOUNDARY SETTING IN EXPERIMENTAL-TYPE EXAMINED PRACTICE INQUIRY

In experimental-type designs, the boundary-setting action process is basically deductive. From this logic structure, the social worker first identifies a population, or what or who will be the object of inquiry. A population is a set of units in which all members have all inclusion criteria specified by the researcher and none of the exclusion criteria that omit members from this group. Thus, the characteristics of the population must be specified in detail including criteria for exclusion. Consider Elton, for example. The social worker expanding a needs assessment to ascertain what is necessary to resolve the problem of reluctance of small business owners to engage in accessibility improvements would have to determine what constitutes a small business, who is included in small business owners, and the scope of concern (e.g., geographic, type of business, and so forth). Who does not belong and thus would not qualify for the study or knowledge generated from it would also be detailed. Second, the decision to use the whole population or to select a sample or subset is made. A sample is part of a population, and thus each member must also have all the inclusion and none of the exclusion criteria. The deductive process of selecting a subgroup or sample is called *sampling*.

SAMPLING PROCESS

The main purpose of sampling is to delimit the scope of a study, most often with the aim of accurately representing the population from a smaller group selected from that population. If the aim of a needs or outcome assessment is to inform local need or outcome only, it is most purposive to select a sample of convenience since inference of findings to a larger group is not the goal. However, if the intent is to broaden the application of the knowledge, even of a local social work activity, sampling which is capable of selecting the group that best represents the population that it represents is indicated. As an example, in examining the outcome of employer behavior as well as the resolution of Elton's problem, only the "case" comprising Elton and his employer was studied. However, recall the larger aim of the social worker who sought to understand what is needed to resolve the problem of small business owner reluctance to implement accessibility measures. Given the scope of this more extensive needs assessment, the population, even when delimited by inclusion and exclusion criteria, might be too large to study. Thus, to set boundaries, a sample would be chosen to represent the population such that the needs assessment study would be feasible.

Within experimental-type design, sampling procedures have been developed to increase the chances of selecting individuals or elements who will be most representative of the population from which they are drawn. The extent to which findings from a sample apply to the population is called *external validity*. While external validity extends the value of knowledge beyond its immediate scope, this rigor criterion may not be desired or possible. As an example, an outcome assessment may be specific and thus delimited to a single client group for whom an intervention was specifically tailored. In this case, external validity would not be a goal. Due to practice constraints and ethics, randomization of sample selection may also not be possible or warranted even when external validity is intended. As in all parts of examined practice, the choice of sampling procedure is guided by purpose, practicality, and ethical considerations.

Consistent with the principles and logic structures underpinning experimental-type thinking and action, the sampling process is sequential and follows specific rules in order to avoid sampling bias, or the unwanted influence of the sampling process on knowledge outcomes. The first step in sampling involves the careful specification of a population. As defined earlier, a population is the complete set of elements that share a common set of characteristics (inclusion criteria also referred to as parameters) and do not possess any characteristics identified as "not to be included" (exclusion criteria). Examples of exclusions in the mobility device study might be persons under the age of 65 or those who are unable to see. The "element" is the unit of analysis included in the population, regardless of its type (e.g., person, device, concept, a study as in meta-analysis, etc.). A population is chosen on the basis of the questions to be answered by the inquiry. Remember that all properly articulated experimental-type questions include the population in which the variables and/or their relationships are being studied.

Given the retrospective nature of experimental-type design, that is to say, its reliance on previously developed theory, if there is no support in the literature for attention to a population parameter, it is not good practice to include or exclude it. Even if the social worker may have a hunch that a parameter is of importance, its relevance must first be studied before assuming that the parameter has further meaning in knowledge development. Consider what can happen if parameters are chosen indiscriminately. Suppose the social worker excluded all people who did not have gray hair from the study of mobility device abandonment, assuming that gray hair color was an indicator of advanced age. Many would be unnecessarily omitted, setting up hair color as a discriminatory parameter. Similarly, what if there is no precedent for examining ethnicity when looking at abandonment? When considering gender, race, class, sexual preference, ethnicity, and so forth, the social worker enacting examined practice is always advised to consult the literature for relevance of these parameters to a particular intervention in order not to unintentionally exclude or introduce essentialism into an inquiry (Epstein, 2007).

The second major step in boundary setting in experimental-type design involves drawing a sample from the specified population through the use of a sampling plan. There are two basic categories of sampling plans: **probability sampling** and nonprobability sampling (Daniel, 2012).

PROBABILITY SAMPLING

Probability sampling refers to plans based on **probability** theory. The two basic principles of probability theory as applied to sampling are as follows: (1) the parameters of the population are known, and (2) every member or element has an equal probability or chance of being selected for the sample (Daniel, 2012). A third rationale, related to probability reasoning but not specific to guiding action, is the theoretical assumption that equal probability of being selected is accompanied by equal probability of being exposed to all influences that could otherwise provide potential confounding factors in an inquiry (DePoy & Gitlin, 2016).

The major principle of probability sampling is that each element included in the study is known, and the possibility for selection is greater than zero. By knowing the population parameters and the degree of chance that each element may be selected, sampling error can be calculated. *Sampling error* refers to the difference between the values obtained from the sample and the values that actually exist in the population. This numeric value reflects the degree to which the sample represents a population. The larger the sampling error, the less representative the sample is of the population and the more limited the external validity is (Daniel, 2012).

To determine sampling error, the "standard error of the mean" is calculated. This number reflects the standard deviation of the sampling distribution and is designated SE_m (see Chapter 12). In essence, the standard deviation is a number that tells a story about the shape or distribution of a set of scores (Pauwels, 2006). Many statistical analytic tools used in experimental-type research are based on an assumption of probability (thus the use of the term *probability sampling*): the assumption that a variable will be distributed in a population along a bell-shaped or "normal" curve. The bell-shaped curve is a graphic depiction of what is expected to occur in a typical group. The bell curve in Figure 10.1 reflects the principle that it is most probable that the majority (68.2%) of observations in a group will be similar and will cluster around the average (within the light gray range). More extreme observations, or those farther from the mean, are expected to be less frequent (medium or dark gray range). The distance of each single score from the mean score is called "deviation."

Sampling error may be caused by either random error or systematic bias. "Random error" refers to errors that occur by chance. Not much can be done about random error at the sampling stage of the inquiry except to calculate the standard error of the mean. "Systematic error" or "systematic bias," within the philosophical framework of experimental-type design, reflects a basic flaw in the sampling process characterized by scores of subjects that systematically differ from the population. Sampling plans based on probability theory are desirable because they are designed to minimize systematic error (Daniel, 2012).

To use probability sampling, a sampling frame must be identifiable. A *sampling frame* is defined as a listing of every element in the target population. *Target population* refers to the group of interest with inclusion and exclusion criteria already specified (Thompson, 2012). As an example, individuals age 65 or older who have been prescribed mobility devices, small business owners, low-literacy web users, and so forth would all be target populations. Specifying a sampling frame from each of these populations could be as simple as identifying all available individuals who meet the inclusion criteria. If more expansive knowledge is the aim, more

Figure 10.1   Bell Curve

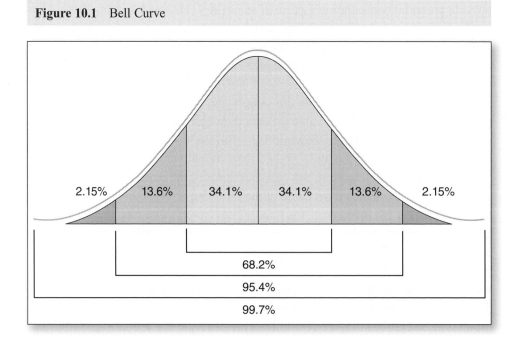

complex methods to identify a sampling frame would be indicated. As an example, looking up the small business owners through Data Universal Numbering System (DUNS) numbers might be a strategy to identify those who are registered and to obtain their locations and contact information. Once the sampling frame is identified, a sampling strategy is used to obtain participants.

As discussed in Chapter 9, randomization is the gold standard of experimental-type designs. The logic for this technique was previously discussed, but just as a reminder, randomization decreases sampling error in that all elements have an equivalent chance of selection and exposure to influences that may affect the study outcome. We suggest that random sampling is most useful and purposive in experimental-type needs assessments that seek to generalize knowledge to a target population who cannot be directly involved in a needs assessment inquiry but will benefit from the knowledge. Similarly, using random sampling in outcome assessment would follow this principle. Consider small business owners as the target for whom the social worker is intending to develop an educational program on improving workplace access and changing attitudes. Randomly selecting a sample of small business owners from a sampling frame would be an efficient way to understand the needs of a large target population. Several types of random sampling have been developed for diverse uses in experimental-type designs (Thompson, 2012).

Simple Random Sampling

Simple random sampling (SRS) is the most basic method used to enhance the representativeness of a sample. In this case, the term *random* does not mean haphazard. Rather, in concert with probability theory, random means that theoretically, every element in the population has an equal chance of being selected for the sample. As we emphasized earlier, theoretically, if elements are chosen by chance, they also have an equal chance to be exposed to all conditions to which all other members in the population are exposed. This random nature of selection therefore decreases the possibility of the sample being selected because of a special trait or of being exposed to one or more influences that render it different from the population from which it was selected. Consider the social worker who is conducting the needs assessment to determine how to best develop a workplace accessibility educational and attitude intervention for small business owners. Recall that the problem was employer reluctance to provide access improvements. When looking upstream at a causal problem statement, the social worker identified limited knowledge and negative attitudes as problems to be addressed through a program of needed education. However, exactly what attitudes and education were necessary framed the needs assessment. The questions to be answered were as follows:

1. What attitudes toward workplace accessibility measures in the workplace are held by small business owners?

2. What knowledge of workplace accessibility strategies and costs are held by small business owners?

The target population was delimited as small business owners in a rural county in the state of Maine, who employed less than 15 full-time workers at a physical site. Exclusion criteria were virtual and online businesses or those that required driving as a primary job function. From this target, a sampling frame was obtained through the online yellow pages. Because there were over 300 businesses that met the inclusion criteria, a simple random sampling technique was used to obtain a purposive sample of 20% of the sampling frame. Using Research Randomizer (Urbaniak & Plous, 2016), the social worker employed the automated random number generator to select 60 participants. This procedure is simple. The online tool generates numbers to be assigned to each element in the sample and then identifies numbers randomly to be chosen for the sample. Thus, each element that has a selected number is recruited as a participant in the needs assessment.

Another consideration is whether or not to randomize with or without replacement. Replacement assures that the selection of a unit will always occur from the total sampling frame. Thus, elements selected for the sample will be put back manually or digitally into the sampling frame before the next selection. Using a table of random numbers typically involves replacement because it is possible to select a number more than once. Random sampling without replacement can be as simple as drawing sample member names from a hat that contains all the names listed on a sampling frame. Replacement should be used with small samples to uphold the equality of opportunity to be selected.

Systematic Sampling

Similar in principle and aim to simple random sampling, systematic random sampling is a more complex approach offering a more efficient method by which to randomly select a precise number of elements, with particular emphasis on not hiding a pattern in the sample that could create nonrandom conditions. As an example, simple random sampling does not consider the geographic distribution of businesses, their size and so forth, and could result in a sample that favored a particular geographic or other pattern in the random selection. If purposive, using a systematic random sampling approach involves determining a sampling interval width based on the needed sample size, then selecting every kth element (referring to the interval as exemplified below) from a sampling frame.

In surveying a sample of 60 small business owners from a total population of 300, a sampling fraction (the interval width), 60:300, or 1 in 5, is derived. Second, a random number between 1 and 5 is selected to determine the first participant in the sampling frame. Every fifth element from this starting point will be selected for inclusion in the sample (i.e., 8th, 13th, 18th, and so on). A number generated from a table of random numbers can also be used to determine the starting point. If the sampling fraction is not a whole number, the decimal is usually rounded upward to the next largest whole number (Thompson, 2012).

Stratified Random Sampling

Systematic sampling and simple random sampling treat the target population as a whole. When there are divisions that are important to consider (e.g., type of business, yearly income), *stratified random sampling* is one way to address these. (We emphasize the importance of selecting these considerations of population parameters on the basis of previous support for their relevance in the research literature.) In stratified random sampling, the population is divided into smaller subgroups, or strata, with support from previous studies regarding their relevance. Then elements are chosen from each stratum in the proportions that are naturally occurring in the target population or in purposive proportions to assure adequacy of representation of each stratum.

Stratified random sampling is a more complex approach than either simple or systematic sampling in that it considers additional variables in the sample selection approach. Stratified random sampling enhances sample representation and lowers sampling error on a number of predetermined characteristics by increasing homogeneity and by decreasing variability in each subgroup.

Once again, we emphasize the importance of ethical and supported selection of strata to avoid essentialism and the perpetuation of change occurrence of differences that may reify inequality. Consider how many irrelevant variables could be used to stratify a sample—shoe size, eye color, and so forth. Without literature support, stratification can be meaningless at best and essentialist, prejudicial, or harmful at worst. As an example, suppose hair color and gender were used to stratify small business owners without support from the literature. A spurious finding in which blond women held the most negative attitudes would only serve to perpetuate stereotypes (Orrell, 2012).

Cluster Sampling

Also referred to as "multistage sampling" or "area sampling," *cluster sampling* is another technique that involves a successive series of random sampling of units

(Thompson, 2012). With cluster sampling, large units or clusters are first identified, in which smaller sampling units are contained. This technique allows the
investigator to draw a random sample without a complete listing of each individual or unit. In the study of small business owners, clusters might be identified by
geographic location without the need to create a complete list of the businesses
themselves.

As introduced previously, random sample selection is methodologically desirable in experimental-type boundary setting. However, it may not be feasible,
purposive, or ethical. Non-probability techniques are thus indicated in these
instances.

NONPROBABILITY METHODS

Non-probability techniques, also referred to as **nonparametric** (Hollander,
Wolfe, & Chicken, 2014) techniques, are often used to assess the direct outcome of local interventions. While nonprobability boundary-setting strategies
cannot support external validity, the aim of the examined practice activity may
not be generalization of knowledge. Much of social work knowledge is based
on non-probability sampling. But remember that expansion of knowledge
derived with non-probability sampling as a boundary-setting method can be
built upon in meta-analysis, in which external validity can be enhanced, as
discussed in Chapter 9 (Borenstein, Hedges, Higgins, & Rothstein, 2009).

In *non-probability sampling,* non-random methods are used to obtain a sample.
Non-random refers to sample members being chosen on criteria other than equal
chance to be selected from a larger sampling frame. Non-probability boundary
setting is used when the parameters of the population are not known or when it is
not feasible or ethical to develop a sampling frame. Several non-probability sampling methods are valuable in examined practice.

Convenience Sampling

Also referred to as "accidental sampling," "volunteer sampling," and "opportu-
nistic sampling," *convenience sampling* involves the enrollment of available subjects or elements until the desired or feasible sample size is reached (Daniel,
2012). It is possible that all participants in a social work intervention would comprise a convenience sample. As an example, the social worker initially working
with Dean would define the target population for substance abuse outcome assessment as all individuals who completed 3 weeks of the intervention. Now consider
how non-probability sampling can be used with nonhuman elements. In the TAP
needs assessment, the social worker identified the sampling frame as all websites

that address smoking prevention or cessation. Not knowing the breadth of sites, the social worker chose a convenience sample to conduct a needs assessment for lowering literacy level. The first 10 websites listed in an Internet search using the key term "smoking prevention and cessation information" served as the sample with the rationale that most web users would not look further than the initial 10 sites derived from a search (Cutts, 2011).

Purposive Sampling

Purposive sampling is another non-probability option. Also referred to as "judgmental sampling," *purposive sampling* involves the deliberate selection of individuals or elements as the basis of predefined criteria. This approach is particularly beneficial to both needs and outcome assessment in that social work interventions are targeted to specific groups and individuals (Thompson, 2012).

Snowball Sampling

Also called "networking," *snowball sampling* involves asking initial participants to provide access to others who may meet criteria for inclusion in a needs or outcome assessment. In the mobility device abandonment needs assessment, initial participants might refer others known to them to the social worker.

Quota Sampling

Quota sampling is the non-probability analogue of stratified random sampling. In *quota sampling,* parameters of a population and their distribution in the population are known (Thompson, 2012). As an example, the social worker might select a geographic scheme to guide the proportional selection of small business owners in the needs assessment for accessibility education intervention.

SAMPLING IN THE VIRTUAL ENVIRONMENT

The Internet and virtual environments bring multiple options to social workers who have the potential to expand boundary-setting options while improving efficiency and decreasing cost. As in any boundary-setting action, the basic thinking and action principles for experimental-type traditions guide the process in electronic environments. However, different from the physical world, the Internet is both far reaching and limited. By far reaching, we refer to the potential to obtain a global sample. Yet the limitations are significant, beginning with access to and comfort with computers as a critical concern and then moving into how to manage sample elements so that the investigator obtains an accurate picture of the population.

For example, Desrosiers (2014) conducted an outcome assessment of an intervention to educate prescribers with new techniques to decrease provider contribution to prescription drug abuse. Providers were accessed through online listings and then tested by electronic survey hosted on the computer. (See Chapter 11 for more detail on virtual data collection.)

The Internet provides many opportunities for non-probability sampling. You can post a request for participation on a content-specific site, send an e-mail or message to a listserv, or even use social networking sites such as Facebook and Twitter to recruit respondents. The boundary-setting options for the Internet are only limited by one's imagination, purpose, budget, and, of course, literature support for selecting a sampling method. Remember, however, that although the techniques may use different technologies, the basic principles for boundary setting in experimental-type design must be followed to enhance rigor.

COMPARING SAMPLE TO POPULATION

As initially stated, the major reason for sampling is to ensure representativeness and the ability to generalize from sample findings to the target population. While this aim can be accomplished to some extent with non-probability sampling, within the experimental-type tradition, the power of probability sampling lies in its capacity to use and generate estimated population parameters from the sample based on statistical theory (DePoy & Gitlin, 2016). As discussed in more detail in Chapter 12, probability or **parametric statistics** rely on the random selection of a sample, although they are often used even when nonrandom samples are being tested. In this chapter, the basic steps and reasoning that underpin probability sampling are provided.

The five steps below link sampling and statistics reasoning. Remember, the logic used to make decisions is deductive, reducing abstraction through smaller parts to measurement. The first step involves stating the hypothesis of no difference (null hypothesis) between the population and the sample being compared. This null hypothesis implies that the values obtained from testing the sample, such as on an attitude toward accessibility scale, are the sample values that would have been obtained if attitudes had been measured in other samples drawn from the same population. Next, a level of significance is set. Level of significance refers to the probability that defines how rare or unlikely the sample data must be before the null hypothesis fails to be accepted. Note the terminology here implies a double negative must be met in order to accept a difference but only within a degree of certainty. We address this point about degree of certainty in Chapter 12. If the significance level is set by the social worker at 0.05, he or she is proposing 95%

confidence in the findings. Because sampling and statistics in the experimental-type tradition are based on probability theory, nothing can be proven, despite the myth that the scientific method proves the truth (Lehmann & Romano, 2010). Once the confidence level is selected, a statistical value to answer the research question is computed (see Chapter 12). The results of the calculated value are then subjected to analysis according to the rules of the particular statistical analytic technique to determine acceptance or failure to accept the null hypothesis. The null hypothesis can be as simple as suggesting that the mean or average of the sample will not differ from the population mean or as complex as understanding the sample as an accurate reflection of complex relationships among variables in the population.

In examined practice, needs assessments often contain larger samples than outcome assessments, in large part because meeting need in social work is typically done through reflexive intervention, not through systematic strategies that can or even need to accommodate large numbers. Sample size is often not calculated at the outcome phase of examined practice with humans since outcome is reserved for those who are undergoing intervention (Gray, Plath, & Webb, 2009). However, for policy initiatives, sample size may be an important consideration in outcome assessment that then may inform a new problem statement and needs assessment areas.

DETERMINING SAMPLE SIZE

Although it is a common belief that large samples provide more accurate evidence than small samples in experimental-type traditions, size is not always the best consideration in sample selection. Because systematic inquiry and knowledge development are embedded within all phases of examined practice, large numbers are often unnecessary, not feasible, or unethical. Once again, determining sample size must be purposive and practical.

Ideally, the number of elements in a sample in experimental-type inquiry is determined after the population and sampling frame have been identified. This decision may be based on availability of participants, the research questions to be answered, or statistical power or the probability of identifying a relationship that exists, or the probability of failing to accept the null hypothesis when it is false. In the experimental-type tradition, power analysis is often seen as desirable practice, although in examined practice it must be purposive. Power analysis is a statistical calculation that reveals the optimal sample size below which a study is not considered adequate (Daniel, 2012). Refer to Chapter 12 for more detailed guidance for conducting a power analysis.

The number in the sample is also determined by the number of units in the sampling frame. Practical considerations, such as time and financial support for conducting the research, may also provide guidelines on the number of units to be included in the sample. Because examined practice is part and parcel of social work action, power analysis as the basis for making a decision about sample size may not even be an option. While the social worker conducting a needs assessment designed to contribute to evidence-based practice may strive to conduct a power analysis as the rationale for sample size, choosing who will partake of social work services is not a statistical decision. Thus, it is unlikely that outcome assessment will rely on power analysis.

To briefly summarize, experimental-type boundary setting is sequential and follows a set of rules designed to eliminate bias and maximize the reach of the knowledge. Many boundary-setting strategies in this tradition are linked to probability theory and statistical analysis in order to study the relationship between the findings from a sample or the likelihood that what is learned from the sample will be relevant, within a degree of certainty, for the population from which the sample was selected. When probability sampling is not possible, external validity cannot be claimed. However, unlike the belief in many models of evidence-based practice that diminish the importance and usefulness of non-probability sampling, the social worker using the examined practice framework uses purpose and pragmatism to guide the boundary-setting process at each stage of the model.

We now turn to naturalistic boundary setting to examine this tool and its use in examined practice.

BOUNDARY SETTING IN NATURALISTIC INQUIRY

Consistent with its philosophical foundations, boundary setting in naturalistic inquiry is a dynamic, inductive process. Because the basic purposes of naturalistic thinking and action are exploration, understanding, description, and explanation, the social worker does not know the specific boundaries of the inquiry or the particular conceptual domains prior to undertaking systematic study. Particularly in needs assessment, the very point of the study may be to discover the specific characteristics that bound or define a group of persons or explain a particular concept or human experience in order to set goals and objectives to guide reflexive action. Unlike experimental-type approaches, the final determination of boundaries for a particular group, concept, or set of constructs may not actually occur until the formal analysis and reporting phases of the inquiry. Nevertheless, setting boundaries is needed in order to conduct an inquiry that is useful in guiding decisions about what to observe, with whom to talk, and how to proceed in other arenas of data collection.

Within naturalistic inquiry, boundaries may be set along a number of dimensions, including but not limited to the setting, the group or experience of interest, the particular concepts that will be explored, the artifacts and images that will be examined, and the ways in which individuals are involved. Note that unlike experimental-type boundary setting, emphasis is not on numbers of units studied. We therefore do not use the term *sample* for naturalistic traditions and suggest that if a sample is present in an otherwise naturalistic study, the design moves to the mixed-methods tradition.

The Setting

Naturalistic traditions may be delimited by a wide range of locations, from virtual settings (e.g., Second Life, Internet chat rooms, blogs, Facebook, websites) to geographic locations and physical settings. Classical ethnographers often traveled to particular isolated geographies to examine contained groups in efforts to discover the universals of human cultures (Nanda & Warms, 2014). Regardless of the setting, there are basic principles for creating boundaries. Choosing the initial boundary or location is a conscious methodological decision often followed by an expansion or change of setting as the inquiry unfolds.

As an example, assessing the outcomes of the mobility device project, the social worker may be interested first in observing device use in the community settings in which users live and then more expansively in diverse geographic locations beyond the immediate residential community, such as travel venues and so forth. Or consider the virtual setting of the TAP project. This context formed the initial boundary for the outcome study, in that the social work team examined website usage in the experimental-type part of the outcome assessment and then expanded the boundaries beyond measuring "website hits" to a conceptual set of boundaries, specifically, what groups were using the setting, how, and why. Recall that this change in boundary setting produced unexpected knowledge regarding the use by immigrant groups who did not speak English as a primary language but who were highly literate in their first languages.

Groups and Experiences of Interest

Defining groups and experiences of interest is another way in which naturalistic boundaries are set. Frequently in social work settings, groups are defined by demographic or service need characteristics (e.g., elderly mobility device users; adults with low English literacy, individual clinical clients, and so forth). Service need may also be a group identifier such as substance abuse clients and rehabilitation clients (Dean and Janice hold memberships in each of these service need groups, respectively). The experience of individuals within groups of interest may be framed as a boundary. For example, the social worker might be interested in bounding a study by perceptions of stigma experienced by mobility device users, loss of function in newly injured or ill persons, limited access to prevention in individuals with limited English literacy, or unemployment due to lack of accessibility in the workplace. Each of these is detailed throughout the book in the examples.

As stated earlier, naturalistic thinking and action have a beginning point at which a decision must be made regarding entry into an inquiry and which direction to take. In the case of elders who use mobility devices, the entry point was the experience of stigma, not the rehabilitation service needs. Thus, the needs assessment moved away from functional need for devices to the experience that in large part was responsible for abandonment of this equipment. The social worker mapped the problem expansively and ruled out other causal or consequential directions for inquiry, ultimately revealing an unmet need. Filling this need resulted in productive intervention that may have not been found using alternative boundaries.

Concepts

Concepts may be used to bound a naturalistic inquiry (Denzin & Lincoln, 2011; DePoy & Gitlin, 2016). In the five examples, concepts were not used specifically to set boundaries. However, Maruyama's work illustrates this point. The concept of interpersonal violence was the entry point into the field and as the inmates conducted the study, the boundaries shifted to the physical location of two prison settings. Several years ago, a group of social work students used the concept of "power uniforms" to examine the experiences of women employed in more traditional men's fields in which uniforms were required. They interviewed women firefighters, policewomen carrying visible weapons, and active female armed service personnel to examine the personal meaning of their uniformed appearance in the context of male-dominated work environments. This study was conducted as a partial needs assessment to determine if clothing choice might be an influence on how women in traditional male professions could improve their esteem and interactions.

Artifacts and Images

Both the uniform study introduced above and the elder mobility device project illustrate the critical importance of image and appearance, areas that are just beginning to be recognized as important in social work literature (DePoy & Gilson, 2012). Bounding research with imagery is an increasingly used method in naturalistic study (Berger, 2009; Rose, 2012). The social worker chooses one or more objects, artifacts, or images to enter a systematic study of need, intervention, or outcome. In the elder mobility project, the initial focus of reflexive intervention was the appearance of mobility devices, not their functionality. Queries about the meaning of the appearance of objects, or what we have referred to as "object reading" from the methodological work of Bennett (2010), Berger (2009), Rose (2012), and Candlin and Guins (2009), emerge from this boundary.

Involving Participants

Involving participants is perhaps the most frequently used approach to boundary setting in naturalistic approaches. It is often believed that social workers who engage in naturalistic needs and outcome assessment select individuals on the basis of convenience or availability. However, the use of a convenience strategy is only one of many ways to recruit participants. Selecting individuals is a purposeful action process, and the social worker must be acutely aware of the implications of his or her selection decisions. As an example, need may be defined differently by distinct groups. Consider the two social workers who engaged with Janice. Each defined her needs from a theoretical perspective, but each had varied interpretations, only one of which produced the desired outcome for Janice. Similarly, how the group of small business owners is delimited and then methods through which individuals are selected to participate in the needs assessment shape the nature of the goals and objectives to guide intervention.

A major factor in deciding who to involve in a naturalistic study concerns the selection of individuals with the potential to illuminate a particular concept, experience, or context. As we noted above, dissimilar to experimental-type design, the number of participants is not as important to the naturalistic process as the amount of exposure to participants and opportunities to explore phenomena in depth. The social worker therefore develops selection strategies that ensure richness of information and complexity of understanding. And recall that we discussed the term *sampling* previously. We prefer the phrase *strategies for involving individuals* over *sampling,* although we often see the word *sample* in naturalistic reports and methods texts (Richie Lewis, Nicholls, & Ormstron, 2014). Sampling techniques in experimental-type designs are based on the deductive premise of representation of a population in which the parameters of the population are already known and determined. Because the logic of boundary setting in naturalistic inquiry is inductive, population parameters are not known, and the term *parameter* is not relevant to inductive methodology. Therefore, using the term *sampling* in inductive processes is misleading and does not capture the intent of the inductive decision-making process within these traditions. As such, there are no specific rules in naturalistic inquiry to assist the social worker in selecting the initial number of persons needed for interviewing or observation in a needs assessment, reflexive intervention, or outcome assessment. Thus, no procedure for naturalistic inquiry is comparable to a power analysis for experimental-type inquiry. However, even with boundary setting as flexible in this tradition, some methods and guidelines can be used to determine the nature and number of participants, informants, objects, and so forth to include.

Maximum variation is one strategy that involves seeking human informants and nonhuman artifacts that are extremely different along dimensions that are the focus of a needs assessment, reflexive intervention, or outcome assessment. In using this variation strategy, the social worker attempts to maximize difference among the broadest range of experiences, information, observations, and perspectives. This type of boundary setting assures breadth rather than homogeneity. As an example, consider the selection of small business owners in informing need for educational intervention. Informants selected for heterogeneity of business location, type, and income would provide the broadest understanding of need.

In contrast to maximum variation, *homogeneous selection* involves choosing informants with similar experiences or features. This approach reduces variation and thereby simplifies the number of experiences, characteristics, and conceptual domains that are represented among participants. Using the small business owner example, restricting variation just to virtual businesses with no physical location would shrink the number of accessibility measures to be addressed in an educational intervention.

It is important to note that the selection of a homogeneous group does not mean that everyone in that group will express and interpret experience similarly or that everything will be interpreted through the same lens. The social worker may discover wide variation and diversity in expression and interpretation of an identified experience or object, even among a group initially selected for similarities. DePoy and Gilson (2011) referred to the assumption that all members identified by one characteristic share others as well as "diversity patina." That is, grouping people by single characteristics that are obvious, such as race, class, gender, disability status, age, and in the example, type of business, may reveal some differences among groups but barely scratch the surface of the diversity within these groups. Thus, proceeding with homogeneous selection does not always result in consensus.

Theory-Based Selection

Theory-based selection involves choosing individuals, concepts, images, or artifacts that reflect a particular theoretical construct for the purposes of expanding an understanding and application of the theory. The mobility device abandonment outcome assessment is a clear example of this approach. The theory to be explored was the expanded view of assistive devices from a purely functional to a material cultural perspective (DePoy & Gilson, 2011; Bennett, 2010). As we discuss in

Chapter 11, in-depth interviews were not only conducted with the elders who used the contemporarily designed device but also with observers, further building the theory of the importance of device appearance.

Confirming and Disconfirming Cases

Confirming cases and *disconfirming cases* are strategies in which the social worker purposively searches for phenomena that will either support or challenge an emerging interpretation or theory. Using disconfirming cases allows the social worker to expand or revise an initial understanding by identifying exceptions or deviations. Using data from sources that may provide alternative views, interpretations, and experiences engages the social worker in a process of elaborating and expanding on an understanding that accounts for a fuller range of social work responses. If attempting to seek divergent perspectives on accessibility measures in small businesses, the social worker might consider selecting one business owner who opposes the ADA and one who supports it or might show imagery of diverse workplace designs to elicit perspectives on access.

Extreme or Deviant Case

In the extreme case, or *deviant* case, the researcher selects a case that represents an extreme example of the phenomenon of interest. Consider Dean as an example. Given his history and current medical picture, he does not neatly fit into the categories of substance abuser or a person with mental illness. His input at the reflexive intervention phase of examined practice would have provided valuable information on how to rethink initial assessment of this client group.

In contrast to the deviant case, a social worker may choose to select a *typical case*, one that typifies a phenomenon or represents the average. Substance abusers would be engaged in reflexive intervention to inform the social worker about the extent to which and how client goals were (or were not) being met.

GUIDELINES FOR DETERMINING "HOW MANY"

In selecting numbers, some basic guidelines can be followed, but these must be judged for adequacy and purpose as naturalistic strategies in examined practice. If the intent is to examine an experience that has been shared by individuals, a homogeneous strategy should be used to obtain study participants. Given that the aim is to minimize variation, only a small number of individuals (e.g., 5 to 10) would form the initial boundary. In contrast, if the intent is to develop a complex theoretical understanding, as exemplified by the approach to mobility device meaning through a material culture lens, larger numbers of informants would be indicated.

A general rule for determining "how many" hinges on data saturation (Denzin & Lincoln, 2011). Saturation refers to the point at which no appreciably new knowledge is revealed from informant sources. When saturation occurs, data collection in a naturalistic study should be completed.

PROCESS OF SETTING BOUNDARIES AND SELECTING INFORMANTS

The process of boundary setting in naturalistic traditions follows several principles.

It begins with the determination of a starting point or what has been referred to in classic studies as *gaining access* (Denzin & Lincoln, 2008). This term was used by ethnographers who classified themselves as etic or outsiders and sought methods to enter an isolated or distant culture in order to study it. As an example, Margaret Mead (1928) as etic gained access to Samoan adolescents by traveling to the island of Ta'ū for her field work. However, over the years, as we have noted, ethnography has taken on many facets beyond exploring contained cultures. Thus, gaining access also takes on a broad meaning in contemporary naturalistic usages. The social worker may gain access to a domain not only through human interaction but through concept, image, and the methods discussed above.

From an entry point, initial information is collected to describe the boundaries. However, after gaining initial access, other issues emerge. For example, although the social worker may be initially accepted into a group or community, it may take a prolonged period before participants will share intimate information or differentiate important from trivial phenomena. Thus, gaining access refers not only to entering the physical or virtual location where the social worker plans to conduct extensive knowledge generation but also to gaining entry to the level of information, meanings, and personal experiences that inform social work and create useful systematic social work knowledge.

In the process of discovery and within the context of the initial access points, further boundaries such as whom to interview, what to observe, what to collect, and what to read are made. There may be an overwhelming number of observation points and potential individuals to interview. Selection decisions are based on the specific queries, practicalities of the social work context, purpose, and ethical dilemmas to be resolved. Expanding, contracting, or remaining on the same course is the next judgment to be made following the initial boundary-setting plan. This decision opportunity presents itself throughout an inductive inquiry. This set of determination processes is referred to as *domain analysis* (Denzin & Lincoln,

2011) in that naturalistic thinking and action inductively aim to understanding the domain or context within the boundaries of an inquiry such that the findings or interpretations are meaningful in building social work knowledge.

ETHICAL CONSIDERATIONS

Ethical dilemmas are not strangers to social workers. Boundary setting is not an exception. We previously discussed the dilemma that could be presented by Dean's involvement in substance abuse intervention. Given the stigma of both substance abuse and delusional thinking, should the social worker approach him for involvement in a formal study of reflexive intervention? Or considering the failure of the initial intervention plan, what might Dean or the social worker experience if asked to reflect on this experience? But without Dean's systematic input, valuable knowledge to revise assessment for such interventions is lost. Other ethical issues in naturalistic approaches involve how to enter and exit the field and how to engage in nonobtrusive methods of observation such that the presence of the social worker has minimal influence on the context.

SUMMARY OF NATURALISTIC BOUNDARY SETTING

Boundary setting in naturalistic inquiry is an ongoing and active process. Decisions and judgments about setting and resetting boundaries are purposive, inductive, flexible, and continuous. The selection strategy used to choose an individual to interview, event to observe, or artifact to review is based on the specific focus of the query. As discussed in more depth in Chapters 11 and 12, boundary setting is influenced and thus concurrent with information gathering and analysis.

A FEW WORDS ABOUT MIXED METHODS

Knowing the rules and conventions for setting boundaries in experimental-type and naturalistic traditions provides the full range of options for setting boundaries in all systematic inquiry. So we will not repeat techniques in this section. However, a major point to consider is the role of boundary setting in mixing methods. Recall that we opposed the term *sampling* for inductive boundary setting despite its frequent use in the methodological and research literature. As we already discussed, using sampling techniques with naturalistic queries, data collection, and analysis is one of the most frequent ways in which investigators mix methods even if they do not describe their studies as such. Purposively and pragmatically using differing logical structures within the same study is, by definition, mixing methods (Tashakorri & Teddlie, 2010), and thus sampling integrated with otherwise naturalistic strategies should be labeled as mixed-method inquiry.

A second point to be made here is that initial inductive boundary setting can move to deduction once queries about the nature and description of a group are known. Thus, within the same study, mixed-method boundary setting may begin with discovery and then move to a more focused affirmation of the accuracy of findings that define a group. Conversely, a study may begin with deductive boundary setting and then move to inductive methods for discovery. The TAP boundary-setting process exemplified this last point, as discovery that the population was more expansive than originally defined was revealed and mined for social work knowledge.

SUMMARY

The term *boundary setting* refers to delimiting and focusing a study. Within examined practice, boundary setting is both purposive and driven by methodological tradition. At each stage of the examined practice sequence, how a systematic activity is focused determines its shape, what come to be known, and what is omitted from knowledge.

Because experimental-type boundary setting most often focuses on obtaining and testing human subjects, we presented the important ethical dilemmas of boundary setting and principles and procedures for protecting human subjects within a study. We then discussed and illustrated boundary setting across the three research traditions and completed the chapter with some considerations for mixing methods within this part of an inquiry.

The main points in this chapter are as follows:

1. Boundary setting is framed within tradition, purpose, and context.

2. Appropriateness and adequacy are two decision factors in setting boundaries in all traditions.

3. Human participants are referred to in numerous ways depending on tradition and design. Each term denotes a particular role and relationship in the research process.

4. Nonhuman boundaries also have diverse names, each indicating a different role and meaning in the process.

5. Protection of human participants should be considered in any systematic inquiry.

6. Principlist ethics guide human subject protection.

7. Boundary setting in experimental-type type design involves specifying a population and determining if the whole population or a sample of it will participate.

8. There are two basic categories of sampling plans in experimental-type design: probability sampling and non-probability sampling.

9. Random sampling is designed to reduce sampling error and improve external validity.

10. In the naturalistic tradition, the final determination of boundaries for a particular group, concept, or set of constructs may not actually occur until the formal analysis and reporting phases of the inquiry.

11. Within naturalistic inquiry, boundaries may be set along a number of dimensions, including but not limited to the setting, the group or experience of interest, the particular concepts that will be explored, the artifacts and images that will be examined, and the ways in which individuals are involved.

12. The process of setting boundaries in naturalistic inquiry is flexible.

REFERENCES

Bennett, J. (2010). *Vibrant matter.* Durham, NC: Duke University.

Berger, A. (2009). *What objects mean.* Walnut Creek, CA: Left Coast.

Borenstein, M., Hedges, L. V., Higgins, J. P. T., & Rothstein, H. R. (2009). *Introduction to meta-analysis.* West Sussex, UK: Wiley & Sons.

Candlin, F., & Guins, R. (2009). *The object reader.* London, UK: Routledge.

Claremont Graduate University. (2014). *History of ethics.* Retrieved from http://www.cgu.edu/pages/1722.asp

Comstock, G. (2013). *Research ethics: A philosophical guide to the responsible conduct of research.* New York, NY: Cambridge University Press.

Cutts, M. (2011). *About search.* Retrieved from https://www.google.com/competition/howgoogle searchworks.html

Daniel, J. (2012). *Sampling essentials: Practical guidelines for making sampling choices.* Thousand Oaks, CA: Sage.

Denzin, N., & Lincoln, Y. S. (2008). *Collecting and interpreting qualitative materials.* Thousand Oaks, CA: Sage.

Denzin, N. K., & Lincoln, Y. S. (2011). *SAGE handbook of qualitative research* (4th ed). Thousand Oaks, CA: Sage.

DePoy, E., & Gilson, S. F. (2011). *Studying disability.* Thousand Oaks, CA: Sage.

DePoy, E., & Gilson, S. F. (2012). *Human behavior theory and applications.* Thousand Oaks, CA: Sage.

DePoy, E., & Gitlin, L. (2016). *Introduction to research* (5th ed.). St Louis, MO: Elsevier.

Desrosiers, C. (2014). *Diversion alert* (Unpublished study).

Epstein, S. (2007). *Inclusion: The politics of difference in medical research.* Chicago, IL: University of Chicago Press.

Fowler, F. (2014). *Survey research.* Thousand Oaks, CA: Sage.

Gray, M., Plath, D., & Webb, S. (2009). *Evidence-based social work: A critical stance.* London, UK: Routledge.

Hollander, M., Wolfe, D. A., & Chicken, E. (2014). *Nonparametric statistical methods.* Hoboken, NJ: Wiley & Sons.

Krug, S. (2014). *Don't make me think, revisited: A common sense approach to web usability.* Upper Saddle River, NJ: Pearson.

Lehmann, E. L., & Romano, J. P. (2010). *Testing statistical hypotheses.* New York, NY: Springer.

Maruyama, M. (1981). Endogenous research: The prison project. In P. Reason & J. Rowan (Eds.), *Human inquiry: A sourcebook of new paradigm research.* New York, NY: Wiley & Sons.

Mead, M. (1928). *Coming of age in Samoa.* New York, NY: William Morrow and Company.

Nanda, S., & Warms, R. L. (2014). *Cultural anthropology.* Belmont, CA: Cenage.

National Association of Social Workers. (2014). *Code of ethics.* Retrieved from http://www.social workers.org/pubs/code/code.asp

National Commission for the Protection of Human Subjects of Biomedical and Behavioral Research. (1979). *The Belmont report.* Retrieved from http://www.hhs.gov/ohrp/humansubjects/guidance/belmont.html

Orrell, D. (2012). *Truth or beauty.* New Haven, CN: Yale University Press.

Pauwels, L. (2006). *Visual cultures of science: Rethinking representational practices in knowledge building and science communication.* Lebanon, NH: Dartmouth.

Richie, J., Lewis, J., Nicholls, C., & Ormstron, R. (2014). *Qualitative research practice: A guide for social science students and researchers.* Thousand Oaks, CA: Sage.

Rose, G. (2012). *Visual methodologies: An introduction to researching with visual materials.* Thousand Oaks, CA: Sage.

Saumure, K., & Given, L. M. (2008). Data saturation. In L. Given (Ed.), *The SAGE encyclopedia of qualitative research methods.* Thousand Oaks, CA: Sage.

Tashakorri, A., & Teddlie, C. (2010). *Handbook of mixed methods in social and behavioral research* (2nd ed.). Thousand Oaks, CA: Sage.

Thompson, S. K. (2012). *Sampling.* Hoboken, NJ: Wiley.

U.S. Department of Health and Human Services. (n.d.). *Institutional review boards.* Retrieved from http://www.hhs.gov/ohrp/assurances/irb

University of Maine. (n.d.). *Research compliance—Institutional review board for the protection of human subjects (IRB).* Retrieved from http://umaine.edu/research/research-compliance/institutional-review-board-for-the-protection-of-human-subjects-irb

Urbaniak, G. C., & Plous, S. (2016). *Research Randomizer.* Retrieved from http://www.randomizer.org

OBTAINING INFORMATION

In this chapter, we detail how information is systematically obtained across the three research traditions. But before we begin, we want to emphasize the importance of asking precise questions in all parts of examined practice by recounting several experiences.

A few years ago, we had the good fortune to travel to China. After having gone to the zoo to see the giant pandas, we were curious about what other types of animals lived in the wild, so we asked several residents, all who spoke English. Each time we asked, we were told that pandas were wild, and that the other animals in the zoo also lived in the wild. Clearly, we were not asking a precise question. So while we may have been speaking the same words as our informants, we were not speaking the meaning that was intended.

A second experience, also from a country in which English is not the national language, further illustrates the importance not simply of asking questions but of reflecting on the asker when a question is answered inaccurately. We were invited to Egypt to lecture at a university near Luxor. Not speaking Arabic, we were reluctant until we were informed that the university held classes primarily in English. However, upon arrival, we found that all classes were held in Arabic. Incredulous, we remarked, "I thought English was spoken here," to which our host replied "Why would we speak English in an Arabic school?" At that point, we noticed ourselves becoming a bit annoyed with what seemed like a flip response. A few hours later, after some self-reflection, we realized that the host perceived us as U.S.-centric, expecting English to be spoken in Egypt. Our intent was to ask why we had received misinformation about the university, but of course, the meaning or even the words in this example did not communicate what we were asking.

Questioning in social interactions is often much less time intensive and easier to repair than inadequate questioning in conducting a systematic inquiry and throughout social work practice. In research involving much effort, one may not have the opportunity to ask again. Therefore, this chapter speaks about systematic inquiry but has a much broader set of lessons to be learned about accuracy of communication. We now return to the world of systematic inquiry.

In examined practice, acquiring information to answer queries and questions is central to all phases and serves multiple purposes. Strategies in needs assessment answer what is necessary to resolve the articulated social problem and further refine intervention as context specific even when evidence-based practice is used. Questions at the need stage inform the development of goals and objectives and thus of expected or desirable outcomes. Consider the elder mobility device example. Had questions about stigmatized appearance of current devices not been asked, goals and objectives would have been framed about decreasing abandonment but would not have included innovative device design as an outcome as well.

Questions in reflexive intervention ask what was done, how, with and to whom, and why. These questions were critical to revising Dean's intervention such that the outcome of reduction of delusions of grandeur was feasible.

Outcome assessment seeks responses to understand what happened as a result of or after all or part of a social work activity. As we discussed previously, if possible questions regarding both anticipated and unanticipated outcomes provide the most useful information, as in the example of the Tobacco Access Portal (TAP) project. The unanticipated utility of the TAP site to immigrant populations would not have been known without opening the questions beyond the stated outcomes.

A major consideration in obtaining information is not only the content but also the form in which it is collected. The nature of data and the methods used to obtain them create a bridge, so to speak, between the research question or query and the analytic strategies. Thus, questioning and the format of responses are fundamental to the knowledge that emerges from any systematic study. Consistent with the philosophical and design features, data collection in experimental-type design is a distinct unidirectional action phase between the thinking processes involved in question formation, development, and the action process of analysis. Instrumentation and measurement in this tradition must be rationalized in the literature review and results in numeric data that then are submitted to statistical analysis to test all or part of the articulated theory on which the study focuses.

In naturalistic inquiry, gathering information is a multidirectional bridge in that this action process stems from the initial query and is more diverse than its experimental-type analogue. For the most part, gathering information across naturalistic designs is embedded in context and is iterative, involving ongoing analysis, reformulation, and refinement of the initial query. Mixed methods may use strategies from both traditions or not, depending on how and which parts of the inquiry are integrated.

PRINCIPLES OF INFORMATION COLLECTION IN ALL THREE TRADITIONS

Three basic principles characterize the process of collecting information across the different research traditions. First, the aim of collecting information, regardless of how, is to obtain data that are both relevant and sufficient to answer a research question or query. Second, the choice of a data collection or information-gathering strategy is based on four major factors:

1. the tradition,

2. the nature of the problem,

3. the type of design, and

4. the practical limitations or resources available.

Third, although the overall data collection strategy reflects a basic philosophical perspective, a specific procedure, such as observation or interview, may be used in either a naturalistic or experimental-type study and of course in mixed methods. As discussed previously, the structure, not the format of information itself, determines what tradition is being used (Agamben, 2009; Audi, 2011). As an example, observation may be used in experimental-type and naturalistic inquiry, but if rated with a preexisting, theory-based scale, it is deductive and thus fits within experimental-type data collection. If treated inductively, observation is often used as the basis for developing or fitting theory within naturalistic inquiry. Collecting data and information with more than one procedure or technique allows the social worker to respond to a question or query in a complex manner. Each of the examples illustrates this point. Consider Dean. Outcome assessment of substance abuse intervention included both deductive and inductive information-gathering approaches.

In general, the systematic action process of collecting information uses one or more of the following strategies: (1) looking, watching, listening, reading, and recording; (2) asking; and (3) examining materials, artifacts or spaces. Each of these strategies can be structured, **semistructured**, or open-ended, depending on the nature of the inquiry, and all can be used in combination with one another (DePoy & Gitlin, 2016).

LOOKING, WATCHING, LISTENING, READING, AND RECORDING

The process of *observation* includes five primary activities, which may be interrelated: looking, watching, listening, reading, and recording (Gillham, 2008). The documentation of information obtained from these activities comprises the data set. Observation may range from being structured to unstructured, participatory to nonparticipatory, narrowly to broadly focused, and time limited to ongoing and fully immersed (Patton, 2012).

In the experimental-type tradition, observation is usually time limited and structured. Criteria to look, watch, listen, read, and record are planned as part of the design before the inquiry is initiated, and data are recorded as a predetermined measurement system. For example, checklists may be used that indicate frequency (or only the presence or absence) of a particular behavior or object being observed. Or a text may be read, and the occurrences of a particular phrase might be counted and recorded. Phenomena other than those specified for observation during the design phase are omitted from documentation.

Looking, watching, listening, reading, and recording take on an inductive quality in naturalistic designs, with varying degrees of participation and interaction between the social worker and the phenomena of interest. Boundaries of observation begin broadly (e.g., the substance abuse treatment program in which Dean participated) and then may move to a more focused observational approach (e.g., Dean's life history during the intervention).

ASKING

Social workers routinely ask a wide range of questions to obtain information for professional purposes. Within examined practice, if systematic and precise asking is purposive throughout the entire process, the foundation for seamlessly integrating practice and inquiry is created. Recall the introductory discussion about the problems with vague asking. As an example, systematically asking Janice about her life history serves both to guide intervention and to act as a platform for knowledge development and sharing. When not asked, the intervention did not facilitate the achievement of Janice's desired outcomes and she did not return.

Similar to observation, questions can vary in structure and content, from unstructured and **open-ended questions** to structured and **closed-ended questions** or fixed-response queries that use a predetermined response set. An example of an open-ended question asked of Janice would be "How have you been feeling this past week?" or "How is life now for you compared to your life before your stroke?" In contrast, an example of a structured or closed-ended question is

"In this past week, how would you rate your mood (select one response that best describes you)?"

Very sad ☐   Somewhat sad ☐   Neutral ☐   Somewhat happy ☐   Very happy ☐

Or to reveal comparative mood states before and after the stroke, the social worker might ask

"Compared to how you generally felt before your stroke, how do you now feel on average (select one that best describes you)?"

Sadder than I did before my stroke ☐   Happier than I did before my stroke ☐

Naturalistic inquiry relies more heavily on open-ended types of asking techniques, whereas experimental-type designs tend to use structured, fixed-response questions or theory-based scoring protocols imposed on open-ended questions. Focused, structured asking is used to obtain data on a phenomenon as articulated and defined in the literature, whereas open-ended asking is used when the purpose is discovery and exploration.

Two primary methods of asking are interview and survey (Gubrium, Holstein, Marvasti, & McKinney, 2012; Fowler, 2014). *Interviews* are interactive, mostly conducted through verbal communication although they may occur through virtual interaction such as e-mail, texting, social media, or even on virtual worlds such as Second Life (Linden Research, Inc., 2015). Interviewing may be structured, semi-structured, or unstructured, conducted with groups or individuals. *Structured interviews* rely on an established questioning protocol (sometimes referred to as an interview schedule) in which maximum control is imposed on the content and sequencing of questions. *Unstructured interviews* typically begin with the presentation of the topic area of the interview to a respondent and proceed with probing questions to obtain the desired level of detailed information (Gubrium et al., 2012).

Surveys are text-based instruments and may be administered face-to-face, by proxy, through the mail, or over the Internet. Similar to interviews, surveys vary as to whether questions are structured or unstructured (Fowler, 2014).

MATERIALS, ARTIFACTS, OR SPACES

Materials, artifacts, and spaces are observable and thus consist of data that already exist. According to Woodward (2007), "Objects have the capacity to do social work" (p. 135). Yet, despite this recognition and growth of the field of material culture over the past several decades, and the importance of object and image within research itself (Pauwels, 2006), social work knowledge in this area is limited and awaiting development. Given the visual culture of the twenty-first century (Rose, 2012), examining observables is not only relevant to understanding and resolving social issues and problems but is required (Meecham, 2013). Using existing materials and spaces as data allows the social worker to view phenomena in the past and over time, which may not be possible with alternative approaches. As detailed below, objects, artifacts, and spaces can be examined in numerous ways in each tradition. Similar to other forms of obtaining information, experimental-type strategies begin with theory acceptance and are deductive, while naturalistic approaches are inductive and seek to develop theory. We now proceed to discuss and illustrate obtaining information in each tradition in detail.

OBTAINING INFORMATION IN THE EXPERIMENTAL-TYPE TRADITION

As we have noted previously, the experimental-type tradition seeks to investigate an objective reality separate and apart from human bias. Therefore, strict adherence to a data collection protocol is one of the ways that bias elimination is proposed.

Within experimental-type approaches, *protocol* has a specific definition. Protocol refers to a series of procedures and techniques designed to remove the influence of the investigator from the data collection process (DePoy & Gitlin, 2016, p. 175). Furthermore, the process of measurement, assigning numerical values to information, is central to experimental-type thinking and action. Measurement is said to promote objectivity by standardizing units as quantitative indicators. Consider weight for example. The subjective observer might judge body size on the basis of appearance and preference. However, standardizing weight in numeric units, pounds, or kilograms, allows assessment and thus comparison of body sizes without opinion.

The debate about the adequacy of numbers to capture human experience within the canon of social work knowledge has already been discussed in previous chapters. We only bring attention to it here so that this debate is refreshed and critically considered as measurement is discussed. **Measurement** is formally defined as the translation of information into numerical values or numbers. It is a vital action process in experimental-type thinking that links abstractions or theoretical concepts to concrete variables that can be empirically or objectively counted and compared.

The process of translating abstracts to measurement is called operationalization. The measurement process involves a series of steps that include both conceptual and operational considerations. Recall that we have emphasized the seminal role of literature in providing a rationale and theory base for experimental-type design. Step 1 involves this conceptual work. Exactly what is to be measured is searched in the scholarly literature, as discussed in Chapter 7, and then precisely articulated.

Consider concepts relevant to the five examples such as employer attitude and functional capacity. Each has been defined in many ways in the research literature. The social worker therefore critically examines the literature to obtain the breadth and depth of theory in the field and then uses purpose, preference, and relevance as the basis for selecting both a theoretical grounding and definition of the concept to be measured.

Next is the development of an operational definition of the concept. This step involves asking, "What kind of an indicator will be used as a gauge of this concept?" or "How will the concept be classified and empirically and numerically represented?" This step involves two sequenced activities: (1) the development of items, either statements or questions that when summed, constitute the entire construct being measured and nothing more and (2) the selection of a structure and numeric scheme (Salkind, 2013). We discuss these in more detail in the section on measurement types.

Recall in the discussion of Hume (2006) in Chapter 1, empirical representation of an underlying concept refers to using and quantifying sense data to examine an abstract. Because, by definition, a concept is never directly observable, the strength of the relationship between an indicator, or its empirical representation, and an underlying concept is critical to the rigor and quality of experimental-type inquiry. This relationship is referred to as **instrument validity**. Recall the definition of validity in Chapters 6 and 9. Applied to measurement, instrument validity refers to the adequacy of a strategy to measure the whole entity it claims to measure and nothing more.

As part of design reliability (see Chapters 6 and 9), the consistency of a measure, or its stability in revealing similar results under similar circumstances, is referred to as its instrument reliability. Reliability and validity are two fundamental rigor properties of indicators. Evaluating their adequacy is a major consideration in determining when and how to use existing measures or if new instrumentation needs to be developed (Salkind, 2013).

Part of the action process of operationalization involves determining the level at which the variable will be measured. *Level of measurement* refers to the properties and meaning of the numbers assigned to an observation. Nominal, ordinal, interval, and ratio are the four types of numbers attributed to observations, each containing different properties and thus serving different functions. **Nominal numbers** are simply labels such as telephone and Social Security numbers. Ordinal numbers provide ranking order, such as largest to smallest, but with no known or equal interval between each. Interval and ratio numbers both have equal intervals between them and thus can be subjected to mathematical functions such as addition, subtraction, multiplication, and division. Ratio numbers have an absolute zero while interval numbers do not (DePoy & Gitlin, 2016). Consider age, for example. People can be categorized nominally as either young = 1 or old = 2, ordinally placed on an ascending scale of 1 to 5 depending on the range in which they fit (1 = 18–35, 2 = 36–55, 3 = 56–65, 4 = 66–75, 5 = 76+) or intervally measured as age in years.

Several principles are used to determine the level of measurement of a variable. (refer to Chapter 6 for discussion of variables). First, every variable must have two qualities. Each must be exhaustive of every possible observation; that is, the variable should be able to classify every observation in terms of one or more of its attributes. Second, the attributes or categories must be mutually exclusive. A simple example is the concept of gender, which most often has been classically defined as either a male or female attribute. These two categories have represented the full range of attributes for the concept of gender. If gender is defined as five or more attributes, then the variable must contain and number five or however many mutually exclusive categories are defined in the construct. If male, female, lesbian, gay, and transgendered categories are named as constituting gender, a respondent must belong only to one category, and these five categories are considered to fully comprise gender and nothing more.

Second, a variable can be characterized as being either discrete or continuous, and thus the nature of the question to be answered through the measurement should be considered along with the intrinsic form of the phenomenon to be quantified. However, even when variables lend themselves to one or the other category, measurement properties can be altered as discussed immediately below. A *discrete variable* is one with a finite number of distinct values. Again, gender is a good example of a discrete variable. Gender, as classically defined, has male or a female value. There is no in-between category. A *continuous variable,* in contrast, has an infinite number of values (Salkind, 2013). Age (measured in years) and height (measured metrically or in feet and inches) are two examples of continuous variables in that they can be measured along a numerical continuum.

In experimental-type design, level of measurement is not inherent in a variable even when a concept seems best measured at a particular level. Rather, it is assigned to reflect the concept and to assure that the statistical analysis necessary to answer the research question can be calculated. Revisit age, for example. Age can be coded with nominal, ordinal, or interval numbers depending on the questions to be answered. If the social worker wants to create groupings by age, then nominal or ordinal data are assigned, such as young and old. If, however, the social worker is interested in knowing how age and function are associated and change or vary together (as one gets older what happens to function), then coding age with interval numbers is most useful. Nominal and ordinal variables can also be statistically treated as interval so that they can be subjected to mathematical functions not possible without continuous data. This technique is referred to as creating "dummy variables." It is an advanced statistical technique, and thus we do not discuss it in this text but rather introduce the term and refer you to sources that detail these procedures. (Frankfort-Nachmias & Leon-Guerrero. 2014).

Measurement Types

Now that the properties of numbers have been discussed, we proceed to the different methods by which data are collected and transformed into numbers in experimental-type inquiry. The choice of measurement tool is of course dependent on purpose, question, and resources. In addition, Corcoran and Fisher (2013) assert that measuring what is intended to be measured in a stable manner (instrument validity and reliability, respectively) is a critical concern that guides measurement approach (see Chapter 6). There are many measurement types. In this chapter we discuss those most useful to social workers. Some lend themselves more readily to surveys and others to interview. However, each format discussed below can be administered through both mechanisms. The key feature is the theory-based operationalization of constructs to be measured and the careful planning of the measurement protocol such that the investigator influence is eliminated from the process of instrumentation to the extent possible. Avoidance of bias is carefully judged to determine instrument validity.

Scales are perhaps the most frequent instruments used for quantitative measurement. This broad category of measures assesses the extent to which respondents possess an attribute or personal characteristic (DeVellis, 2012). As an example, scales would be well suited to examine small business owners' attitudes toward workplace accessibility.

Although there are variations, three scaling formats are most frequently used: **Likert-type**, Guttman, and semantic differential scales. The Likert-type scale consists of a series of items (usually between 10 and 20) worded favorably and unfavorably regarding the underlying construct to be assessed. Respondents indicate a level of agreement or disagreement with each statement by selecting one of several response alternatives (usually five to seven) (DeVellis, 2012).

Attitude measures, such as the one that the social worker would use to test perspectives about workplace accessibility changes on the part of small business owners, are often formatted as Likert-type scales. Look at how Popovich, Scherbaum, Scherbaum, & Polinko (2003) discuss the instrument that they developed and that the social worker used to examine what type of intervention is needed to resolve unnecessary unemployment for individuals such as Elton.

> We designed this 25-item scale to assess individuals' beliefs about the reasonableness of common workplace accommodations for persons with disabilities. Participants rated the items on a 7-point Likert-type scale ranging from very reasonable (1) to very unreasonable (7). (Popovich et al., 2003, p. 166)

Likert-type scales may be considered nominal, ordinal, or interval, depending on what is being measured and which analytical procedures are selected. A disadvantage of Likert-type scaling is that there is no way to ensure that all respondents have an equivalent understanding of the magnitude of each response (DeVellis, 2012). So two people may choose a response of strongly agree for the same item but still may have widely varying perspectives.

The Guttman scale is referred to as "unidimensional" or "cumulative." (DeVellis, 2012). It typically contains a small number of items that relate to one concept. The items form a homogeneous or unitary set and are cumulative or graduated in intensity of expression. In other words, the items are hierarchically arranged so that endorsement of one item means an endorsement of those items below it, which are expressed at less intensity. The value of this type of scaling is that knowledge of the total score is predictive of the individual's responses to each item. If the attitude scale discussed above was modified as a Guttman scale, the items could be organized from least to most favorable such that the item selected by respondents would represent the most positive attitude held by each.

The semantic differential scale could also be used to assess need by the social worker, as it is typically seen as a psychological measure to assess attitudes and beliefs (DeVellis, 2012). This approach involves a series of rating scales in which the respondent is asked to give a judgment about something along an ordered dimension, usually of seven points. Ratings are "bipolar" in that they specify two opposite ends of a continuum (e.g., good–bad, happy–sad). Instead of a seven-point scale in which the respondent is asked about level of agreement (Popovich et al., 2003), attitude items on this type of scale would be stated in binary terms, asking the respondent to place an *X* on a line to denote his or her opinion. Semantic differential scaling is most useful when natural phenomena can be categorized in opposite or contrary positions. However, this format limits the range of responses to a linear configuration.

Scaling is not the only type of measurement used in experimental-type thinking and action. Social science researchers use a vast array of options, so we delimit our discussion to those that best serve social workers at each stage in the examined practice sequence.

Self-Report

Self-report involves asking persons to rate themselves using a standard. This approach is often used in clinical settings to examine progress over time. As an example, Janice could rate herself on engagement in desired activities such that the social worker could judge the magnitude or progress at different outcome intervals.

Proxy

The use of a proxy, or informant, is another important source of information, particularly in the clinical setting. This type of instrumentation involves asking a family member, professional, or an individual familiar with the subject to rate that person on the phenomenon of interest using a standard measure. As an example, to verify Janice's engagement in activity, a family member might be asked to rate her, allowing the social worker to verify Janice's own perception of outcome.

Observation

Consistent with its philosophical grounding, experimental-type observation tends to be highly structured in order to produce numerical ratings (DePoy & Gitlin, 2016).

Performance-based measures in which the social worker observes and rates behavior fit into this category of instrumentation. As an example, in the reflexive intervention phase, Dean's participation in substance abuse programming would be observed and scored by the social worker.

Recording Information in Experimental-Type Traditions

Recording information is a structured process within this tradition. The purpose of recording is to organize numeric findings so that they can be subjected to statistical analysis. Computer-hosted spreadsheets are widely available for purchase as well as in open source formats. We discuss this process in more detail in Chapter 12, but for now we highlight the importance of recording and entering data into spreadsheets in a manner such that questions can be answered through statistical manipulation of scores.

OBTAINING INFORMATION IN NATURALISTIC TRADITIONS

Gathering information in naturalistic forms of inquiry involves a set of investigative actions that are quite divergent in purpose, approach, and process not only from experimental-type instrumentation but even within the range of naturalistic designs themselves. Generally gathering information in naturalistic inquiry serves to uncover multiple and diverse perspectives or underlying patterns that describe, relate, and even predict the phenomena under study within the context in which they occur (Denzin & Lincoln, 2008). This tradition is therefore extremely relevant for capturing ongoing occurrences, such as activity within the reflexive intervention stage, as it is proceeding. Context is broadly conceptualized referring not simply to a physical space but rather to physical, virtual, intellectual, social, economic, cultural, spiritual, emotive, and other types of environments in which human experience unfolds.

Consistent with the diversity of the tradition, there is wide variation of information-gathering techniques that fit under naturalistic inquiry. While sources of data similar or equivalent to those in experimental-type action may be obtained (observation, interview), what makes them naturalistic is the inductive logic structure used to engage the data (Agamben, 2009). As an example, rather than imposing a preexisting coding scheme on observations, as in the example of Dean's participation in the substance abuse intervention, the social worker would observe without a predetermined theory, set of variables, or numeric scoring protocol. Doing so allows knowledge to emerge from the data set. We now turn to principles that guide naturalistic information gathering in examined practice.

Four Information-Gathering Considerations

Although the processes differ across the types of naturalistic inquiry, four basic considerations provide guidance for social work action:

1. the nature of involvement of the social worker;

2. the inductive, abductive process of gathering information, analyzing the information, and gathering more information;

3. time commitment; and

4. the use of multiple data collection strategies.

Involvement

Active involvement and participation (to a greater or lesser degree) with people and other sources of information, such as artifacts, written historical documents, virtual text and image, and pictorial representations are characteristic of the naturalistic tradition (Creswell, 2013). Thus, dissimilar from experimental-type rules, naturalistic approaches espouse subjectivity and thus reject the possibility of objectivity and the creation of controlled conditions apart from the practice setting designed to eliminate investigator influence (DePoy & Gilson, 2009). The quality of the data collected therefore is dependent on the generalist social work skills of engagement, trust, rapport, and mutual respect among those participating (Marlow, 2011). Thus, the social worker as a data-gathering tool is a logical extension of the primary aim of naturalistic inquiry as well as of the social work process itself. As noted, the level and nature of the investigator's involvement with people and other sources of information depend on the specific type of naturalistic design pursued as well as purpose and constraints.

Consider reflexive intervention with Dean. In the reflexive intervention stage, in addition to measurement, Dean's log of his activity and responses to the substance abuse program were used as data by the social worker who was also conducting the intervention. Moreover, as is often the case in social work, the social worker used supervision to reflect on use of self in the social work interaction with Dean. These data were analyzed throughout the process, revealing that substance abuse treatment might not be the appropriate intervention.

To review level of involvement, revisit Chapter 9 in which naturalistic design is described.

Information Collection and Analysis

In naturalistic inquiry, the act of gathering information is intimately connected to analysis—that is, collecting data and conducting analysis reciprocally inform one another and co-occur. Thus, once a systematic process has been initiated, the social worker evaluates the information obtained through observation, examination of artifacts and images, recorded interviews, and participation in relevant activities. These initial analytical efforts detail the "who, what, when, how, and where" aspects of the context, which in turn are used to further define and refine subsequent data collection efforts and directions.

Time Commitment

The amount of time spent in a systematic naturalistic data collection process varies greatly across the types of design and parts of examined practice. In some systematic activities, understanding a natural or virtual setting can be time consuming because of the complexity of the initial query and the context being studied. However, when integrated into daily social work practice with client groups, naturalistic strategies may be accomplished by enacting deliberate methods to systematically obtain information as social work is proceeding (DePoy & Gilson, 2009). As an example, well-structured clinical notes taken by the social workers practicing with both Dean and Janice can serve as both practice notes and data for formal analysis.

The amount of time spent in systematic inquiry may vary from hours to years. Regardless of the time duration, the point at which sufficient information has been obtained needs to be determined such that a final analytic or interpretive process can be implemented, and the knowledge gained can be shared. As we introduced, the judgment to terminate systematic data collection because no new learning is occurring is referred to as saturation (Denzin & Lincoln, 2011). As an example, in the elder mobility device project, studying the reasons for device abandonment and thus defining need was terminated at the point of repetition by new informants of what had already been learned.

Multiple Information-Gathering Strategies

The naturalistic tradition is often characterized by the use of numerous data collection methods in a single inquiry. Because different strategies are designed to derive information from varied sources, the use of multiple approaches to obtain information enhances the complexity and richness of understanding of the phenomenon under study. For example, collecting data both through interview and observation not only provides multiple forms of data, but one source can confirm the other (or not). It is therefore common practice to use more than one data collection strategy even if a query is small in scope (Fortune, Reid, & Miller 2013). Throughout and at the end of the data collection process, all sources of information are analyzed to ensure that they support a rich descriptive or interpretive scheme and set of conclusions.

As expected within naturalistic traditions, there is no standard approach available to indicate which strategy should be used and when it should be introduced. Data collection decisions are specific to the purpose, query, preferred way of knowing, and the contextual opportunities and limitations that emerge.

INFORMATION-GATHERING PROCESSES

Unlike experimental-type information gathering, because of its underlying logic structures of induction and abduction, there is no single set of rules to guide systematic data collection in naturalistic inquiry. As we indicated, generally, the process starts the identification of a context and query and proceeds to an entry point such as a concept, geography, or informant. However, the purpose as well as constraints of context and the element in examined practice delimit and guide how data collection unfolds.

INFORMATION-GATHERING STRATEGIES

Many information-gathering strategies are used in naturalistic inquiry. The main techniques—observing, asking, and examining materials—have a different purpose and structure when used in naturalistic inquiry than when used in experimental-type designs.

Observing: Looking, Watching, and Listening

In the naturalistic tradition, the processes of looking, watching, and listening are often referred to as "observation" (Lofland, Snow, Anderson, & Lofland, 2006). In this data collection strategy, the social worker ranges in involvement on a continuum from passive to fully participatory.

Although the term *participant observation* has been used to describe a classical anthropological research of an etic researcher collecting information through immersion in a distant culture (Creswell, 2013), we find more recent models of participant observation most relevant for examined practice. This process, as characterized by Denzin and Lincoln (2011), is systematic but occurs as a complex human interaction in which meaning and knowledge are generated by all involved. Thus, rather than being a passive observer, the social worker practices active engagement in context, which is a valued source of knowledge and analysis. Participant observation is natural within social work intervention and thus is an excellent approach to systematic information gathering within the natural context and sequence of examined practice. Consider the practice context with Janice,

Dean, and Elton. Simultaneous social work intervention along with systematic observation and analysis already were occurring and thus illustrate how intervention itself is knowledge generating within reflexive intervention.

Some systematic activities warrant less investigator participation as illustrated in the classic study conducted by Maruyama (1981). Less extreme than the endogenous nature of Maruyma's study but still not fully immersed, is non-participatory observation in which the social worker is not directly involved in the daily intervention process. This type of research is particularly relevant to situations in which more active participation interferes with progress in examined practice and knowledge acquisition. Consider the needs assessment study to determine the educational needs of small business owners regarding workplace accessibility. Exploring attitudes might not be free from social desirability responses if the employers perceived a preferred position on the part of the social worker. Observation of the nonhuman environment, such as doorways, and even who is present in a physical setting could be added to an attitudinal scale to elicit important findings not tested through other methods.

Asking

Asking in the form of interviewing is a critical social work skill (Marlow, 2011) that also is a powerful method of data collection. Unlike observation, asking involves direct or mediated contact with persons who are capable of providing information (Rubin & Rubin, 2012). Thus, collecting data by asking requires the establishment of a relationship appropriate to the purpose and level of involvement with the informant and a clear systematic sequence of inquiry. Four steps guide naturalistic asking:

1. access,

2. description,

3. focus, and

4. verification.

Asking must begin with access to someone who is not only willing to answer but whose responses are purposive and useful. It is therefore important to know the reasons someone is willing to participate and to select informants to meet the aim of the inquiry. In the elder needs assessment study, elders as well as observers were sought as participants. The recruitment plan was therefore designed to obtain access to elders and others who were expected to possess knowledge about mobility device use and nonuse as well as perceptions on the meanings of these devices to users and casual lookers.

After access is obtained, the initial goal of asking is broad description. Open-ended questions such as "Tell me about . . ." are useful in breaking the ice, so to speak, while not constraining the interaction in a desired direction (Rubin & Rubin, 2012).

On the basis of emerging descriptive knowledge, asking becomes more focused and probing. Asking questions requires intense listening and demonstration of interest in each aspect of what the informant is saying (Rubin & Rubin, 2012).

Finally, verification is the process of checking the accuracy of impressions with informants. Statements that repeat understandings back to informants to check the social worker's accurate receipt of the message communicated by the informant should be incorporated into every naturalistic asking approach. This technique is referred to as *member checking* and thus serves as both a data collection and rigor strategy (Lofland et al., 2006). As an example, in the elder study, the social worker stated to one group of informants, "So what I think I hear is that reluctance to use a mobility device has to do with the stigma you feel when using one."

What and how long to continue asking, who to ask, where, and how are all decisions that influence the knowledge obtained from answers to well-crafted questions. Given the range of philosophical and design approaches in the naturalistic tradition, it is not surprising that asking can take many forms, from an informal, open-ended conversation to a focused or long in-depth interview. Moreover, asking can occur as a one-to-one interaction or in a group. Characteristic of naturalistic inquiry in general is the purposive and nonprescriptive timing of interview (Rubin & Rubin, 2012). Consider the elder mobility device project. Asking elders about usage and preference accompanied observation as a major strategy in needs assessment.

Remember that asking may occur face-to-face or may be mediated by human or nonhuman sources (e.g., language interpretation or computer mediated as illustrated in the TAP outcome assessment). Asking can cover a range of time from an instant, to a full life, or even to the history of a culture. Of particular relevance to examined practice in clinical settings is life history, or biography (Paquin, 2009). This form of naturalistic interview chronicles an individual's life within a social context. The social worker elicits information not only on the important events or "turnings" that influence a life trajectory but also on the meaning of those events within the contexts in which they occur (Denzin & Lincoln, 2011). As an example, Janice's life history was a crucial piece of knowledge not only in informing intervention by the second social worker but in adding to the knowledge repository of clinical practice with individuals who experience sudden loss of function.

One frequently used asking strategy, particularly in the needs assessment phase of examined practice, is the focus group. This method is useful when interactions and group discussions are expected to yield more meaningful understandings than single, independent interviews. Focus groups can be orchestrated in different ways depending upon purpose. Typically, a group of six to 12 individuals is purposively chosen and convened to address the specified topic. Guiding probes or questions are proposed by the investigator to stimulate interaction among the members (Liamputtong, 2011).

Recall that group interview was one method used by the social work team during reflexive intervention in the elder mobility device project. As we noted, several groups were conducted, one comprising elders who did not use prescribed equipment, one with elders who did use prescribed equipment, and one of observers. In each group, specific questions regarding meanings of the appearance of the device aesthetic were posed with photographic props to elicit depth of response.

Examining Materials

As we have already introduced, within the past several decades, material and visual culture have become important fields of study in themselves. Examined practice has much to gain from this scholarship as visuals and images take on increasing centrality in the twenty-first century (Meecham, 2013). Examining materials such as texts (records, diaries, journals, e-mails, articles, narratives, letters), images (photographs, logos, signs, spaces, architectures, and so forth), and objects is an essential strategy in examined practice. Things and appearances are not simply materials and their properties respectively but hold meaning to those who possess, create, and observe them (Rose, 2012; Miller, 2010).

Similar to looking, watching, listening, and asking, review of materials typically begins with a broad examination of things and images and then becomes more focused to explore recurring themes and emerging patterns of meaning. Object reading (Candlin & Guins, 2009) has been applied to understanding phenomena through visualizing things, their design, placement, use, and meaning. This approach may be overt or covert. Covert observation has been referred to as unobtrusive data collection in which identity of the individuals who create or possess observed materials is not revealed or in many cases sought at all. Unobtrusive data span a continuum from individual possessions to big data (Cukier & Mayer-Schonberger, 2013). Big data, the huge repositories of information often generated through the Internet or other computer-assisted methods, exemplify not only knowledge available for mining without consent but also for visualizing trends and patterns across the globe. We do not discuss these methods further here as they are beyond the scope of the text. However, because big data collection and analysis are major contemporary methods, they may have much to contribute to examined practice, answering questions through visual maps of health and economic disparities, drug abuse patterns, and so forth (Sicignano, 2012).

We suggest that object and image analysis feasible for all social workers to accomplish within examined practice be added to the skills that social workers typically learn and practice on a daily basis. The elder mobility device study is a prime example of objects as it reveals that their visual meaning often trumps safety and health concerns. Thus, the object and material world must be part of social work information.

RECORDING OBTAINED INFORMATION

Unlike experimental-type approaches where numbers are recorded on a spreadsheet for immediate analysis, documentation of naturalistic data such that this vast array of information can be used in examined practice is a critical concern.

Field notes have served as a staple so to speak to document data in naturalistic methods. Generally, field notes have two basic components: (1) recordings of what is observed (watching, listening, looking, and asking) and (2) recordings of the personal perspective of the observer. Different from historical field notes in which ethnographers would record copious notes and transcripts (Nanda & Warms, 2014), current descriptive notes include voice and video recording, photography, scanning, and even speech-to-text translation (Creswell, 2013).

Unlike data organization in experimental-type designs, there is no prescriptive format to record data. Rather, documentation methods are purposive and must conform to ethical standards to protect human subjects. Because of the capacity to obtain and store multiple formats, the ease of organization and manipulation, and the most seamless input into qualitative analysis software, digital tools are particularly useful. As an example, a single device such as a tablet or smartphone can record voice, photo, video, and text, and can scan documents that can be imported into a laptop or tablet app for analysis. Some are even capable of creating three-dimensional images that can be printed into objects on 3D printers and then analyzed. Coding for type of observation or impression can be as simple as placing a symbol or color code on each type of data. Automated links among devices and apps such as calendars and photos have reduced the time and effort for documentation in the naturalistic tradition.

ACCURACY IN COLLECTING INFORMATION

Accuracy or rigor in experimental-type thinking refers to validity and reliability. Some authors use the experimental-type terms validity and reliability to refer to rigor in naturalistic inquiry (Creswell, 2013). However, for us, because of its logic structures, absence of defined variables, and unstructured research questions, these two terms are not relevant to naturalistic methods and only serve to confound rigor.

The concept of "trustworthiness" makes more sense as it refers to the accuracy and credibility of data to support claims (Denzin & Lincoln, 2011). Several strategies have been used, all or some of which can be used in examined practice.

Multiple Thinkers

One technique is the involvement of two or more people in the data-gathering and analytical process. This technique checks the accuracy of the observations; more than one pair of eyes and ears are examining and recording the same context (Denzin & Lincoln, 2008).

Triangulation (Crystallization)

Another technique that increases the accuracy of information gathering is called *triangulation*. To reflect the complexity of multiple approaches and reject the two-dimensional image of a triangle, some have suggested replacing the word *triangulation* with *crystallization* (Ellingson, 2008). Regardless of the name, this technique involves the collection and analysis of multiple sources of data to inform the same phenomenon. As an example, interview, observation, and object analysis were all used in the needs assessment informing the elder mobility device project.

Saturation

This term has already been introduced. *Saturation* refers to the point at which sufficient information has been obtained for a full understanding of the phenomenon under study. As previously discussed, when the information gathered does not provide new insights or understandings, it is a signal that saturation has been achieved (Denzin & Lincoln, 2011).

Member Checking

Member checking, illustrated above, is a well-used skill in social work. Also referred to as active listening and message paraphrasing (Weger, Castle, & Emmett 2010), this technique involves asking informants to verify description as well as analytic impressions. This type of affirmation decreases the potential for misinterpretation.

Reflexivity

As discussed earlier, and as a major part of examined practice, reflexivity refers to looking in on self to examine how knowledge has been influenced by those who generate it. Reflexivity may be ongoing and formally recoded as impressions and reactions to description or may be more sporadic (Gilgun, 2010). Although deliberately emphasized in the intervention phase, reflexivity is part and parcel of all steps in examined practice. Without reflecting on what problem was identified, what was needed to address it, what was done, why, by whom, where, and how, valuable knowledge and the potential to attribute outcome to social work activity are lost from both the immediate social work initiative as well as the canon of social work knowledge.

Audit Trail

An audit trail involves leaving a path of thinking and action processes so that others can clearly follow the logic and manner in which knowledge was developed (Creswell, 2013). By sharing the thinking and action processes, the social worker makes the process of knowledge generation transparent so that the reader or consumer has a complete understanding not only about the data on which claims are based but also about how they were obtained and analyzed.

MIXING METHODS

Any of the strategies discussed above in both traditions can be integrated and combined in mixed-method inquiry. As we have indicated, through a pragmatic philosophical framework, integrating the thinking and action of both classical traditions can eliminate gaps in knowledge caused by limitations of single-tradition data collection. For example, consider how open-ended interview compliments closed-ended, theory-based questioning or how following theory-generating data collection with theory-testing information and analysis can enrich knowing. In Chapter 13, each example illustrates the value of mixing data collection methods.

Moreover, consider social work practice in general. Within the course of examined practice, it would be unusual for a social worker to use only one source of knowledge to inform practice decisions and thus, mixing methods fits well in all phases of examined practice. As an example, consider reflexive intervention phases with Janice, Dean, and Elton. Multiple approaches to document practice and how each client experienced the social work process were used, without which a well-rounded understanding of the social work action could not be obtained.

SUMMARY

In this chapter, principles and methods for collecting information across all three traditions were discussed. The primary methods for obtaining information in all systematic categories are (1) looking, watching, listening, reading, and recording; (2) asking; and (3) examining materials, artifacts, or spaces. The logic structure determines which tradition is being used, the processes to implement, and the rigor criteria to be followed.

Measurement forms the primary data within all experimental-type processes. Consistent with philosophical monism and deduction, methods to obtain information are planned before any action takes place. The data collection plan is designed to minimize bias introduced by the investigators. Information is recorded as numeric data awaiting statistical analysis and reporting.

Naturalistic strategies for obtaining information fall into categories of observation (defined broadly) and reflection. There are numerous approaches for obtaining and recording data. For the most part, naturalistic inquiry relies on more than one data collection technique.

Methods for integrating and preserving rigor in each tradition were also discussed. The chapter concluded with a brief discussion of mixing methods from both experimental-type and naturalistic traditions to serve examined practice.

The main points in the chapter are as follows:

1. Content and format are both critical in asking for and obtaining information.

2. Data collection in experimental-type design is a distinct, unidirectional action phase between the thinking processes involved in question formation and the action process of analysis.

3. In naturalistic inquiry, gathering information is multidirectional in that this action process stems from the initial query and is diverse.

4. The sequence of data collection in each tradition differs according to the underlying logic structure.

5. Measurement is the sole data recording strategy in experimental-type design, although it can be enacted through multiple structures. Measurement precedes analysis.

6. Data collection in naturalistic inquiry co-occurs with analysis.

7. Although frequently articulated, we suggest that the rigor criteria for experimental-type design are not relevant and thus should not be used to judge the efficacy of naturalistic data collection.

REFERENCES

Agamben, G. (2009). *The signature of all things: On method.* New York, NY: Zone Books.

Audi, R. (2011). *Epistemology.* New York, NY: Routledge.

Candlin, F., & Guins, R. (2009). *The object reader.* London, UK: Routledge.

Corcoran, K., & Fisher, J. (2013). *Measures for clinical practice* (5th ed.). New York, NY: Oxford University Press.

Creswell, J. (2013). *Qualitative inquiry and research design: Choosing among five approaches* (3rd ed.). Thousand Oaks, CA: Sage.

Cukier, K., & Mayer-Schonberger, V. (2013). *Big data: A revolution that will transform how we live, work, and think.* New York, NY: Houghton Mifflin Harcourt.

Denzin, N., & Lincoln, Y. (2008). *Collecting and interpreting qualitative materials.* Thousand Oaks, CA: Sage.

Denzin, N., & Lincoln, Y. (2011). *SAGE handbook of qualitative research* (4th ed.). Thousand Oaks, CA.

DePoy, E., & Gilson, S. (2009). *Evaluation practice.* New York, NY: Routledge.

DePoy, E., & Gitlin, L. (2016). *Introduction to research* (4th ed.). St Louis, MO: Elsevier.

DeVellis, R. F. (2012). *Scale development* (3rd ed.). Thousand Oaks, CA: Sage.

Ellingson, L. (2008). *Engaging crystallization in qualitative research.* Thousand Oaks, CA: Sage.

Fortune, A. E., Reid, W. J., & Miller, R. L. (2013). *Qualitative research in social work.* (2nd ed.). New York, NY: Columbia University Press.

Fowler, F. (2014). *Survey research.* Thousand Oaks, CA: Sage.

Frankfort-Nachmias, C., & Leon-Guerrero, A. (2014). *Ryan Beaumont* (7th ed.). Thousand Oaks, CA: Sage.

Gilgun, J. (2010). Reflexivity and qualitative research. *Current Issues in Qualitative Research, 1*(2).

Gillham, B. (2008). *Observation techniques: Structured to unstructured.* New York, NY: Bloomsbury Academic.

Gubrium, J. F., Holstein, J. A., Marvasti, A. B., & McKinney, K. D. (2012). *The SAGE handbook of interview research: The complexity of the craft.* Thousand Oaks, CA: Sage.

Hume, D. (2006). *An enquiry concerning human understanding.* Stilwell, KS: Digireads.com.

Liamputtong, P. (2011). *Focus group methodology.* Thousand Oaks, CA: Sage.

Linden Research, Inc. (2015). *Second Life.* Retrieved from http://secondlife.com

Lofland, J., Snow, D., Anderson, L., & Lofland, L. H. (2006). *Analyzing social settings* (4th ed.). Belmont, CA: Wadsworth.

Marlow, C. (2011). *Research methods for generalist social work* (5th ed.). Belmont, CA: Brooks Cole.

Maruyama, M. (1981). Endogenous research: The prison project. In P. Reason & J. Rowan (Eds.), *Human inquiry: A sourcebook of new paradigm research.* New York, NY: Wiley & Sons.

Meecham, P. (2013). Social work: Museums, technology, and material culture. In K. Drotner & K. C. Schroder (Eds), *Museum communication and social media* (pp. 33–53). New York, NY: Routledge.

Miller, D. (2010). *Stuff.* Malden, MA: Polity.

Nanda, S., & Warms, R. L. (2014). *Cultural anthropology.* Belmont, CA: Cenage.

Paquin, G. (2009). *Clinical social work: A narrative approach.* Alexandria, VA: CSWE Press.

Patton, M. Q. (2012). *Essentials of utilization-focused evaluation.* Thousand Oaks, CA: Sage.

Pauwels, L. (2006). *Visual cultures of science: Rethinking representational practices in knowledge building and science communication.* Lebanon, NH: Dartmouth.

Popovich, P. M., Scherbaum, C. A., Scherbaum, K. L., & Polinko, N. (2003). The assessment of attitudes toward individuals with disabilities in the workplace. *Journal of Psychology: Interdisciplinary and Applied, 137*(2), 163–177.

Rose, G. (2012). *Visual methodologies: An introduction to researching with visual materials.* Thousand Oaks, CA: Sage.

Rubin, H. J., &. Rubin, I. S. (2012). *Qualitative interviewing: The art of hearing* (3rd ed.). Thousand Oaks, CA: Sage.

Salkind, N. (2013). *Tests & measurement for people who (think they) hate tests & measurement.* Thousand Oaks, CA: Sage.

Sicignano, M. (2012). *Big data analysis and quality improvement in social services.* Retrieved from http://www.socialjusticesolutions.org/2012/12/21/big-data-analysis-and-quality-improvement-in-social-services

Weger, H., Castle, G. R., & Emmett, M. C. (2010). Active listening in peer interviews: The influence of message paraphrasing on perceptions of listening skill. *International Journal of Listening, 24*(1), 34–49.

Woodward, I. (2007). *Understanding material culture.* Thousand Oaks, CA: Sage.

Chapter 12

ANALYSIS

The primary objective of this chapter is to discuss methods of analyses across all three traditions as they are most useful throughout examined practice. We begin with experimental-type design, identifying the logic of choosing a statistical approach. The action processes of statistical calculation central to experimental-type inquiry are then discussed before we move on to analysis in naturalistic inquiry and mixed methods.

WHAT IS STATISTICAL ANALYSIS?

A formal definition of statistical analysis is the organization, interpretation, and presentation of data according to well-defined, systematic, and mathematical procedures and rules (DePoy & Gitlin, 2016). As discussed in Chapter 11, the term *data* within the experimental-type tradition refers to information obtained through measurement, answering questions such as, "How much? How many? How long? How fast? How similar? and How different?" In statistical analysis, data are represented by numbers. The benefits of numerical representation lie largely in the clarity of numbers, a property which, according to logical positivists, cannot always be exhibited in words due to their interpretive nature. Thus, within experimental-type approaches, numeric data comprise the precise language to describe, relate, or predict phenomena. Statistical analytic tools are methods for systematically analyzing and drawing conclusions to tell a quantitative story.

In concert with the linear sequence of experimental-type designs, statistical analysis occurs after all the previous steps of the inquiry, including the level of knowledge development, research problem, research question, study design, number of study variables, assignment of level of measurement, sampling procedures, and sample size have been completed. Each of these steps logically leads to and should justify the selection of appropriate statistical actions.

Statistics can be divided into three broad analytic categories: descriptive, inferential, and associational. Each level of analysis corresponds to the particular level of knowledge about the topic, the specific type of question asked, and whether the data are derived from the population as a whole or from a subset or sample. Because experimental-type inquiry ultimately aims to predict the causes of phenomena, the three analytic levels form a hierarchy consistent with this goal as the levels of questioning discussed in Chapter 8 proceed from descriptive to predictive.

Descriptive Statistics

Descriptive statistics, the most basic level of analysis, are used to reduce large sets of observations into more compact and interpretable forms (Frankfort-Nachmias & Leon-Guerrero, 2014). If an entire population is participating in an inquiry, descriptive statistics form the primary analytic strategy. However, descriptive statistics can also be used to summarize the data derived from a sample. Description, the first step of any analytical process, typically involves counting occurrences, proportions, or distributions.

Inferential Statistics

The second level of statistics, inferential statistics, involves making inferences about a population on the basis of what was found in the sample selected from that larger group. Inferential statistics are also used to examine group differences within a sample (Trochim, 2006). If the subjects are a sample, both descriptive and inferential statistics can be used. However, because of their formal purpose and their design to account for errors that can occur when using a small group to determine conclusions about the larger group it represents, using inferential statistics may not be necessary when analyzing results from an entire population.

Associational Statistics

Associational statistics are the third level of analytic tools (Frankfort-Nachmias & Leon-Guerrero, 2014). These statistics comprise a set of procedures designed to identify relationships between and among multiple variables and to determine whether knowledge of one set of data allows the investigator to infer or predict the characteristics of another set. The primary purpose of these multivariate types of statistical analyses is to make causal statements and predictions (Pelham, 2013). We now detail and illustrate the basic statistical procedures in each of the three levels.

LEVEL 1: DESCRIPTIVE STATISTICS

Consider all the numbers that are generated in a survey as we proceed through this discussion. Each number provides information about an individual phenomenon but does not provide an understanding of a group of individuals as a whole and thus cannot accomplish this major aim of experimental-type research. Recall the discussion in Chapter 11 about the four levels of measurement (nominal, ordinal, interval, and ratio). Large masses of unorganized numbers, regardless of the level of measurement, are not understandable and cannot in themselves answer a research question that seeks to know something about a group.

Descriptive statistical techniques provide tools to reduce large sets of data into smaller, comprehensible sets without sacrificing critical information. This action process, referred to as data reduction, entails the summary of data and their reduction to numerical scores that can be interpreted to answer the research questions.

A descriptive analysis is the first action undertaken to understand the full set of data that have been collected. Basic and most typically used descriptive techniques include frequency distribution, measures of central tendency (mode, median, and mean), variances, contingency tables, and correlational analyses. All involve direct measures of characteristics of the actual group studied.

Frequency Distribution

The first and most basic descriptive statistic is the *frequency distribution*. This term refers to both the distribution of values for a given variable and the number of times each value occurs. The distribution reflects a simple tally or count of how frequently each value of the variable occurs in the set of measured objects. Frequencies can be used to check the accuracy of data entry into a spreadsheet (referred to as cleaning the data set) and to describe the nature of a variable.

Frequency distributions are usually arranged in table format, with the values of a variable arranged in a structure that is most useful and transparent in both answering the questions and sharing the findings. Two basic aspects of the data collected are displayed in frequencies; (1) the most frequently occurring class of scores and (2) any pattern in the distribution of scores. In addition to a count of the raw scores, *relative frequencies*, or frequencies converted into percentages, may also be useful to compute and report. This calculation immediately presents the percentage of subjects that has a score on any given value.

As an example, frequencies and relative frequencies could be calculated to quickly visualize the range of attitude scores regarding workplace accessibility on the instrument administered to small business owners. To conduct the needs assessment informing a pilot intervention, the social worker administered the 25-item Likert-type scaled instrument developed and validated by Popovich, Scherbaum, Scherbaum, and Polinko (2003) to test the attitudes toward the reasonableness of workplace accommodations held by a convenience sample of 10 small local business owners in a small urban area. Respondents rated each of the items on a 1 to 7 scale from least favorable to most favorable. To analyze the findings, the social worker entered the scores into the SPSS spreadsheet. SPSS software is a powerful and widely used computer program that provides tools from simple to the most complex statistical analysis and graphics (IBM, n.d.). The social worker began the analysis by computing frequencies on the 25-item scores and on the total attitude score. These calculations served to clean the data (i.e., to identify and correct errors in entry into the spreadsheet). Data were also collected on the size of each business (recording the number of employees and dollar amount of yearly net income averaged over the past 3 years).

As briefly introduced in Chapter 11, an investigator can assign the level of numbers (nominal, ordinal, interval, ratio) to a variable to achieve the purpose of an inquiry. In this example, the social worker decided to treat the 1 to 7 scaling as interval. We revisit this choice below in more detail. But for now, note that this decision allows for mathematical manipulation of the data such as calculating averages. In part, the social worker made this decision because it is difficult to derive any immediate understanding from a table with a large distribution of numbers. Consider how many numbers are reflected in a table with 10 scores on 25 individual items and then a total score. The total number of scores is 260.

Figure 12.1   Pie Chart Example

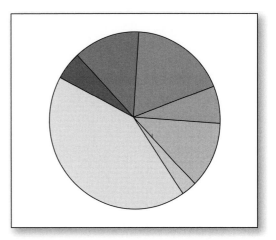

In addition to a table format, frequencies can be visually represented by graphs, such as a pie chart, histogram, or bar graph, and polygon (dots connected by lines). For each of the seven responses, Figure 12.1 depicts a pie chart of the distribution of the scores by percentage of responses in each category (relative frequency).

Scores can also be visually represented using a polygon graph. A dot is plotted for the percentage value, and lines are drawn among the dots to yield a picture of the shape of the distribution, as well as the frequency of responses in each category (Figure 12.2).

Frequencies can be described by the nature of their distribution. There are several shapes of distributions. Distributions can be symmetrical in which both halves of the distribution are identical (referred to as a normal distribution in Figure 12.3) or nonsymmetrical (positively or negatively skewed as in Figures 12.4 and 12.5, respectively).

A distribution can also be characterized by its width and height, or what is called *kurtosis*. This descriptor is either characterized by its flatness (platykurtic; Figure 12.6) or peakedness (leptokurtic; Figure 12.7).

A bimodal distribution (Figure 12.8) is also possible, in which scores are characterized by two high points.

Besides being good practice for more advanced statistical decision making, these elegant visual depictions of a distribution have much to tell (Orrell, 2012). For example, Figure 12.1 (pie chart) of total scores shows that the largest number

Figure 12.2   Polygon

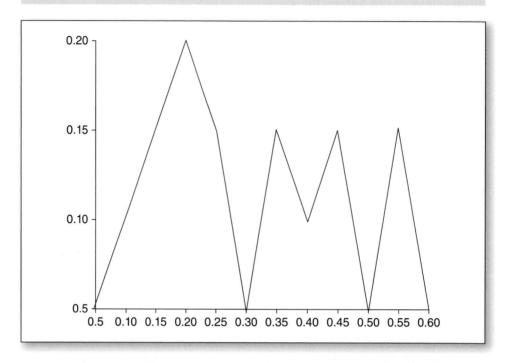

Figure 12.3   Normal Curve

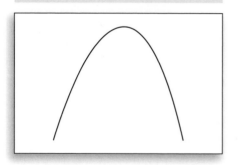

Figure 12.4   Positively Skewed

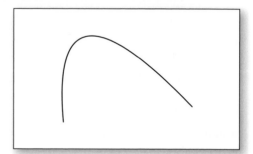

Figure 12.5   Negatively Skewed

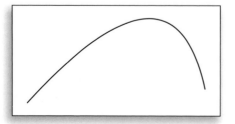

Figure 12.6   Platykurtic

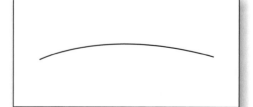

of respondents scored a 5, indicating general negative attitudes toward workplace accommodations. If the distribution were platykurtic (flat), the social worker would conclude that there was not a great deal of agreement in attitude. Similarly, if the curve were bimodal, the social worker would visualize two camps, one with positive attitudes and one with negative attitudes.

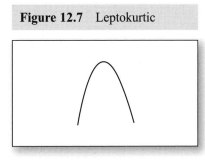

Figure 12.7 Leptokurtic

Measures of Central Tendency

A frequency distribution reduces a large collection of data into a relatively compact form. Although terms can be used to describe these charts and figures (e.g., bell shaped, kurtosis, or skewed to the right), scores can also be summarized by using specific numerical values, called *measures of central tendency.* In concert with the aim of experimental-type inquiry to characterize a group, this class of statistics provides important information regarding the most typical or representative scores within a group. The three basic measures of central tendency are the mode, median, and mean.

Mode

In most data distributions, observations tend to cluster heavily around certain values. One logical measure of central tendency is the value that occurs most frequently. This value is referred to as the *modal value* or the *mode.* For example, consider the following total scores on the attitude scale:

3, 4, 4, 5, 5, 5, 5, 5, 6, 6, 7

Figure 12.8 Bimodal Distribution

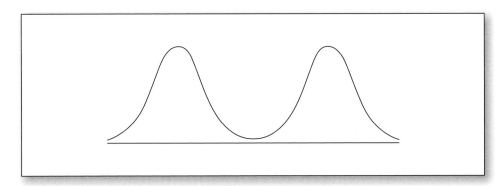

In this distribution of scores, the modal value is 5 because it occurs more often than any other score.

In a distribution based on data that have been grouped into intervals, the mode is often considered to be the numerical midpoint of the interval that contains the highest frequency of observations. For example, consider the social worker's measurement of the net income. The ranges provided were 1 = under $10,000; 2 = $10,001–$20,000; 3 = $20,001–$30,000, and 4 = >$30,000 (measured as average income in dollars over the past 3 years). The mode for the total sample was 3, indicating that most respondents had an average net income of $20,001–$30,000. This number could then be expressed as a mode of $25,000, the midpoint of the range.

Median

The second measure of central tendency is the median, the point on a scale above or below which 50% of the cases fall. It lies at the middle of a distribution. To determine the median, a set of observations is arranged from lowest to highest in value. The middle value is then identified as the number below and above which 50% of the observations occur. The median of the total attitude scores provided above is 5 because half the scores fall below, and half are above. In an odd number of values, the median is always one of the values in the distribution. However, when an even number of values occurs in a distribution, the median may or may not be one of the actual values, because there is no middle number, so the average between the two middle numbers (in the example, 5 and 5) would be calculated as the median.

In the case of a frequency distribution based on grouped data, the median can be reported as the interval in which the cumulative frequency equals 50% (or midpoint of that interval). The major advantage of the median is that it is insensitive to extreme scores in a distribution.

Mean

The *mean*, as a measure of central tendency, is the most fundamental concept in statistical analysis used with continuous (interval and ratio) data. Different from the mode and median, which do not require mathematical calculations (with the exceptions discussed), the mean is derived from manipulating numbers mathematically. Thus, the data must have the properties that will allow them to be subjected to addition, subtraction, multiplication, and division. For this reason, the social worker assigned interval level properties to the 1 to 7 rating scale.

The mean serves two purposes. First, it is a data reduction technique in that it provides a summary value for an entire distribution. As an example, the mean score of the total attitude scores above is 5. Second, the mean provides the building block for many other statistical techniques. As such, the mean is of the utmost importance, and thus, it is not surprising that there are several symbols to depict it as presented in Table 12.1.

The major advantage of the mean over the mode and median is that in calculating the mean, the numerical value of every observation in the data distribution is considered and used. When the mean is calculated, all values are summed and then divided by the number of values. However, this strength can be a drawback with highly skewed data in which there are outliers or extreme scores that pull the mean away from the median or middle score. In such cases, the average may not be central at all.

Which Measure(s) to Calculate?

Although all three measures of central tendency for continuous (interval or ratio) data are often computed, which one or ones to select depends on the purpose of the analysis and the nature of the distribution of scores. In a normal or bell-shaped curve, the mean, median, and mode are in the same location as illustrated by the sample scores above. In this case, it is most efficient to use the mean, because it is the most widely used measure of central tendency and forms the foundation for subsequent statistical calculations. However, in a skewed distribution, the three measures of central tendency fall in different places, and thus examining all three measures is warranted to tell an accurate story (Yau, 2011).

Consider the following example. Instead of the normal distribution above, what if the total attitude scores were bimodal, at 2 and 6, but still yielding a mean of 5? If the social worker neglected to examine the mode and assumed that the mean of 5 depicted generally negative attitudes, an inaccurate assumption of need would inform goals, objectives, and intervention.

Measures of Variability

While single numerical indices, such as the mean, median, or mode, can be used to describe central tendencies in a large frequency of scores, these statistics are limited in that used only by themselves, these numbers cannot represent how the scores are

Table 12.1   Symbols Used to Denote the Mean Score

M_x = mean of variable x
M_y = mean of variable y
M = mu, mean of a sample
μ = mean of a population

distributed. Most groups of scores on a scale or index differ from one another, or have what is termed *variability* (also called *spread* or *dispersion*). Variability is another way to summarize and characterize data sets. This term simply refers to the degree of *dispersion,* or the differences among scores. If scores are similar to one another within a distribution, there is little dispersion as in the visual of the leptokurtic curve (Figure 12.7). However, if scores are dissimilar, there is a high degree of dispersion as in the platykurtic visual (Figure 12.6) (Yau, 2011).

Even though a measure of central tendency provides a numerical index of the average score in a group, the inability of that single indicator to depict the actual distribution shows the importance of knowing how the scores vary or how they are dispersed around the measure of central tendency. Measures of variability provide additional information about the scoring patterns of the entire group (Frankfort-Nachmias & Leon-Guerrero, 2014). Thus, to describe a data distribution more fully, a summary measure of the variation or dispersion of the observed values is important. Most relevant to examined practice are the five basic and frequently calculated measures of variability: range, interquartile range, sum of squares, variance, and standard deviation.

Range

The *range* represents the simplest measure of variation. It refers to the difference between the highest and lowest observed value in a collection of data. The range is a crude measure because it does not take into account all values of a distribution but rather reports only the lowest and highest. In the distribution above, the range is 3 to 7 or a spread of 4.

Interquartile Range

A more meaningful measure of variability is called the *interquartile range* (IQR). This number represents the middle 50% of subjects and thus describes the middle of the sample or the range of a majority of subjects. By using the range of 50% of subjects, extreme scores or outliers are ignored. The IQR for the ten scores above is 5 given that the middle 50% of scores is 5.

Sum of Squares

Another way to interpret variability is by squaring the difference between each score and the mean. Using squares ensures that positive and negative numbers, when added, do not cancel each other out and limit the ability to use the universe of scores obtained. This value is not typically reported but instead serves as the basis for calculating other statistics.

Variance

Variance is simply the mean or average of the sum of squares. The larger the variance, the larger is the spread of scores. Similar to the sum of squares, this value is rarely reported by itself as it too serves as the foundation for other statistical tools, in particular the standard deviation.

Standard Deviation

The *standard deviation* (SD) is the most widely used measure of dispersion. It is an indicator of the average deviation of scores around the mean or, simply, the square root of the variance. In reporting the SD, researchers often use lowercase sigma (σ) or SD. Similar to the mean, SD is calculated by taking into consideration every score in a distribution. The SD is based on distances of sample scores away from the mean score and equals the square root of the mean of the squared deviations. SD is derived by computing the variation of each value from the mean, squaring the variation, and taking the square root of that calculation. There are several formulas for calculating the standard deviation that can be found online or in a basic research or statistics text (Frankfort-Nachmias & Leon-Guerrero, 2014: Gravetter & Wallnau, 2011; (University of Surrey, n.d.). We do not include them here because these statistics are rarely computed by hand. Rather, SD is such a basic and frequently used statistic that it can be computed in simple spreadsheets such as Excel or Open Office Spread Sheet or in an online app. In all of these formulas, the first step is to compute deviation scores (the difference between individual scores and the mean) for each score. Second, each deviation score is squared. As we noted earlier, if the deviation scores were added without being squared, the sum would equal zero, because the deviations above the mean always balance the deviations below the mean. The standard deviation overcomes this problem by squaring each deviation score before adding. Third, the squared deviations are added; the result is divided by one less than the number of cases, and then the square root is obtained. The square root takes the index back to the original units; in other words, the standard deviation is expressed in the units that are being measured.

We entered the numbers above into the standard deviation calculator provided for free on Mathportal.org (Petrović, n.d.), derived a standard deviation of 1.09545, and rounded it to 1.1.

In a normal curve, by definition, approximately 68% of the means from samples in a population will fall within one standard deviation from the mean of means, 95% will fall within two standard deviations, and 99% will fall within three standard deviations, thus, the use of the word standard. Standardizing dispersion allows the comparison of curves across data sets. For example, if the raw value of SD from Group 1 is larger than that of Group 2, you can say that the Group 1 scores are more dispersed than Group 2 scores. So if the social worker was planning workplace accessibility intervention for each group, he or she would use different techniques for each group based on the varied attitudes in Group 1 and the more homogenous attitudes in Group 2.

The mean and SD are often reported together in a data table. As a reporting example, the social worker would include the following table in the needs assessment report:

$$M = 5$$

$$SD = 1.1$$

These numbers would indicate that 68% of the scores fall between 3.9 and 6.1 within a range of 3 to 7 and a possible range of 1 to 7. From these basic numbers, the social worker knows that the group of respondents holds relatively similar negative attitudes and thus might consider one set of goals and objectives for the group of respondents.

Bivariate Descriptive Statistics

Another major set of questions in examined practice relates to relationships among variables. For example, in the needs assessment study, the social worker wanted to know if there could be an association between income and attitude score, or between number of employees and attitudes. This knowledge would illuminate the correlates (variables that are related but not known to be causal) of attitudes such that social work intervention would be well informed with additional factors to be considered.

Contingency Table

One method for describing a relationship between two variables (bivariate relationship) is a contingency table, also referred to as a cross-tabulation. This visual is analyzed and presented as a two-dimensional frequency distribution that is primarily used with categorical (nominal) data. In a contingency table, the attributes of one variable are related to the attributes of another (Frankfort-Nachmias & Leon-Guerrero, 2014). If the social worker were examining the relationship between longevity of business ownership and negative or positive attitudes, both variables could be recoded as nominal. To accomplish this aim for attitudes, a cut-off score between positive and negative attitudes was established for the total score at 4. Thus, any score at 4 or below was considered to be negative, and any score above 4 was considered to be positive. Similarly, for longevity, short and long categories would be created by establishing a cut-off point (under 5 years considered to be short and 5 or more years considered to be long). The contingency table is shown below as Table 12.2.

Recall the scores from the 10 respondents above (3, 4, 4, 5, 5, 5, 5, 5, 6, 6, 7). Reflected in the contingency table is the disproportionately high number of negative scores on employers in the long category. Just these few descriptive statistics suggest that there is a difference between employer groups related to length of time in business ownership. However, before jumping to conclusions on the basis of description, the extent to which these findings are a chance occurrence should be tested through one of a number of statistical tests discussed later in this chapter.

Correlational Analysis

Correlational analysis examines the extent to which two variables are related to each other. Determining the statistical procedure to compute depends primarily on the level of measurement and sample size. In a correlational statistic, an index is calculated that describes the direction and magnitude of a relationship.

Three types of directional relationships can exist among variables: positive correlation, negative correlation, and zero correlation (no correlation). A positive correlation indicates that as the numeric values of one variable increase or decrease, the values for the other variable also change in the same direction. Conversely, a negative correlation indicates that numeric values for each variable are related in an opposing direction; as the values for one variable increase, the values for the other variable

Table 12.2 Contingency Table

	Positive Attitude Score	*Negative Attitude Score*
Short ($n = 5$)	5	0
Long ($n = 5$)	2	3

decrease. As an example, the relationship between age and height in children younger than 12 years demonstrates a positive correlation, whereas the relationship between weight and hours of exercise represents a negative correlation.

To indicate the magnitude or strength of a relationship, the value calculated in correlational statistics ranges from −1 to +1. This value provides two critical pieces of information: the absolute value denoting the strength of the relationship and the sign depicting its direction. The value of −1 indicates a perfect negative correlation, and +1 signifies a perfect positive correlation. By "perfect," we mean that the calculated values for each variable change at the equivalent rate. As an example, a perfect positive correlation between years of education and reading level would be written as +1. This absolute value indicates that for each year (measured as a single unit) of education, reading level will change 1 unit (measured as a score on a literacy test). The +sign indicates that both move in the same direction.

A zero correlation is reflected as 0 and indicates no association between the variables. As an example, self esteem score and age were measured in a group of adults over the age of 18, revealing no association. Thus, the closer the absolute value is to 1, the stronger the correlation. As the absolute value moves toward 0, the association weakens.

Two correlation statistics are most frequently used in social work inquiry: the Pearson product-moment correlation, known as the Pearson *r*, and the Spearman *rho*. Both statistics yield a value between −1 and +1. The Pearson *r* is calculated on interval level data, whereas the Spearman *rho* is used with ordinal data.

To illustrate the use of the Pearson *r*, as part of the needs assessment, the social worker looked for the relationship between attitudes and number of employees. A Pearson r = .7 revealed that a greater a number of employees was highly associated with negative attitudes. (Recall that attitude was measured on a 7-point scale with ascending scores indicating more negative attitudes.) Thus, the social worker found that human resources in small businesses were related to attitude. Why this was the case was an area for further exploration.

Other statistical tests of association are used with different levels of measurement. We refer you to online sources or statistical texts to explore these statistics in detail (Frankfort-Nachmias & Leon-Guerrero, 2014).

LEVEL 2: DRAWING INFERENCES

Descriptive statistics are useful for summarizing univariate and bivariate sets of data obtained from either a population or a sample. In many experimental-type inquiries, however, the aim is to determine the extent to which observations of the sample are representative of the population from which the sample was selected.

Inferential statistics provide the action processes for drawing conclusions about a population, based on the data obtained from a sample (Frankfort-Nachmias & Leon-Guerrero, 2014).

Statistical inference, which is based on probability theory, is the process of generalizing from samples to populations from which the samples are derived. The tools of statistics help identify valid generalizations and those that are likely to stand up under further study. Inference testing is particularly critical for evidence-based practice since this structure of knowledge is intended to be used to inform the development of standard interventions with predictable outcomes. Inferential statistics include statistical techniques for evaluating many properties of populations, such as differences among sets of data and predicting scores on one variable by knowing about others.

Two major concepts are fundamental to understanding inferential statistics: confidence levels and confidence intervals. Because inference focuses on estimates and predictions about a larger group from observations drawn from a subset of that group, the extent to which observations of the sample are accurate for all members of the larger group is determined by conducting these procedures. By specifying a confidence level and a confidence interval, a prediction is made regarding the expected range of values and their accuracy for the population, respectively. This set of predictions also specifies the degree of acceptable error and guides the interpretation of statistical findings (Petrović, n.d.).

A *confidence interval* is defined as the range of values observed in a sample and the expectation that this range accurately reflects the population from which the sample was selected. Consider the following example. In the elder mobility device intermediate outcome assessment, a sample was selected from a population of elders who had abandoned prescribed mobility devices. Two months into the intervention, consisting of being given the newly designed device and a fitness plan, monitoring revealed that 80% are using this equipment, and 60% are using it in the prescribed fitness plan. Should the social work team expect that 80% and 60% respectively of the population would follow the same pattern? The sample percentages would be a best guess, but they are derived from a subset of population members. Therefore, the estimates should be expanded to specify intervals of scores to include the "true value" of the larger population—in this case, an interval of 70% to 90% and 50% to 70%, respectively.

However, deriving a confidence interval is only the first step. Because probability theory underpins inferential statistics, specifying a confidence interval must contain a statement about the level of uncertainty as well. A *confidence level* is simply the degree of certainty (or expected uncertainty) that the confidence interval is accurate for the population. This interval is set by the investigator (Frankfort-Nachmias & Leon-Guerrero, 2014). In the previous example, if the social worker specified a confidence level of 99%, that number would indicate 99% certainty that 70% to 90% of the population would be using adaptive equipment, and 50% to 70% would be using it as specified in the fitness plan, 3 months after discharge from the rehabilitation unit. The degree of assuredness, or level of confidence, that sample values are accurate for the population is what constitutes the confidence level.

The example above inferentially tests only the single variables of use and compliance. However, changes over time, differences between groups, associations, and multivariate modeling can be subjected to inference as well. In all cases, the aim is to generalize from the sample to the population.

In the example above, note that the sample was not randomly selected. Recall that we discussed random sampling in Chapter 10. Because randomization is anchored on probability theory, it is one of the basic principles of inference testing. However, resulting from the difficulty in obtaining random samples in examined practice, social workers often use inference testing and agree to violate the randomization criterion. When random sample selection is not possible, the social worker can treat the group tested as a population, and thus inference testing is not necessary, or the social worker may identify the lack of random sampling as a limitation of the knowledge. Because of their ability to answer predictive questions, inferential statistics are often used without randomization, in which case, sharing the knowledge must state this omission so that it is transparent.

How to Use Inferential Statistics

To use an inferential statistic, five action processes are followed in sequence.

Action 1: State the Hypothesis

Stating a hypothesis is both simple and complex. In experimental-type designs that test the differences between population and sample, a working hypothesis or hunch of what is expected is stated. For statistical analysis, however, a working hypothesis is transformed into the null hypothesis, a statement of no difference between or among groups.

In the example above, the social worker hopes to reject (formally referred to in the language of probability theory as fail to accept) the null hypothesis, thereby finding a difference between the sample and the population. Such findings will reveal that the intervention has most likely changed the sample so that its members are no longer representative of the population of elders who abandoned mobility devices. Why is the null hypothesis used? Theoretically, it is impossible to prove a finding. Thus, when using probability, it is only possible to negate the null hypothesis or the hypothesis of "no difference." Nonsupport for the null hypothesis is similar to stating a double negative. If it is not "not raining," it logically follows that it is most likely raining. Applied to the inquiry, if there is no "no difference among groups," differences among groups can be assumed, although not proven (Frankfort-Nachmias & Leon-Guerrero, 2014).

Action 2: Select a Significance Level

A level of significance defines how rare or unlikely the sample data must be before the null hypothesis will fail to be accepted. The level of significance indicates degree of confidence that the findings are not attributed to chance. For example, selecting a significance level of 0.05 denotes 95% confidence that the statistical findings did not occur by chance. Similarly, a confidence level of 0.1 indicates that the findings may be caused by chance 1 of every 10 times. A smaller number indicates more confidence in the findings and improves the credibility of the results. Because of the nature of probability theory, findings can never be 100% accurate, and thus, research cannot prove but can only support a claim within a degree of assuredness. Significance levels are selected by the researcher on the basis of sample size, level of measurement, and conventional norms in the literature. As a general rule, the larger the sample size, the smaller the numerical value in the level of significance. If the sample size is small, the risk in obtaining a study group that is not highly representative of the population from which it was selected is increased, and thus the confidence level as well as credibility drops (Frankfort-Nachmias & Leon-Guerrero, 2014).

One-Tailed and Two-Tailed Levels of Significance

Consider the shape and distribution of scores in a normal curve (see Figures 12.3, 12.6, and 12.7). The extreme scores occurring to either the left or the right of the bell shape are referred to as "tails." If a hypothesis is nondirectional, it usually assumes that extreme scores can occur at either end of the curve or in either tail. If this is the case, a two-tailed test of significance will be used. If, on the other hand, the hypothesis is directional, a one-tailed test of significance is indicated. In this case, the portion of the curve in which statistical values are considered significant is on one side of the curve only, either the right or the left tail. It is easier to obtain statistical significance with a one-tailed statistical test, but the risk of a Type I error (see below) is high in this case. A two-tailed test is a more stringent statistical approach (DePoy & Gitlin, 2011).

Type I Errors

A *Type I error*, also called an "alpha error," refers to failing to accept the null hypothesis when it is true. In other words, significance is claimed when, if the entire population were measured, there would be no difference. Because the probability of making a Type I error is equal to the level of significance, reducing the level of significance will reduce the chances of making this type of error. Unfortunately, as the probability of making a Type I error is reduced, the potential to make a Type II error increases (Trochim, 2006).

Type II Errors

A *Type II error,* also called a "beta error," occurs if the null hypothesis is mistakenly accepted when it should be not be. In other words, differences fail to be detected when they have occurred. The probability of making a Type II error is not as apparent as making a Type I error. The likelihood of making a Type II error is based in large part on the power of the statistic to find group differences (Trochim, 2006).

Action 3: Compute a Calculated Value

To test a hypothesis, a statistical formula is chosen and calculated. The selection is based on the research question, level of measurement, number of groups being described or compared, and sample size. Inferential statistics fall into two primary classifications: parametric and nonparametric procedures. Both are similar in that they (1) test hypotheses, (2) involve a level of significance, (3) require a calculated value, (4) compare the calculated value against a critical value, and (5) conclude with decisions about the hypotheses. But each differs according to the principles for use (DePoy & Gitlin, 2016).

Parametric Statistics

Parametric statistics are mathematical formulas that test hypotheses on the basis of three assumptions. First, data must be derived from a population in which the characteristic to be studied is distributed normally (in the shape of a bell curve). Second, if more than one group is involved, the variances within the groups must be homogeneous. Homogeneity is displayed by the scores in one group having approximately the same degree of variability as the scores in another group. Third, the data must be measured at the interval level (DePoy & Gitlin, 2016).

Parametric statistics can test the extent to which numerous findings about a sample are reflected in the population. For example, some statistics test differences between only two groups, whereas others test differences among many groups. Some statistics test main effects (i.e., the direct effect of one variable on another), whereas other statistics have the capacity to test both main and interactive effects (i.e., the combined effects that several variables have on another variable). Furthermore, some statistical action processes test group differences only one time, whereas others test differences over time. Because parametric tests are the most robust, they are the tools of choice when possible (DePoy & Gitlin, 2016).

Although we cannot present the full spectrum of parametric statistics, in this chapter we examine three statistical tests used frequently in examined practice: t-test, one-way analysis of variance (ANOVA), and multiple comparisons (DePoy & Gilson, 2009). These techniques are used to compare two or more groups to determine whether the differences in the means of the groups are large enough to assume that the corresponding population means are different.

t-Test

The t-test, the most basic statistical procedure in this grouping, is used to compare two sample means on one variable (DePoy & Gitlin, 2016). Consider the following example. Because they wanted to know if mobility device use differed between men and women in the needs assessment, the social work team conducted a t-test in which they divided the sample into two separate groups by gender (male and female) and hypothesized no difference between genders. The null hypothesis was accepted, and thus it was concluded that no difference in use between men and women was apparent. Informed by this knowledge, the social work team concluded that it was not necessary to develop gender-specific devices.

Three principles influence the t-test. First, the larger the sample size, the less likely a difference between two means is a consequence of an error in sampling. Second, the larger the observed difference between two means, the less likely the difference is a consequence of a sampling error. Third, the smaller the variance, it is less likely that the difference between the means is also a consequence of a sampling error (Trochim, 2006).

The t-test can be used only when the means of two groups are compared. Similar to all parametric statistics, t-tests must be calculated with interval level data and should be selected when the assumptions for the use of parametric statistics have not been violated. But once again, recall the example above in which the sample was not randomly selected from the population, even when a primary assumption of parametric statistical use is randomization. Because the t-test is a powerful indicator of group difference, it is frequently used even when randomization is violated. The t-test yields a t value that is reported as "$t = x, p = 0.05$"; x is the calculated t value, and p is the level of significance. When the calculated value of t is smaller than the computed "critical" value at the level of probability selected, a significant finding (one not caused by change) is affirmed.

There are two types of t-tests. One type is for independent or uncorrelated data, and the other type is for dependent or correlated data. Independent data sets are created when the two comparison groups are distinct from one another as in the example above examining gender differences in mobility device use. Thus, each set of scores is generated once. Correlated data emerge from the same group generating scores on two occasions, such as pre- and posttesting.

One-Way Analysis of Variance

The "one-way" ANOVA, or "single-factor" ANOVA, (also referred to as the F test) serves the same purpose as the t-test but can accommodate more than two groups. The null hypothesis for an ANOVA, as in the t-test, states that there is no difference between or among the means of two or more groups. The procedure is also similar to the t-test. The original raw data are entered into a formula to obtain a calculated value. The resulting calculated value is compared against the critical value, and the null hypothesis is not accepted if the calculated value is larger than the tabled critical value or accepted if the calculated value is less than the critical value. Computing the one-way ANOVA yields an F value that may be reported as "$F(a,b) = x, p = 0.05$"; x is the computed F value, a is group degrees of freedom, b is sample degrees of freedom, and p is level of significance. *Degrees of freedom* refers to the "number of values, which are free to vary" in a data set. These are linked to sample size and number of groups being compared (Frankfort-Nachmias & Leon-Guerrero, 2014).

There are many variations of ANOVA. Some test relationships when variables have multiple levels, and some examine complex relationships among multiple levels of variables. If three gender groups were compared on the elder mobility device needs assessment, male, female, and LGBT, the one-way ANOVA would be the statistic of choice.

Multiple Comparisons

When a one-way ANOVA is used to compare three or more groups, a significant F value means that the null hypothesis fails to be accepted. However, the F value, in itself, does not indicate which of the group means is significantly different; it only indicates a difference. Several procedures, referred to as multiple comparisons (also referred to as **post hoc** comparisons because they are computed following a significant F-test) are used to determine which group difference is greater than the others. These procedures are capable of identifying which group or groups differ among those being compared.

Nonparametric Statistics

Nonparametric statistics are formulas used to test hypotheses when the data violate one or more of the assumptions for parametric procedures. If variance in the population is skewed or asymmetrical, if the data generated from measures are ordinal or nominal, or if the size of the sample is small, the researcher should select a nonparametric statistic.

Each of the parametric tests mentioned has a nonparametric analogue. For example, the nonparametric analogue of the t-test for categorical data is the chi-square. The chi-square test is used when the data are nominal and when computation of a mean is not possible. This procedure uses proportions and percentages to evaluate group differences. The Mann-Whitney U test, a powerful nonparametric test, is similar to the t-test in that it is designed to test differences between groups, but it is used with data that are ordinal.

Action 4: Obtain a Critical Value

Before the widespread use of computer analytic software, critical values could be found in tables appended at the end of statistics books. The *critical value* is a criterion related to the level of significance, indicating what number must be derived from the statistical formula to have a significant finding at the selected level of probability (Frankfort-Nachmias & Leon-Guerrero, 2014). However, as we noted, although using the same logic, statistical software reports findings differently. Rather than identifying a probability level and then examining the critical value, the software will indicate the probability at which the calculated value is a critical value (IBM, n.d.). So, rather than looking at the calculated value, significant findings are identified by searching for levels of probability that are equal to or smaller in value than the selected p value. For example, the t-test for gender differences in the elder mobility needs assessment yielded a probability of 0.13, a probability much higher than 0.05 chosen by the social work team. Thus the finding was not compelling enough to assert a difference.

Action 5: Reject or Fail to Reject the Null Hypothesis

The final action process is the decision about whether to reject or fail to reject the null hypothesis. Recall that the sequence begins with the selection of a statistical formula and level of significance. The formula is then calculated, yielding a numeric value and a probability. The probability value, not the calculated statistical value, is the final step in the decision process. As noted above, if the probability is equal to or smaller than the criterion selected in Step 1, the finding is significant and *vice versa*.

LEVEL 3: ASSOCIATIONS AND RELATIONSHIPS

The third major role of statistics is the identification of relationships between and among variables and whether knowledge about one set of data allows inference or prediction of characteristics about another set of data. These statistical tests include factor analyses, discriminant function analysis, multiple regression, and modeling techniques. Common among these tests is that all seek to predict one or more outcomes from multiple variables. Some of the techniques can further identify time factors, interactive effects, and complex relationships among multiple independent and dependent variables.

To illustrate this level of statistical analysis, consider the elder mobility device needs assessment. Given the complexity of why people abandon devices, the prediction of maximum use is not an easy task. In the literature, geography, diagnostic condition, degree of mobility impairment, age, activity level, social support, and perception of stigma, among other variables, have been theorized as influencing device use. To analyze this complex data set, multiple regression, a statistical procedure that can reveal predictive relationships and their strength, was selected. Multiple regression can predict the effect of multiple independent (predictor) variables on one dependent (outcome or criterion) variable but only when all variables are measured at the interval level (recall the brief discussion above about assigning level of measurement). In the case of nominal data such as gender, dummy variables can be created at the interval level of measurement. We refer you to Frankfort-Nachmias & Leon-Guerrero (2014) for further discussion of how this technique is conducted and used.

Discriminant function analysis is a similar test used with categorical or nominal dependent variables. Other techniques, such as modeling strategies, are frequently used to understand complex system relationships. These techniques, once learned, are simple to compute using software such as SPSS (IBM, n.d.) and even freeware such as PSPP (GNU PSPP, 2016) hosted online. In particular, these statistics are very useful when surveys with large samples are used to generate need statements. We refer you to online and print resources for a more detailed discussion of these appended techniques.

Geospatial Analysis: GIS

Geospatial analysis is a very useful tool in examined practice. This approach recognizes the role of place in knowledge generation and use. Consider the elder mobility device project once again here to illustrate. While geospatial analysis was not used, it would have been extremely valuable to understand the role not only of physical geography in creating barriers for device use but also of urban-rural differences that might suggest that different device styles would be important to consider. If, for example, a device was prescribed to a farmer who had no access to smooth ground, the use of a wheeled walker would not fit the safety needs of this individual. Or perhaps stigma would be perceived differently in diverse neighborhoods in which the visual takes on importance.

Geographic information system (GIS) is a computer-assisted action process that has the capacity to handle and analyze multiple sources of data, providing that they are relevant to spatial presentation. GIS relies on two overarching spatial structures, raster and vector. Raster GIS carves geography into mutually exclusive spaces and then examines the attributes of these. This type of analysis would be relevant to questions about comparative attributes of specific locations. Vector GIS is relevant to determining characteristics of a space that is defined by points and the lines that "connect the dots" (ESRI, n.d.).

GIS maps are constructed from data tables, and because GIS software allows the importation of data from frequently used spreadsheets and databases such as Excel, Access, and even SPSS, combining visual and statistical analytic techniques is a relatively simple and powerful action process. Below, we provide an example of the use of GIS in examined practice. In order to determine what type of prevention needs were present in rural communities in a large rural state, GIS analysis was used to examine substance abuse rates as well as the location of substance abuse services. The initial problem statement preceding this inquiry was "drug abuse and addiction are increasing." From this statement, a problem map was created pointing to the need to address both causes and consequences. The GIS study was enacted to identify the areas of "high abuse" and services within them. Substance abuse data generated by the state and locations of services were located on state vector and raster mapping.

As the maps below indicate, small population areas with limited services had disproportionately high rates of abuse. Moreover, areas close to the Canadian border were also identified as high abuse locations. From the GIS analysis, different prevention programs were developed and implemented in different geographic areas. For more detail on this valuable set of analytic techniques, we refer you to the multiple websites and texts on GIS for specific techniques.

Other Visual Analysis Action Processes

Mapping is only one type of visual analysis. In statistical analysis, image is primarily used to represent numeric data (Orrell, 2012). Visuals such as graphs and charts have been used to display and analyze information since the inception of statistics in the mid-seventeenth century. As illustrated above, similar to numeric analysis, visuals such as pie charts and polygons reduce data to comprehensible forms. Consider the normal curve, polygons, and bar charts. Each tells an analytic story, translating statistical analysis into a visual form. According to Tufte (2001), "of all methods for analyzing and communicating statistical information, well-designed data graphics are usually the simplest and at the same time, the most powerful (p. 9)." Visuals can be used for many levels of analysis, from simple

Figure 12.9   Frequency of Primary Programs by Minor Civil Divisions

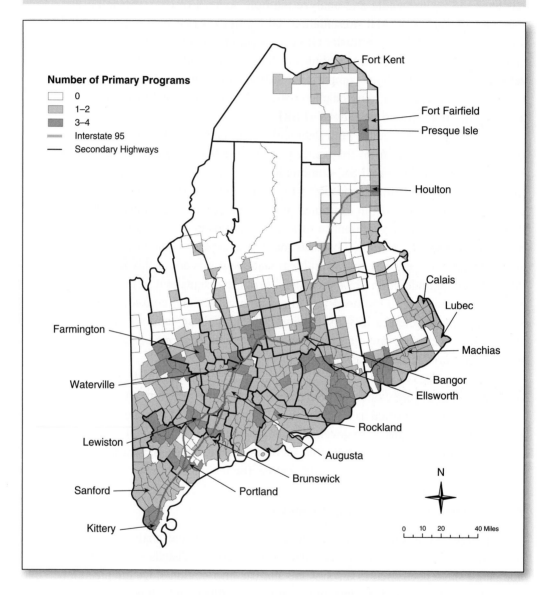

univariate description through multivariate prediction. One of the more recent types of visual analysis involves big data previously introduced. With the widespread use of computers, numeric data can be transformed instantaneously into a variety of images (Sicignano, 2012). As an example, Photo 12.1 depicts the complex web of networking on Facebook.

Photo 12.1 Complex Web of Networking on Facebook

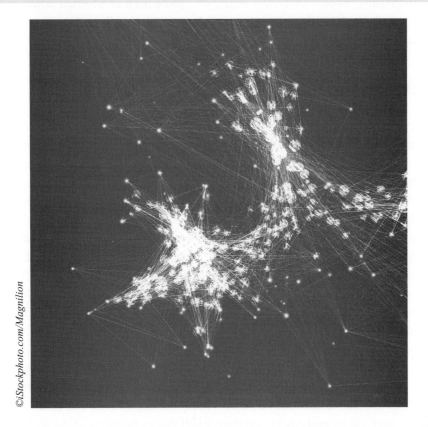

©iStockphoto.com/Magnilion

In summary so far, we realize that even this short section on data analysis is complex but also realize that it presents only basic data analytic strategies with a smattering of more advanced action processes introduced. Visuals in presenting data are irreplaceable as they can be manipulated for emphasis as well as recognition by those who are intimidated or not knowledgeable in statistical symbols.

The selection of technique and the methods of sharing are guided by purpose, social worker skill, the research questions and the audience intended as recipients of the knowledge generated. We now turn to naturalistic data analysis, a process that is distinct from statistical analysis in logic structure and sequence.

Naturalistic Data Analysis

Unlike experimental-type analysis, naturalistic analytic activities tend to be dynamic and iterative processes. Thus, although all analytical strategies reflect a logical approach, there is no planned sequence to be followed in naturalistic inquiry. Because diverse analytical strategies can be used at different points in the process, analysis depends on the type of data that are collected (e.g. narrative, observational, visual, musical, diaries, or other data formats).

STRATEGIES AND STAGES IN NATURALISTIC ANALYSIS

Many purposes inform the analytical process in naturalistic inquiry. The selection of a particular approach to analysis depends on the primary purpose, scope, and design in each step of examined practice. Some naturalistic analytical strategies are extremely unstructured, such as in phenomenology, heuristic approaches, and some ethnographic studies. Other analytical strategies are highly structured, as in grounded theory. Still other types of naturalistic inquiry may incorporate numerical descriptions and may vary in the type of analysis used, as in certain forms of ethnography, endogenous approaches, and participatory action research. Further, some forms of naturalistic inquiry are highly interpretive but use a specific analytical strategy, such as in life history or object reading. Each analytical approach provides a different vantage point from which understanding of the phenomenon under study is developed.

Although each type of naturalistic design uses a different analytical strategy, the common processes can be conceptualized as occurring in two overlapping, interrelated stages. The first stage, occurring at the inception of the inquiry, involves the attempt to make immediate sense of what is being observed and heard. At this stage, the purpose of analysis is descriptive and theory building, yielding hunches or initial ideas that guide subsequent data collection. The second stage, following the conclusion of data collection, involves a more formal review and analysis of all the information that has been collected.

STAGE ONE: INCEPTION OF INQUIRY

As discussed in previous chapters, the process of naturalistic inquiry is iterative. Within Stage 1, analysis occurs immediately as the study is initiated. Analysis is the basis from which all subsequent decisions are made: who to interview, what to observe, where to find information, and which information to further explore. Each collection-analysis sequence builds successively on the previous action.

This initial set of analytical steps involves four integrated thinking and action processes: (1) deliberate thinking about the data, (2) developing categories, and (3) finding taxonomies.

Deliberate Thinking

In most designs, one of the first analytical efforts requires active engagement in the intentional search of an organizational system that emerges from initial data. This step guides as well as provides a scaffold for subsequent data collection and analysis. If existing theory is used as the basis to guide open-ended data collection, we would classify the inquiry as mixed-method, in that a deductive thinking process is used (DePoy & Gitlin, 2016).

Consider the example of the needs assessment in which small business owners are surveyed and interviewed. Despite the interviews being open-ended, the social worker is looking for attitudes as already defined in theoretical literature. It is therefore possible to use both inductive as well as deductive reasoning in that the social worker is open to unexpected insights not theorized as attitudinal. Or the process may be abductive as well. In that case, the social worker begins inductively but then with some initial information may formulate a working hypothesis, which is examined for fit with the data generated from interview (Fetterman, 2009).

Developing Categories

The second step common to many designs in naturalistic inquiry is the development of categories in which data can be placed. This basic action process in naturalistic analysis guides examination of data without imposing concepts, labels, categories, or meanings *a priori*. Thus, categories emerge from inductive interactions with the data and the initial information that is obtained and synthesized. Preliminary categories are developed and become the tools used to sort and classify subsequent information as it is received (Miles, Huberman, & Saldaña, 2014).

Categories can classify people, objects, concepts, meanings, social and cultural traditions, and so forth. For example, in the mobility device project needs assessment, emergent categories from interview data about the causes for abandonment included:

Lack of perceived need

Inconvenience

Inability to use

Appearance as barrier

Perception of dependency

People stare

Pitied

The first level of analysis involved reading transcripts until statements emerged that could be grouped by commonality. The analytical strategy involved using a pile-sorting technique (Anthrostrategist, 2011) in which two members of the team independently read each statement about the devices generated by elders in interviews. These comments were independently sorted into categories based on perceived similarities and differences. The categories reflected the underlying topics expressed in statements. (A statement about a "walker" device, such as, "if it did not look so ugly, I might use it," and similar types of comments were categorized as "appearance as barrier"). Next, the two analyzers compared their summary lists of the categories. Differences were discussed, and the identified categories were negotiated and refined. A final comprehensive list was prepared and reviewed by the team. This process yielded seven basic topics or categories of meaning and subcategories as we discuss below in the section on taxonomy.

As the data collection activity proceeds, the original categories are used as the basis for analyzing new data. New data either are classified into existing categories or may serve to modify or create new categories to depict the phenomenon of interest accurately (Miles et al., 2014). Data placed in the descriptive categories answer "who, what, where, and when" queries and do not involve interpretation. Analytical or more interpretive categories answer "how and why" queries (DePoy & Gitlin, 2016). Any one datum can be categorized in several ways. Thus, cross-coding (referencing the same excerpt or piece of information in multiple ways) adds another level of complexity to the coding process (Miles et al., 2014). Consider the appearance category for example. This level of analysis is both descriptive and interprets meaning of the device to the user.

The development of categories is accomplished through repeated review and examination of narrative, video, object, image, or other types of information that have been obtained. Codes are assigned to each category such that diverse analytic methods can be used. Computer software programs (e.g., Nudist, Zyindex, Ethnograph, NVivo, Atlas.ti) facilitate the coding process for large data sets and can accelerate the analysis as well. These programs automatically assign codes to similar passages or keywords first identified by the analyzer. For example, the software may be configured to assign the code "descriptive appearance barrier" to every reference with color and shape in it. Keywords can be selected based on categories that arise from the data set, and the computer can be programmed to assign codes automatically based on a keyword list.

Developing Taxonomies

A *taxonomy* is a system of categories and relationships. Taxonomies have also been called "typologies" and "mindmaps" (Miles et al., 2014). Problem mapping (presented in Chapter 2) is a prime example of a taxonomy as it provides a relational visual image of categories of cause and consequence (DePoy & Gilson, 2009). Developing a taxonomy, referred to as **taxonomic analysis**, comprises two processes: (1) organizing or grouping similar or related categories into larger categories and (2) identifying differences between sets of subcategories and larger or overarching categories.

Related subcategories are grouped together in the taxonomic process. For example, basic categories such as "whales" and "dogs" belong to the larger category of "animals"; basic categories such as "blocks" and "dolls" belong to the larger category of "toys." In a taxonomy, sets of categories are grouped on the basis of similarities of members. In the elder mobility device needs assessment study shown in Figure 12.10, the following taxonomy emerged.

This simple taxonomy reflects the analysis of statements from the interviews and provides a rich image of the relationship of nonuse to appearance. Also illustrated are the divisions (within the thinly lined black borders) of the major themes (contained within the borders identified by heavily lined borders.).

STAGE TWO: FORMAL REPORT PREPARATION

Analysis is a critical and active component of the data collection process in naturalistic inquiry. As noted, it begins early in the action process of data collection and continues after the completion of data collection. The main objective of this latter action process is to consolidate the understandings and impressions developed earlier by preparing one or more products to be shared as part of social work knowledge. In interpretive analysis, this reporting effort involves a self-reflective process.

Figure 12.10   Taxonomy From Elder Mobility Device Needs Assessment Study

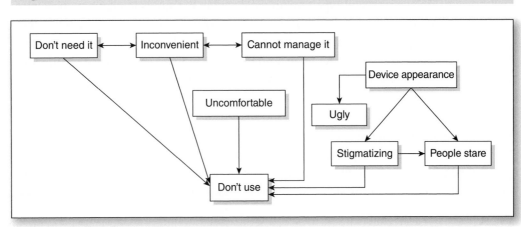

The ease of Stage 2 action across all analytic strategies in this tradition often depends on how well the social worker initially organizes and cross-references the voluminous records and notes. In this more formal analytical stage, the materials and refined categories, taxonomies, and themes are reexamined; interpreted if indicated; refined; and illustrated with quotations, images, or other types of examples from the data. Selections of exemplars are both illustrative and chosen for depth of understanding. Examples function to

1. ensure adequate and compelling representation of the interpretation or themes to be conveyed,

2. reflect the voices and experiences being referenced, and

3. accurately depict the context in which the data are embedded (Miles et al., 2014).

In the final stage, the social worker moves beyond each datum or piece of information to suggest an understanding of the "whole" through theory development or a detailed presentation of the themes and general principles that emerge.

ACCURACY AND RIGOR IN NATURALISTIC ANALYSIS

Given the flexibility and fluidity of this tradition, questions regarding the accuracy and rigor of naturalistic strategies have been raised, in particular by investigators and professionals who hold clinical trials and true experimentation as the primary type of method to develop evidence-based practice. As indicated throughout the book, we see both experimental-type and naturalistic traditions as interpretative in some sense. The difference lies in what is interpreted and when the interpretation occurs. In experimental-type thinking and action, the aim is to eliminate bias introduced by research procedures and investigator bias. However, we agree with others (Sim, 2011) who would argue that the viewpoints and preferences of the investigator influence knowledge the moment theory is determined and chosen as important for testing. Thus, the interpretive piece of experimental-type inquiry occurs even before the literature review begins and then proceeds through the selection of theory and method. Conclusions interpret the analysis in light of the specific theory tested. In naturalistic inquiry, interpretation occurs throughout the process, but unlike experimental-type approaches, is central to the process. However, experimental-type thinking and action by the nature of the sequenced design and use of numbers to standardize analysis strive for reliability such that replication of the work under similar circumstances results in similar findings. Such is not the case with naturalistic designs that may yield vastly different interpretations of a data set. So the question about whether the naturalistic findings reflect the object or subject of inquiry or the opinions of the investigator must be addressed.

As we presented in previous chapters, trustworthiness and credibility are naturalistic analogues to the rigor criteria in experimental-type design. Using a rather structured approach, strategies by which confidence in the accuracy of the findings from naturalistic inquiry can be enhanced are followed (Denzin & Lincoln, 2011). The concern with credibility of an account or interpretive scheme is similar to the issue of internal validity in experimental-type designs. In reading a report involving naturalistic inquiry, two primary questions are asked: (1) To what extent are the biases and personal perspectives of the investigator identified and considered in the data analysis and interpretation? and (2) What actions have been taken to enhance credibility?

Six Basic Actions Are Conducted for This Purpose

Triangulation, more recently referred to as *crystallization* as discussed above, is a basic aspect of data gathering that also shapes the action process of data analysis (Ellingson, 2008). In triangulation, one source of information is checked against one or more alternative types of sources to determine the accuracy of hypothetical understandings and to develop complexity of understanding. As in the example of the elder mobility device project, the approach to triangulation involved the comparison of a narrative from an interview with published materials from visual object reading research. Triangulation enables the investigator to validate (or not) a particular finding by examining whether different sources provide convergent information. The term *crystallization* has been applied to reflect the multidimensional understanding that occurs as a result of the comparison of different and diverse sources to explain a phenomenon.

Saturation refers to the point at which an investigator has obtained sufficient information from data collection. We have already discussed this process in Chapter 11.

As discussed previously, *member checking* is a technique similar to active listening. The social worker checks an assumption or a particular understanding with one or more informants. Affirmation of a particular insight from a participant strengthens the credibility of the interpretation. This technique is often used throughout the data collection process. It is also introduced in the formal stage of analysis to confirm the accuracy of specific accounts and investigator impressions (Denzin & Lincoln, 2008).

Reflexivity

As we have indicated throughout the book, reflexivity is central to the examined practice model in all steps but named specifically in the intervention phase, given the importance of use of self and constant monitoring in social work. As previously defined, reflexivity refers to examination of the self and context. In his classic work, Schon (1983) integrated the concept of reflexivity into professional practice by characterizing the reflective practitioner as an individual whose activity involves regular and deliberate self-monitoring and correction. We borrowed reflexivity from Schon (1983), who appropriated it from naturalistic inquiry. In inquiry, reflexivity therefore is the process of examining the influence of the investigator, observer, or interpreter on the knowledge created. The inability to eliminate bias is therefore not considered a limitation in naturalistic knowledge development as the investigator identifies his or her fingerprints in the knowledge process.

Another way an investigator can increase accuracy is by using an **audit trail**, or a detailed and transparent path of thinking and coding decisions (Creswell & Clark, 2011). Revealing logic and support for interpretations is one of the beauties of all systematic knowledge generation in any tradition as it allows the receiver to evaluate the development process, not just the final claims.

Peer debriefing involves peers in the analytical process. A group of peers reviews an audit trail and emerging findings to evaluate the logical structure and adequacy of evidence to support claims. Peer debriefing may occur at various junctures in the analytical process (Denzin & Lincoln, 2011).

Some Words About Mixed-Method Analysis

Mixing analytic methods is dependent on the nature of data, the process by which they are collected, and the logic structure applied to making sense of information. In order to mix analytic methods, data must be available that lend themselves to diverse approaches. For example, it is not feasible to mix analytic traditions within an exclusive true-experimental design.

Mixing analytic methods may occur within naturalistic inquiry itself by using diverse techniques such as thematic analysis and object reading, or it may occur across traditions through integrating statistical and inductive strategies. In Chapter 13, we illustrate mixed-method analysis in each of the exemplars.

SUMMARY

This chapter presented data analytic techniques across the three traditions. Experimental-type designs rely on numeric analysis, each which tells a different story about a distribution of numbers within and between groups. From description, inference, or the expansion of what is expanded from a sample to the population from which it was selected, can be accomplished. Inference occurs with a degree of certainty and thus statistical analysis cannot prove or disprove hypotheses. Rather they can accept or fail to accept null hypotheses within a degree of confidence set by the investigator.

Naturalistic analysis co-occurs with data collection. Consistent with inductive logic structure, analysis is iterative and fluid. For the most part, analysis seeks themes emergent from data, although fitting theories to data may also occur.

Both experimental-type and naturalistic traditions require the application of rigor criteria relevant to their own traditions.

We concluded with analysis within mixed-method designs.

The main points in this chapter are as follows:

1. Statistical analysis tells a story in numbers but does not prove theory.

2. Although violating the criterion of randomization, inferential statistics are frequently used without random sampling to examine group differences in scores generated in a study. Limitations of this approach should be noted in sharing findings.

3. Visuals used to present data are irreplaceable as they can be manipulated for emphasis as well as recognition by those who are intimidated or not knowledgeable in statistical symbols.

4. Final data analysis is followed by reporting findings, entering the sharing phase of examined practice.

5. Naturalistic analytic activities tend to be dynamic and iterative. These processes are interspersed with data collection.

REFERENCES

Anthrostrategist. (2011). *Pile sorting techniques for ethnographers*. Retrieved from http://anthrostrategy.com/2011/08/06/pile-sorting-techniques-for-ethnographers

Creswell, J., & Clark, V. P. (2011). *Designing and conducting mixed methods research*. Thousand Oaks, CA: Sage.

Denzin, N., & Lincoln, Y. (2008). *Collecting and interpreting qualitative materials*. Thousand Oaks, CA: Sage.

Denzin, N. K., & Lincoln, Y. S. (2011). *SAGE handbook of qualitative research* (4th ed.). Thousand Oaks, CA.

DePoy, E., & Gilson, S. (2009). *Evaluation practice*. Belmont, CA: Brooks-Cole.

DePoy, E., & Gitlin, L. (2011). *Introduction to research* (4th ed.). St Louis, MO: Elsevier.

DePoy, E., & Gitlin, L. (2016). *Introduction to research* (5th ed.). St. Louis, MO: Elsevier.

Ellingson, L. (2008). *Engaging crystallization in qualitative research.* Thousand Oaks, CA: Sage.

ESRI. (n.d.). *What is GIS?* Retrieved from http://www.esri.com/what-is-gis

Fetterman, D. M. (2009). *Ethnography: Step-by-step.* Thousand Oaks, CA: Sage.

Frankfort-Nachmias, C., & Leon-Guerrero, A. (2014). *Social statistics for a diverse society.* Thousand Oaks, CA: Sage.

GNU PSPP. (2014). Retrieved from https://www.gnu.org/software/pspp

Gravetter, F. J., & Wallnau, L. B. (2011). *Essentials of statistics for the behavioral sciences.* Belmont, CA: Wadsworth.

IBM. (n.d.). *SPSS 22.0 software.* Retrieved from http://www-01.ibm.com/software/analytics/spss/products/data-collection

Miles, M. B., Huberman, A. M., & Saldaña, J. (2014). *Qualitative data analysis: A methods sourcebook* (3rd ed.). Thousand Oaks, CA: Sage.

Orrell, D. (2012). *Truth or beauty.* New Haven, CT: Yale University Press.

Pelham, B. (2013). *Intermediate statistics.* Thousand Oaks, CA: Sage.

Petrović, M. (n.d.). *Calculators :: Statistics calculators :: Standard deviation Calculator.* Retrieved from http://www.mathportal.org/calculators/statistics-calculator/standard-deviation-calculator.php

Popovich, P. M., Scherbaum, C. A., Scherbaum, K. L., & Polinko, N. (2003). The assessment of attitudes toward individuals with disabilities in the workplace. *The Journal of Psychology: Interdisciplinary and Applied, 137*(2): 163–77. Retrieved from http://www.tandfonline.com/doi/abs/10.1080/00223980309600606?journalCode=vjrl20

Schon, D. (1983). *The reflexive practitioner.* New York, NY: Basic Books.

Sicignano, M. (2012, December 21). *Big data analysis and quality improvement in social services.* Retrieved from http://www.socialjusticesolutions.org/2012/12/21/big-data-analysis-and-quality-improvement-in-social-services

Sim, S. (2011). *The Routledge companion to postmodernism.* London, UK: Routledge.

Trochim, W. (2006). *Inferential statistics.* Retrieved from http://www.socialresearchmethods.net/kb/statinf.php

Tufte, E. (2001). *The visual display of quantitative information.* Cheshire, CT: Graphics Press.

University of Surrey. (n.d.). *Formulae for the standard deviation.* Retrieved from http://libweb.surrey.ac.uk/library/skills/Number%20Skills%20Leicester/page_19.htm

Yau, N. (2011). *Visualize this: The flowing data guide to design, visualization, and statistics.* Indianapolis, IN: Wiley.

Chapter 13

PUTTING THE MODEL TO WORK

M uch conceptual and applied ground has been traveled in this book. In this final chapter, the examined practice examples that were used to illustrate each thinking and action process are reconstituted and integrated throughout a full sequence. Before the examples make their final appearance, the principles that guide examined practice, introduced in Chapter 1, are reviewed.

Table 13.1   Principles of Examined Practice

1. Social work practice and systematically developed knowledge (following diverse traditions in research) are inseparable.

2. Professional knowledge building and use are value-based and thus evaluative.

3. Research in social work is evaluative of the extent to which and how social problems are encountered and resolved.

4. Engaging in examined practice in all contexts and domains is an ethical obligation for all social workers.

As encountered in each chapter, by now it should be clear that social work thinking and action are equivalent to systematic thinking and action. Social workers act (or should act) on the basis of well-developed knowledge and, thus, in making practice decisions, dip into this reservoir for guidance as well as to replenish it. However, as indicated throughout, given that social work is a value-based profession, social work thinking and action occur within evaluative boundaries. Thus, the knowledge used and developed as examined practice proceeds is professionally evaluative as well. And, of course, examined practice asserts the ethical obligation for all social workers to be engaged in systematic thinking and action that uses legitimate knowledge and to generate and share it throughout all practice and professional activity.

While the examples are presented according to the sequence that organized the book, recall that examined practice is not linear but rather is overlapping and not always neat. For instructive purposes, however, each example is presented in order from problem identification through outcome and final sharing. As we address below, however, all social work action within the examined practice model is initiated to resolve or change a social problem or situation. From the articulated problem, many needs can arise to change or respond to the problem. Once a need is empirically verified, goal-directed professional activity is enacted, during and following which an assessment of the value of action processes and outcomes is made and, in this model, shared. As a result of sharing, relevant and contemporary social work knowledge is continuously built.

THEMES

Several important themes were woven throughout the book. We summarize them here. First and foremost, social work practice is based on legitimate professional sources of knowledge, those that are generated and supported with systematic evidence. While the nature of the evidence is not prescriptive, systematically developed knowledge is required.

Second, examined practice begins with the premise that social work is practiced to resolve or make changes to social problems, even when not clearly articulated or cast as problems. It is therefore obligatory for social work at any point in the examined practice sequence to specify what is to be accomplished, changed, or improved by social work activity.

Third, purpose emerges in every activity. Intended purposes shape social work practice and the knowledge that both supports and emerges from it.

Fourth, social work occurs within context. Therefore, knowledge used and generated cannot be separated from the human, social, institutional, economic, and other environments in which the knowledge is produced and applied. Related to context are resources available to social work. The type of knowledge used and created are dependent on time; fiscal assets; and intellectual, built, and other assets availed throughout examined practice.

Finally, we assert that all systematic activity in examined practice, whether characterized as practice or research, is evaluative, and thus, systematic evaluation of what is needed to resolve problems, to implement goals and objectives, and to assess the efficacy and goodness of outcomes is the model of inquiry that best serves social work. Each of our exemplars illustrates the principles and themes summarized above. We turn to them now.

EXEMPLAR #1—JANICE

At the age of 46, Janice, an accomplished author, was taken to the emergency department of her local hospital in a semicomatose state. She was diagnosed with cerebrovascular accident (CVA), resulting in right hemiparesis, decrease in visual and auditory acuity on her right side, ataxia, and loss of coordination. She was referred to a clinical social worker for the problem of depression.

Problem Statement

As a result of functional losses resulting from a CVA, Janice is depressed.

Figure 13.1   Initial Problem Statement

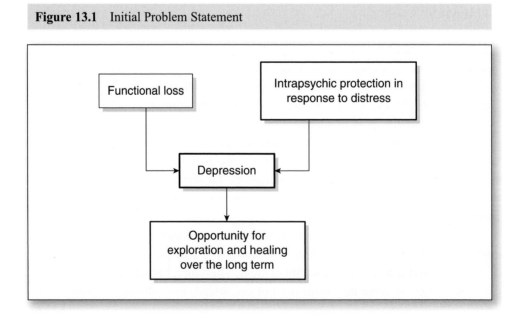

Recall that the first social worker proceeded to frame Janice's problem through a Jungian theoretical lens. The problem map in Figure 13.1 depicts this thinking. Boxes outlined with heavy lined borders mapped the thinking and knowledge use path.

Social Work Intervention #1

According to the social worker relying on Jungian theory to guide thinking and action, Janice's depression was caused by a protective mechanism to deal with functional loss, and thus the consequence of depression, although uncomfortable, was an opportunity for growth through prolonged engagement in therapy.

Need Statement

Proceeding from the problem statement, the social worker who initially saw Janice believed that long-term intervention was needed as the basis and opportunity for exploration and intrapsychic healing. The social worker proceeded to organize goals and intervention from a Jungian theoretical position, a well developed and tested body of literature.

Literature Support

Within Jungian literature, brief intervention is not indicated, as depression is seen as a signifier for depth of analysis and slow, long-term healing of historical wounds (Wilde, 2011).

Reflexive Intervention

Over several weeks of social work intervention, Janice became frustrated, not receiving the guidance that she sought on how to resume life with changes due to stroke. When the social worker continued to work with Janice through a Jungian theoretical lens, Janice left to obtain help from another social worker. One of the factors that produced a negative outcome and thus termination of intervention with this social worker was Janice's lack of alliance or trust in the social worker's plan of action.

Outcome Assessment #1

Not completed.

Social Work Intervention #2

In this interaction, the second social worker asked Janice to state what she saw as the problem, which Janice perceived as lack of knowledge on how to regain the activity that made her life worth living.

Consulting the literature on stroke rehabilitation did not suffice to guide the intervention, and, thus, the social worker turned to literature in progressive disability theory to understand alternatives for redefining the problems of depression and poor adaptation. Figure 13.2 presents the alternative problem map.

Problem Statement

The revised problem statement is poor adaptation.

Figure 13.2   Revised Problem Statement

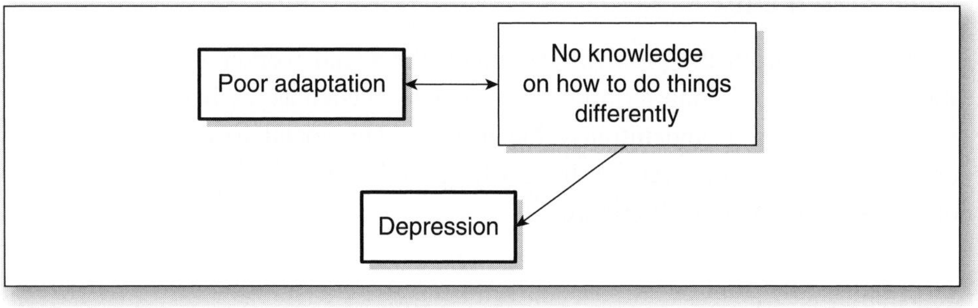

Need Statement

The social worker used two sources to establish and systematically support need: life history and literature. First, Janice was asked to construct her life history so that the social worker could systematically elicit what was meaningful to her over time. From the narrative, it was clear that Janice valued physical activity and intellectual involvement throughout her life, and thus, the social worker used this information to identify relevant literature to further inform need necessary to craft goals and objectives as well as intervention strategies.

Second, the social worker searched several sources of literature. He looked to adaptive sports and kinesiology to find methods to help Janice resume outdoor fitness. What he found was not satisfactory, and thus he consulted knowledge on fabrication of adaptive equipment. From the literature on disability theorized as barriers to access, the social worker revised the need away from depression intervention to involving Janice in a centered process in which she identified and learned how to resume her valued activities. The need was therefore articulated as acquisition of resources and strategies to facilitate Janice's return to meaningful activity.

Goals and Objectives

Goals and objectives were developed to meet the need. The overarching goal was for Janice to regain meaning in her life. Objectives included collaborating with Janice and others to find and obtain equipment, identify locations, and organize people to support Janice in adaptive sports.

Reflexive Intervention

Janice worked with the social worker to accomplish the objectives. Because the literature did not contain systematic inquiry on the availability of equipment or methods to aid ambulatory individuals with mobility barriers to engage in cross-country skiing, the social worker proceeded to conduct his own investigation on how Janice might proceed to regain this valued part of her life. Throughout the social work intervention, Janice was asked to document her experience, once again in narrative form. This data source served as evidence for reflexive intervention as well as for part of the outcome assessment.

Characteristic of reflexive intervention is monitoring and self-examination. Because Janice's social worker was also concerned with large system issues, he consulted with an engineering department at the local university to advocate for the development of adaptive equipment for clients who had needs similar to Janice's but who similarly remained unserved.

Outcome Assessment

Narrative assessment revealed that Janice was adapting and learning to regain esteem as she learned new ways to engage in valued endeavors.

Sharing

The social worker sought permission to publish his practice knowledge, and thus, his practice joined the social work canon to inform others who might encounter similar clients and needs. Based on his future expansive work, he wrote a scholarly article on social work collaboration with mechanical engineering, adding innovative reflexive intervention to the knowledge base of social work.

EXEMPLAR #2—DEAN

Dean, a jazz musician in his early 20s, was hospitalized after he sustained a complex fracture of his left hip. When interviewed in the emergency department, Dean reported that he believed that he could fly and was injured in an attempt to take off from a second story window in his home. After his orthopedic needs were evaluated and addressed, Dean was referred to a social worker for intervention.

Problem Statement

The initial problem statement was articulated as Dean sustained a serious injury. The problem map to identify the locus for change appears in Figure 13.3.

The boxes outlined with heavy lined borders comprised the initial problem statement used to ascertain need. The "Delusions of grandeur" box was the point selected for social work action.

Need Statement

The need for psychiatric treatment was determined as the point for entering and structuring goals and objectives for intervention. Dean was immediately placed on the short-term psychiatric floor of the general hospital where he was seen by the mental health care team. During his intake interview with the social worker, Dean indicated that he had some experience with cocaine and other "recreational drugs" but not within the past few weeks. He reported previous episodes of believing that he could fly. After a routine social work intake in which Dean's narrative responses to an interview schedule were recorded, Dean was referred to substance abuse

Figure 13.3   Initial Problem Map

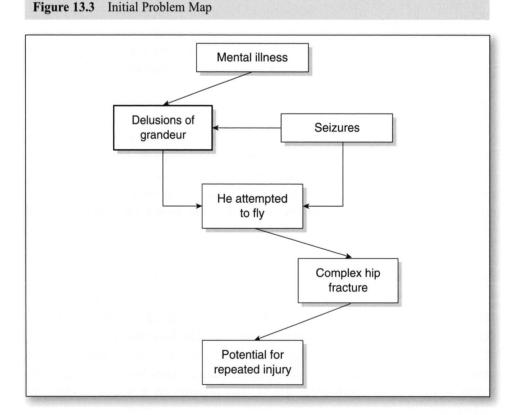

rehabilitation, further refining the need statement. There, the physician started him on risperidone, an antipsychotic medication for the treatment of delusions, and Dean was enrolled in substance abuse counseling with a social worker. In efforts to avoid future injury, Dean complied with all recommendations.

From Dean's initial presentation, it was certainly feasible that reduction or elimination of substance use was a primary need in order to resolve the problem of delusions of grandeur resulting in dangerous behavior. Given evidence-based practice guidelines, it was not only feasible but also appropriate to identify a need for substance abuse intervention.

Goals and Objectives

Dean's assumed need for psychiatric and substance abuse intervention produced two goals: (1) sobriety and (2) prevention of further injury through decreasing and ultimately eliminating Dean's substance abuse. Objectives included enrollment in a substance abuse treatment program, completion of the program, attainment of evidence-based short-term and intermediate milestones, and the final outcome of elimination of substance-produced delusions.

Reflexive Intervention

Dean attended the evidence-based substance intervention. Dean's attendance was monitored, and he participated in regular mixed-method assessments to systematically document his progress. Measures included clinical notes scanned into the database, a record of Dean's attendance, Dean's log of his own activity, and measured responses on evidence-based indicators of expected outcomes. Moreover, as is often the case in social work, the social worker used weekly peer supervision to reflect on use of self in the social work interaction with Dean. Reflexive intervention, however, revealed that despite Dean's compliance, regular attendance, and engagement in substance abuse counseling, the outcome objective was not met. The social worker used this knowledge to identify the failure of the intervention strategy and to obtain additional data on which to craft an alternative problem and new need statement. Once revised, the need for medical intervention was established and goals and objectives were revised.

Outcome Assessment

Dean's social worker used well-documented outcome assessment tools to examine Dean's goal attainment in substance abuse intervention. When the empirical findings did not document absence of delusions and no further injury, it became clear that the problem was not accurately or completely articulated.

Revised Problem and Need Statement

Over the course of substance abuse intervention, Dean gained 20 pounds, and was anxious and unable to concentrate on practicing or performing music. At 4 months following enrollment, he again was hospitalized for fractures sustained in a fall after he tried to fly out his second story window. A new problem statement was created to redirect need and subsequent intervention. Figure 13.4 presents the revised problem map. Note that the failure of substance abuse treatment is conceptualized as a problem but not one to be addressed as it relates to Dean. However, the knowledge about failure is important and should be heeded by the social worker as the basis to formatively evaluate individual and agency practice.

Note that given that substance abuse treatment did not resolve the problem of injury, mental illness (see initial map) was eliminated from the new problem map as irrelevant. From the new problem statement, the need was narrowed to evaluating Dean's medical status. He was referred for medical intervention. The medical

Figure 13.4   Revised Problem Map for Dean

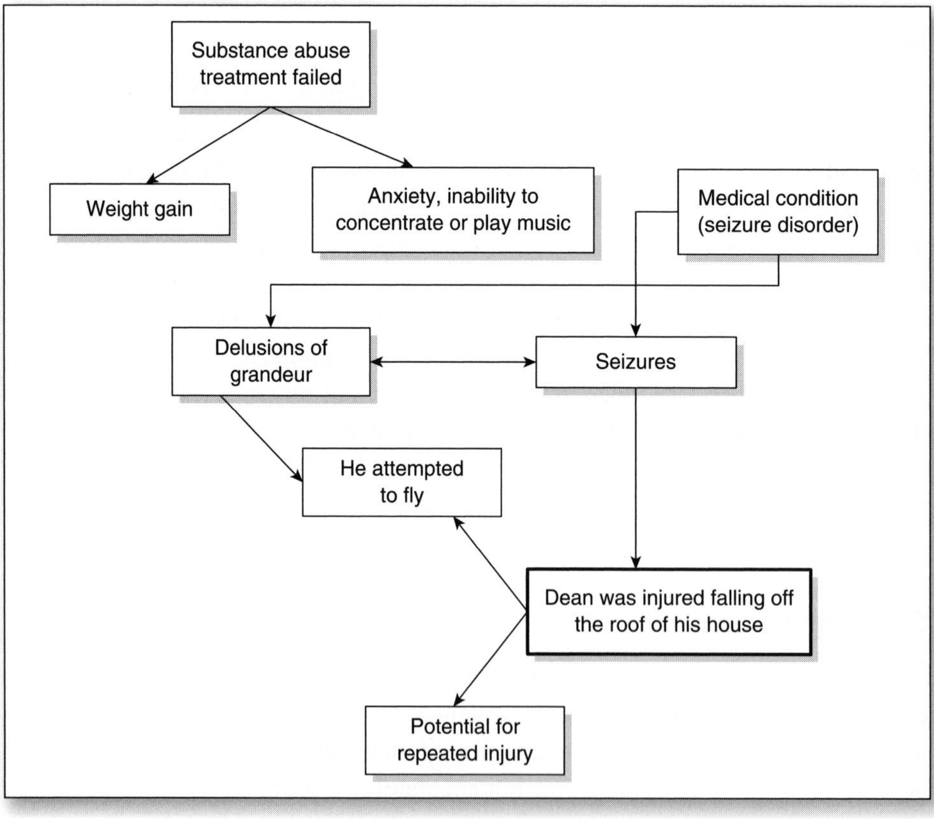

nature of the problem eliminated the need for social work intervention, and thus, Dean was discharged from social services.

Sharing

The social worker shared this work in peer supervision.

EXEMPLAR #3—TOBACCO ACCESS PORTAL (TAP)

Problem Statement

People with low literacy levels are at disproportionately greater risk for smoking related illness and fatality.

The map in Figure 13.5 depicts the complexity of this problem and the multiple ways in which it could have been addressed. Because the social work team members approached this large issue from a macro stance and were able to amass the resources necessary to accomplish a broad purpose, their initial consideration focused on the right to health information.

Figure 13.5   TAP Problem Map

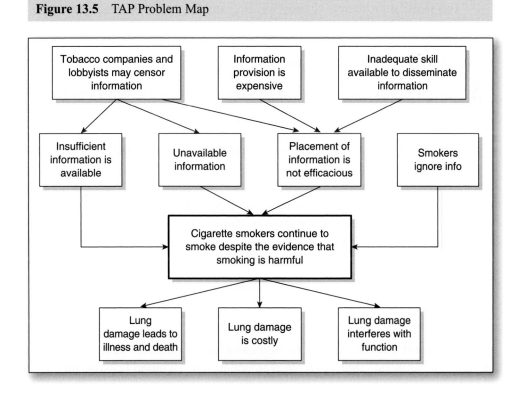

The problem revealed the following values: Smoking related illness and fatality are undesirable. Equal access to health information is a right.

Recall that a problem is a local or individual value statement. Thus, it is important to acknowledge and be prepared for different perspectives on what constitutes a problem. As an example, the part of the social work team's problem that highlights the fatal effects of smoking may not be espoused in the value bases of corporations that produce and sell cigarettes and other tobacco products. However, the right to information may be supported by the tobacco industry, and thus odd bedfellows might emerge with creative thinking.

To further clarify the problem and to identify assets that could be exploited for social change, the social work team conducted a force field analysis using the following statement:

> Available information to the public about the negative primary, secondary, and tertiary health and environmental consequences of smoking is not accessible to many, including those with low literacy. The following were identified as driving forces:

1. The potential and diversity of electronic information delivery systems

2. Reasonable costs of disseminating information on the Internet

3. Extensive information already existing on the negative consequences of smoking

Restraining forces included the following:

1. Diverse methods of information consumption among the target population

2. Limitations of print material for the diverse target population

3. Lack of skilled professionals who can make information available in multiple formats

A major restraining force, "diverse methods of information consumption among the target population," identified the failure of a single approach to providing public information. Doing so excluded too many individuals who consume knowledge in ways that rendered current information inaccessible. The action agenda of expansive access to information was therefore formalized.

Needs Assessment

To document that a website with automated literacy translation was needed to resolve the problem, the social worker conducted a comprehensive literature review and also collected data on the readability level of existing smoking prevention and cessation websites.

The literature revealed the following principles:

1. Access to prevention knowledge contributes to healthy decision making.

2. Limited access to information does not provide individuals with knowledge on which to make informed substance use decisions.

3. Limited access to information in the state in which the needs assessment was conducted is caused by limited literacy and inability to comprehend electronic information.

4. There is an inverse relationship between smoking rates and literacy level.

Needs Assessment Sampling

The TAP needs assessment sampling frame comprised all websites that address smoking prevention or cessation. Not knowing the breadth of sites, the social worker chose a convenience sample to conduct a needs assessment. The first 19 websites listed in an Internet search using the key term "smoking prevention and cessation information" served as the sample supported by the data-based rationale that most web users would not look further than the initial 10 sites derived from a search (Cutts, 2011). The readability and accessibility of the sites listed on the lead page of the search were presented as evidence (Table 13.2 on page 294).

Synthesizing literature with data from Table 13.2 provided a compelling argument for the need as it was conceptualized by the social work team.

Goals and Objectives

To achieve the goal of expansive access to tobacco prevention and cessation information, the team established the objectives, timeline, and assessment approach presented in Table 13.3 on page 295. Note that reflexive intervention monitoring and strategies for assessment of intended outcomes were listed in the table adjacent to each objective. This table clearly illustrates that establishing clear objectives for social work activity organizes meaningful systematic assessment as well. Process (P) and short- and long-term outcome (O) objectives both appear and are designated.

Reflexive Intervention

As specified in Table 13.3, intervention was conceptualized as the development and launch of the website. The process objectives guided the team in activity as well as systematic monitoring of the project. Specific formative objectives inserted into the plan assured that the team would not only engage in careful and timely self-examination, but also document their responses to feedback.

Outcome Assessment

A mixed-method study was used to assess outcome. The last two objectives formed the experimental-type assessment of intended outcomes. Two research questions were posed to guide this systematic activity:

1. What level of use is realized on the TAP website?

2. To what extent did access and use of the website produce positive attitudes toward smoking cessation?

To answer question #1, the team returned to the literature to select lexical and operational definitions of use. From the literature, they found many definitions, ranging from simply viewing to spending time engaging in interactive functions. They chose to define use as both viewing and time spent on the site. The literature further pointed to automated strategies that could be integrated into the website design to obtain data on both measures of the use variable (Krug, 2014).

Table 13.2   Flesch-Kincaid Raw Scores and Grade Level Readability and Compliance With 508 Access Guidelines

Site	Readability score (0–100)	Grade Level	508 Accessibility
Quit Smoking Support (quitsmokingsupport.com)	45	12	No
American Lung Association	15	14	No
Smoke Free Housing (tenants)	45	11	No
Center for Tobacco Independence	30	14	No
Healthy Maine Partnerships	17	17	No
Maine Lung Association	48	9	No
Maine Public Health	7	18	No
Smokefree.gov	45	12	No
HHS-Tobacco cessation	32	14	No

Table 13.3 Objectives, Timeline, and Assessment Approach for the TAP project

Objectives	Timeline	Assessment Strategy
1. Determine expertise to be assembled (P)	Month 1	Areas of expertise identified and names assembled
2. Convene project team (P)	Months 1–3	Agreements and team assignments completed
3. Develop a work and funding plan (p)	Months 3–12	Funding and work plan for prototype completed
4. Identify the content to be disseminated (p)	Month 12	All materials are completed and documented
5. Develop automated literacy translation software (O)	Months 12–18	Complete and host prototype website
6. Link the text translation software to text to voice and language translation portals (o)	Month 18	Completion of linkages
7. Pilot test the system (P)	Months 18–22	Conduct mixed-method trials
8. Conduct focus groups to determine website design preferences (needs assessment)	Months 18–22	Complete focus groups with diverse users and report
9. Develop website design (P)	Months 22–24	Finalize design and functionality
10. Pilot test website (P, O)	Months 24–28	Test functionality, preference, and use in diverse user groups
11. Revise website based on pilot test findings (P)	Months 28–30	Complete web design and navigation in response to pilot testing
12. Host formal website, and disseminate it widely to diverse user audiences (O)	Months 30+	Completely functional website hosted, tracking analytics and broad dissemination Design research on web use and tobacco prevention learning in target populations
13. Achieve widespread use of the website	Months 30+	Record website use statistics
14. Improve web users' attitudes toward smoking cessation (O)	Months 30+	Online survey

To structure conditions necessary to answer question #2, groups with and without access to the website were created by randomly selecting first wave participants and then staggering participation. The outcome objective of attitude change was measured at two intervals for both groups, before anyone was exposed to the website and then after only one group accessed and used it. By using a waiting list, the social worker was able to follow the rules of true experimentation while being assured that this intervention would be available for all users in the long run.

In conducting research on website use, the social work team found that immigrants who had high levels of literacy in their native language were the most frequent but totally unanticipated user group. Through interview, the team then found that immigrants coming to the United States as smokers found smoking both expensive and stigmatizing. They comprised an unanticipated population who benefitted from this site as much if not more than the planned target group. Further unanticipated outcomes included low-literacy English text being easier to read and digest than text on higher-literacy sites. Moreover, the totally unexpected outcome of higher accuracy of automated translation from English to other languages on Babelfish and Google Translate was revealed. The unanticipated use of the website by immigrants who spoke English as a second language prompted a new literature review to inform how to better recruit and meet the prevention and cessation information needs of this subpopulation group.

Sharing

Several purposes framed the dissemination strategy. First, in order to produce this entity, funding was necessary. However, in the long term, the substantive public health information remained free, but the programming methods were kept as proprietary. So in order to successfully obtain funding, the problem statement, compelling systematic evidence that the website would fill an essential unmet need, and plans on how the project would be carried out were shared through a research grant proposal format. However, limited technical information was made available in order to keep a balance between privacy and adequacy of information for judgment and favorable funding response.

Second, because this project was central to our own professional activity and research agendas, a major purpose of dissemination was contributing to professional knowledge. Third and most important was the purpose of improving equality of access to public health information for all population segments and individuals. So the multiple scholarly, outcome, and proprietary purposes guided strategies for the timing, locations, and formats for knowledge dissemination in this project.

EXEMPLAR #4—AESTHETIC MOBILITY DEVICE PROJECT

Problem Statement

Elders abandon prescribed walking devices, resulting in sedentary lifestyles and related negative consequences of inactivity.

The impetus for this project emerged from the personal experience of the social worker who herself had contracted encephalitis, resulting in balance and motor planning difficulties. When confronted with the need to use a walker, the social worker did so in the hospital but abandoned it upon discharge. Her experience of using a stigmatized medical device was the knowledge that initiated the problem statement discussed earlier.

The problem map in Figure 13.6 visually depicts the complexity of abandonment and the area where this social worker chose to concentrate her efforts. Note once again that values framed the examined practice sequence from problem definition and expansion through sharing.

Figure 13.6   Problem Map—Mobility Device Abandonment

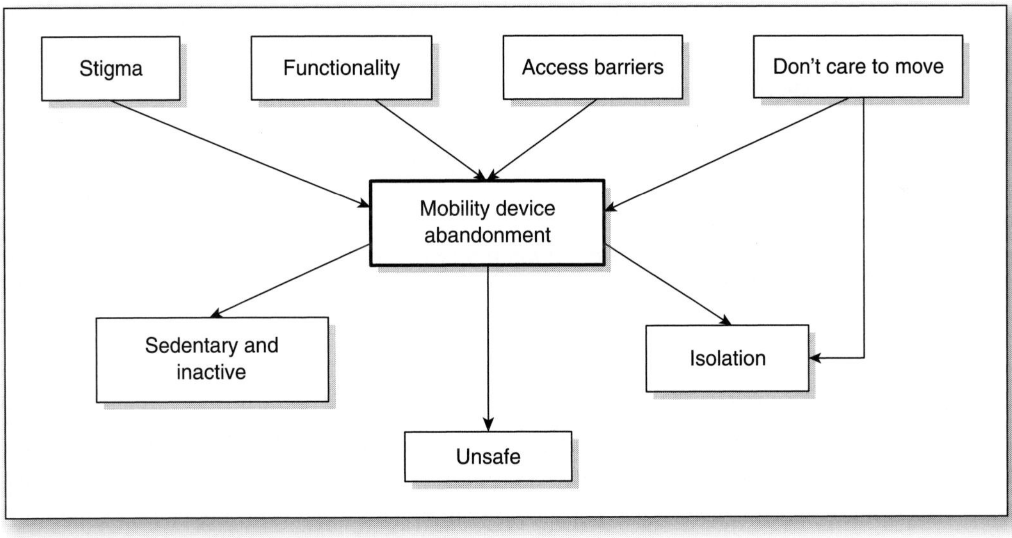

Needs Assessment

A substantive needs assessment was planned to meet several purposes. First, given the personal nature of the problem, it was necessary for the social worker to affirm that others perceived similar barriers in using mobility devices. Second, because this social work innovation would require significant resources and testing, the needs assessment was designed to provide a clear, well-researched need statement and rationale for this direction.

The social worker initially conducted a comprehensive literature review to examine the scope of research on the reasons that elders abandon needed mobility devices. There was widespread documentation of the increasing risk of falling as one ages, particularly in the presence of mobility instability or other impairment. However, the causes of abandonment theorized in the literature were incomplete (Bateni & Maki, 2005), leading to its continuation even in the presence of efforts to convince device users that they needed walking supports to be safe.

Combined with knowing derived from theoretical and artistic counterparts of Cohen and Miller (Candlin and Guins, 2009; Pullin, 2009), the literature and subsequent artifact review crafted the rationale to support research that investigated the role of appearance and perceived stigma resulting from use of medicalized-appearing mobility equipment typically prescribed for mobility support. Thus, in addition to functional disappointment, appearance was empirically verified as the major barrier that needed to be overcome in order to promote adoption and use of mobility devices by those who needed them for safety, balance, and so forth (DePoy & Gilson, 2010).

Based on the literature review, a mixed-method design was selected to both verify theory and provide more precise guidance for social work intervention.

Quasi-experimental design was used to answer the following research questions:

1. What are the articulated reasons for nonuse of mobility equipment among elders?

2. What is the relationship between age of user and abandonment of mobility device?

To answer question #1, interviewing was used, with responses numerically coded for frequency. Because they wanted to know if mobility device use differed between men and women in the needs assessment, the social work team conducted a t-test in which they separated the sample by two gender groups and hypothesized no difference between groups. The null hypothesis was accepted, and thus, it was concluded that no difference in use between men and women was apparent. Informed by this knowledge, the social work team concluded that it was not necessary to develop gender-specific intervention.

The naturalistic element of the needs assessment was designed to inform need from the perspective of elders. The query that guided the entrance into the study was "What is the meaning of mobility device appearance to elders who have been prescribed such devices?"

From the group of elders who were receiving outpatient rehabilitation following hip replacement, the social work team entered as etic to seek knowledge from members. Face-to-face, open-ended interviews and object reading were conducted with consenting informants, the elders themselves. Participants were asked to reflect on how the use of the mobility device made them feel, what it meant to them to be using a walker, and how the use of this device affected their lives. Several of the informants noted that using a walker made them feel old, one informant indicated that she did not like the way she looked when she saw her gait with the walker in the mirror, and several others said that they were embarrassed to be using this device.

Thematic analysis revealed the following categories from interview data about the causes for abandonment:

Lack of perceived need

Inconvenience

Inability to use

Appearance as barrier

Perception of dependency

People stare

Pitied

The device function was secondary to a majority of the informants. Thus, the primacy of the material symbol, the walker, had diverse meanings to those interviewed. Illustrating flexibility, this unanticipated knowledge led the social work team to rethink the needs assessment to ask about aesthetic preferences and assume diverse pluralistic responses. When asked, elders had many preferences for activity and appearance of a mobility device. Further illustrating flexibility, a group was then convened to observe illustrations of potential designs, eliciting multiple meanings for the visual symbols. Narrative data were analyzed to reveal commonalities to guide theory development.

Goals and Objectives

A major goal of the intervention was to improve the safety and mobility of elders who needed adaptive devices by decreasing abandonment due to stigmatizing design. A second goal focused on social change by addressing the recognized problem of device abandonment through user-generated knowledge. Objectives related to each goal were both formative and summative and guided both reflexive intervention and outcome assessment.

Reflexive Intervention

Over the course of year, the social work team collaborated with engineering faculty and students to develop and test the usability and potential for adoption of a stylized mobility assistive device. When the first prototype was fabricated, focus group methodology was used by the social work team to investigate formative objectives of creating a relevant, nonstigmatizing design. Several groups were conducted, one comprising elders who did not need prescribed equipment, one with elders who did need prescribed equipment, and one of observers. In each group, specific questions regarding meanings of the appearance of the device were posed with photographic props to stimulate depth of response, yielding valuable knowledge to guide intervention. Thematic analysis of all three groups suggested that device redesign was not only viable but was an innovation that was apt to produce the desired outcome of improvement in adoption and use of mobility devices.

Outcome Assessment

To study the outcome of the project and to verify the theory regarding the importance of considering and building functional devices with relevant and non-stigmatizing aesthetic designs, the following research question was posed:

To what extent do elders abandon an aesthetically designed mobility device compared to a typical "medicalized walker" with equivalent functionality?

It was hypothesized that abandonment of the aesthetically designed device would occur significantly less frequently than the use of typical wheeled walkers with a medical appearance. The mobility device was named as the independent variable. Abandonment, defined as nonuse and operationally defined by frequency of use per week, was compared for both devices.

Given that the object of the study was abandonment, the research design was structured with a comparison rather than a control group. Elders were selected purposely from a population of clients in an outpatient rehabilitation practice who had just received hip replacements. To reduce bias related to assignment of elders to one group or the other based on person preference, time of day, and so on, each participant was randomly assigned to one of two groups and provided with instructions for use of the device. Randomization with replacement was used as the technique to equalize assignment opportunity. Over a month-long period, elders were asked to document the frequency and duration of use of the device on an indoor public track. The track was selected to (1) eliminate the influence of extraneous variables such as weather and (2) enhance reliability through creating equivalent and stable testing conditions. Note that the sample was one of convenience, and thus, the results of the study were specific to that group only, limiting external validity. Results revealed that 80% were using this equipment, and 60% were using it in the prescribed fitness plan.

Sharing

The project is being disseminated widely and shared for funding support.

EXEMPLAR #5—WORKPLACE ACCESSIBILITY

Problem Statement #1

As a result of the reasonable accommodation standard of the Americans With Disabilities Act (ADA) and the ADA Amendments Act (ADAAA), workplace accommodations have been insufficient to maintain Elton in his job as janitor. He is unemployed and facing eviction and homelessness.

Because he did not know why Elton was terminated, the social worker conducted a systematic interview with the employer and Elton to understand the context and associated factors that prevented Elton's retention on the job. Answers to his questions revealed Elton's recent exacerbation of Parkinson's disease, resulting in his difficulty walking. An examination of the evidence suggested that Elton's employer, responding to Elton's use of a rolling walker, assumed that he would be required to erect ramped access inside and outside of the building. The second and most illuminating influence revealed by systematic interview was employer and employee ignorance of other accommodation strategies so that Elton would be able to navigate the small building. The employer's assumption of a high cost of providing Elton with an accommodation resulted in Elton's unemployment. Undue financial hardship that allows some employers to refuse accommodations is legally sanctioned within the ADA.

Needs Assessment

The social worker ascertained two major needs: immediate response to Elton's fiscal hardship and long-term educational action for small business owners. Many other needs related to this complex tangle of rights, fiscal responsibilities, and human need could have emerged from a complex problem map depicted in Figure 13.7. Targeting individual client need, returning Elton to his previous gainful employment position, was undertaken first with specific objectives of finding accommodations that would be within the budget of the employer and could be used by Elton when he was rehired. In the empirical needs assessment, literature on cost and availability of navigation options was examined, revealing a large choice of inexpensive products. The goal guiding intervention was gainful employment for Elton with specific objectives of compiling a list of options, costs, and funders for navigation accommodations; sharing them with the employer; and negotiating Elton's return to work. While potentially seamless, reflexive intervention revealed employer reluctance to rehire Elton because of fear that Elton would become ill and be costly in time lost and high health insurance premiums. Documenting this interaction, the social worker revised the objectives to include education about Parkinson's disease for the employer and a 6-month trial period during which time the social worker would stay engaged in the workplace in case plans needed to be renegotiated.

Goals and Objectives

To meet the goal of gainful employment and thriving for Elton, the social worker crafted objectives to find resources, share them with the employer and Elton, and work with the employer over a 6-month monitored trial period to secure Elton's return to work with adaptions.

Reflexive Intervention

The monitoring plan during this social work action involved several areas. First, the social worker was concerned not only with employer knowledge but also with attitudes toward improving accessibility features. Attitudes and unsubstantiated beliefs about cost on the part of both the employer and Elton could have created barriers to a successful outcome for Elton's return to work. So the social worker provided knowledge and resources to the employer that were assistive to Elton and readily affordable for the employer.

The second major area of reflexivity during intervention focused on cost-benefit analysis. The inputs of social work effort involving time and cost of finding and working with Elton's employer could be calculated using time, supplies, equipment, and expense equations. Outputs were conceptualized as the number of visits to the employer and trials of access equipment. However, cost benefits of the intervention could be substantial if considered from a more complex and long-term stance. Variables such as public savings resulting from not having to pay Elton safety net support along with Elton's continued contribution through paying taxes and his productivity would have clearly been illustrative of the cost-benefit value

Figure 13.7 Problem Map for the Initial Statement

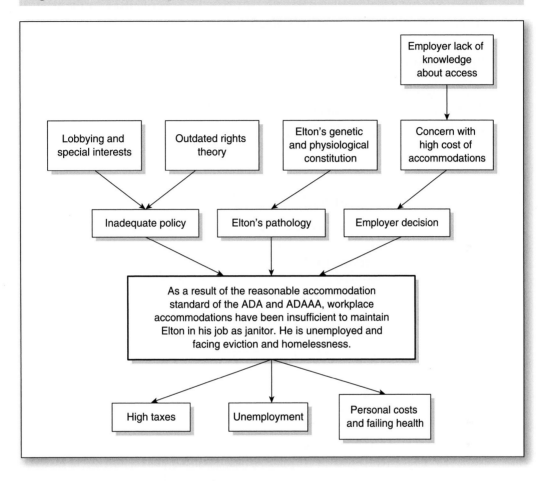

of this local social work intervention for a single individual. Further theorizing and systematically examining social-return-on-investment for the expansive long-term goal of ADA policy change, while much more complicated and debatable, could be undertaken as a collaborative project during reflexive intervention.

Outcome Assessment

The immediate outcome assessment of returning Elton to gainful employment did not require measurement. Elton's maintenance job required simple technological solutions to reduce his physical effort. Targeted to navigation access, the social worker, working online with an access consultant, was able to find inexpensive, lightweight portable ramps for Elton's walker that easily provided access even when stairs were present. The total cost of this access feature was $143, and because it was purchased for Elton, the employer did not have to expend additional funds to keep Elton employed. However, once Elton was employed, the problem statement for this social worker shifted to the macro-sphere, initiating a new examined practice sequence.

Problem Statement #2

As a result of the reasonable accommodation standard of the ADA and the ADAAA, workplace accommodations have been insufficient to maintain Elton in his job as a janitor. He is unemployed and facing eviction and homelessness.

The new problem map (Figure 13.8) highlighted problem statement #2.

Figure 13.8 Problem Map for the Second Statement

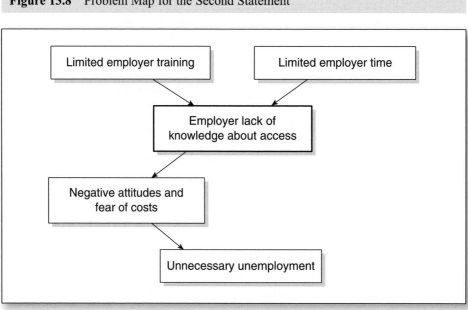

While formal force field analysis was not indicated to address the employer's concern with the high cost of accommodation, the social worker still used this thinking strategy to identify driving and restraining forces to further inform the issue. The increasing production of navigation options was determined to be a major driving force and was thus factored into needs assessment.

Needs Assessment

Formal needs assessment involved surveying and interviewing small business owners to answer the following research question:

What attitudes and knowledge of workplace accommodations are held by small business owners?

Interviews were open-ended but deductive in that the social worker looked for attitudes as defined in theoretical literature. In addition, the social worker administered the 2-item Likert-type scaled instrument developed and validated by Popovich, Scherbaum, Scherbaum, and Polinko (2003) to test the attitudes toward the reasonableness of workplace accommodations held by a convenience sample of 10 small local business owners in a small geographic area. Respondents rated each of the items on a 1 to 7 scale from least favorable to most favorable. Information on the size of each business (recording the number of employees and dollar amount of yearly net income averaged over the past 3 years) was also obtained.

Measures of central tendency were calculated revealing the following findings:

$M = 5$

$SD = 1.1$

These numbers indicate that 68% of the scores fall between 3.9 and 6.1 within a range of 3 to 7 and a possible range of 1 to 7. Groups differences between short- and long-term business ownership were also calculated using a contingency table and chi square statistic (see Table 13.4). This analytic strategy was undertaken because of the small purposive sample. To accomplish the aim of analyzing attitudes for this small sample, a cutoff score between positive and negative attitudes was established for the total score at 4. Thus, any score at 4 or below was considered to be negative, and any score above 4 was considered to be positive. Similarly, for longevity in business, short and long categories were created by establishing a cutoff point (under 5 years was considered to be short, and 5 or more years was considered to be long). The contingency table is shown in Table 13.4.

Initially, the nonsignificant chi square indicated to the social worker that there were no differences between groups, and thus, a single intervention could be planned. However, the Pearson r correlation coefficient was also calculated from raw interval level scores. The value of 0.7 ($r = .7$) revealed that an increasing

Table 13.4   Contingency Table

	Positive Attitude Score	*Negative Attitude Score*
Short (*n* = 5)	5	0
Long (*n* = 5)	2	3

number of employees were highly associated with negative attitudes. Thus, the social worker found that the magnitude of human resources in small businesses was a factor related to attitude. Thus, the social worker took this finding into consideration and decided to conduct a larger study before planning an intervention.

CONCLUSION

The five exemplars have worked throughout the book to illustrate examined practice in diverse practice arenas, from clinical practice with individuals through macropractice in policy, employer education, and the development of innovations to achieve health and safety of elders. Our purpose in writing this book was fivefold:

1. To propose a flexible model that seamlessly integrates practice and research

2. To illustrate the model

3. To propose and illustrate evaluation research as the science and art of empirically informed practice

4. To assert the obligation of all social workers to contribute to social work knowledge

5. To illustrate how all social work thinking and action, if enacted systematically, forms the basis for legitimate social work knowledge

The book began with a detailed discussion of each of the steps in the examined practice sequence and then turned to a focus on how each of the research traditions is used in each step. In this book, we also chose examples that demonstrate professional innovations as well as conventions. We are confident that using this model, whether in clinical practice or in large systems, will advance social work in the twenty-first century context.

REFERENCES

Bateni, H., & Maki, B. (2005). Assistive devices for balance and mobility: Benefits, demands, and adverse consequences. *Archives of Physical Medicine and Rehabilitation, 86*, 134–145.

Candlin, F., & Guins, R. (2009). *The object reader.* London, UK: Routledge.

Cutts, M. (2011). Matt Cutts: Technologist. *Ted Talks.* Retrieved from https://www.ted.com/speakers/matt_cutts

DePoy, E., & Gilson, S. (2010). Disability by design. *Review of Disability Studies, 6*(3), 53–62.

Krug, S. (2014). *Don't make me think, revisited: A common sense approach to web usability.* Pearson.

Popovich, P. M., Scherbaum, C. A., Scherbaum, K. L., & Polinko, N. (2003). The assessment of attitudes towards individuals with disabilities in the workplace. *Journal of Psychology, 137*(2), 163–177.

Pullin, G. (2009). *Disability meets design.* Boston, MA: MIT Press.

Wilde, D. (2011). *Jung's personality theory quantified.* New York, NY: Springer.

GLOSSARY

Audience: an individual or group of individuals who have a role in some or all thinking and action processes of an evaluation, including the initiation, receipt, and use of findings

Audit trail: explanation of how method was conceptualized and implemented, what evidence was used, and how it was used to support and verify an inductive claim

Bias: unplanned influence that confounds the outcome of a study

Closed-ended question: one that poses a limited range of responses from which the respondent chooses, all of which are posited by the researcher

Code: numbering assigned to observations of variables

Concept: abstraction of observed or experienced phenomena

Connotative: describes the meaning symbolized by the visual

Control: a set of processes to eliminate sampling or experimental bias

Culture: the set of explicit and tacit rules, symbols, and rituals that guide patterns of human behavior within a group

Deductive reasoning: applying a general principle to explain a specific case or phenomenon

Denotative: describes the image, object, or observed phenomenon

Dependent variable: outcome variable

Emic: see **Insider**

Error: inaccurate claim based on limitations in various parts of the research design

Ethics: guidelines for moral thinking and action processes

Etic: the perspective of a researcher who is external to the context of the object or subject of inquiry

Experimental-type design: research design based in positivist, logico-deductive philosophical framework and which relies on reduction and interpretation of numeric data

Ex post facto **designs** (literally translated as "after the fact"): methods to examine phenomena of interest that have already occurred and cannot be manipulated in any way

External validity: Extent to which findings from a sample can be generalized to the population from which the sample was selected.

Force field analysis: a planning tool that provides a diagrammatic picture of all influences that maintain or impact a situation at a given moment

Formative evaluation: use of data about intervention input, conduct, and output to inform intervention improvement

Frequency: the number of times a value occurs in a data set

GIS: Geographic information systems are a set of computer-based analytic techniques that provide mapped images of a geographically bounded space

Goals: broad statements about the ideal or "hoped for"

Grounded theory: an inductive approach to theory generation relying on the constant comparative method of data analysis

Idiographic: an approach to design that reveals individual phenomena within a specified context

Independent variable: phenomenon that is presumed to cause an outcome

Indicators: an empirical representation of an underlying concept

Insider: investigator who occupies an integral role in the delivery of intervention being examined

Instrument validity: the relationship between a concept and its measurement

Internal validity: The extent to which a research design can answer the research question.

Intervention processes: the set of actions that occurs to meet the goals and objectives of intervention

Likert-type scale: closed-ended response format in which the respondent is instructed to select one of five or seven categories, such as "strongly agree," "agree," "uncertain," "disagree," or "strongly disagree," to indicate his or her opinion or experience

Listserve: electronic format used to distribute a body of information

Literature review: the thinking and action step of critically examining literature and resources as a basis for formulating questions and approaches to answer them

Mean: the average value of a group of scores

Measurement: the translation of observations into numbers

Monitoring (also called formative evaluation): a set of thinking and action processes to ascertain, characterize, and document the relationship between articulated objectives and what occurs during an intervention, which factors impact the intervention, who is involved, and to what extent resources are used

Needs statement: an empirical understanding of what is necessary to resolve all or part of a problem

Nominal numbers (also called categorical): numbers assigned to phenomena for the purpose of labeling only

Nomothetic: an approach to design that reveals commonalities within and/or among groups

Non-experimental designs: experimental-type designs in which the criteria for true-experimental design (random selection, control, and manipulation) cannot be met

Nonparametric: statistical formulas used to analyze nominal and ordinal data in which the tenets of random selection, homogeneity of variance, and sufficient sample size are not present

Objectives: operationalized goal statements

Object Reading: the primary method of analyzing meaning of visuals

Open-ended question: one in which the respondent is asked to offer his or her comments on a topic without being directed to specific answers

Outcome: the result of being acted upon by or participating in an action process

Outcome assessment: a set of thinking and action processes to ascertain and document what occurs as a result of being voluntarily or involuntarily exposed to a purposive process; the application of rigorous research design to inquiry about intervention efficacy in producing desired results

Parametric statistics: data analytic procedures to ascertain population characteristics in which numeric data are homogeneous, interval, or ratio and have been generated through probability methods or distributions, and in which the minimum sample size criterion for use has been met

Passive observation designs: methods used to examine phenomena as they naturally occur and to discern the relationship between two or more variables

Population: the group of people (or other units of analysis) that are delimited by the investigator

Post hoc: after the occurrence of the phenomenon

Probability: theory that focuses on the likelihood of occurrence of an event

Probability sampling: sampling based on probability theory

Problem: a value statement, an undesirable that needs to be reduced or eliminated

Problem mapping: a method in which one expands a problem statement beyond its initial conceptualization by asking two questions repeatedly: What caused the problem? and What are the consequences of the problem?

Random: without bias

Random group assignment: probability method of placing subjects in groups as a means to eliminate bias and error

Random sample: sampling method in which all individuals in the studied population (or other units of analysis) have an equivalent chance of being selected for a study sample

Reflexivity: self-examination for the purpose of ascertaining how one's perspective influences the interpretation of data

Reliability: the rigor criterion that specifies the stability of an inquiry approach

Sample: a smaller number of units of analysis than those in the population, possessing the characteristics of the population and not possessing any of the exclusion criteria named by the inquirer, that are selected to directly participate in a study

Saturation: in naturalistic inquiry, the point at which new data do not provide any new insights

Science: a philosophical, theoretical, and epistemological lens through which one systematically examines phenomena, collects evidence, and uses evidence to develop, support, or refute a knowledge claim

Semistructured: a data collection technique in which the respondent is delimited to a set of answers without being forced to choose an existing response

Single-case design: use of multiple methods of data collection to examine change in a single unit of analysis

Stability: longitudinal accuracy of a measure

Subjectivity: the perspective of an individual, given his or her biases

Survey designs: methods used primarily to measure characteristics of a population, including their knowledge, opinions, and attitudes

Surveys: questionnaires that are administered to ascertain the characteristics of a population or phenomenon

Target: individual, group, or unit that is expected to demonstrate a desirable outcome as a result of participation in intervention

Taxonomic analysis: inductive technique in which relationships among themes in a data set are identified

Theory: description, explanation, or prediction of phenomena through a set of interrelated concepts, constructs, and principles that can be verified or falsified by empirical approaches

Triangulation: the use of multiple approaches to investigate a single phenomenon

True-experimental design: classic two-group (or variations thereof) design in which subjects are randomly selected and randomly assigned (R) to either an experimental or control group condition

Validity: rigor criterion that assesses the relationship between concept and evidence

Values: beliefs and opinions about what is desirable or undesirable, important or unimportant, and correct or incorrect

Variable: a concept or construct to which a numeric value is assigned. By definition, a variable must have more than one value, even if the investigator is interested in only one condition

Index